Hip-Hop as Philosophical Text and Testimony

Philosophy of Race

Series Editor: George Yancy, Emory University

Editorial Board: Sybol Anderson, Barbara Applebaum, Alison Bailey, Chike Jeffers, Janine Jones, David Kim, Emily S. Lee, Zeus Leonardo, Falguni A. Sheth, Grant Silva

The Philosophy of Race book series publishes interdisciplinary projects that center upon the concept of race, a concept that continues to have very profound contemporary implications. Philosophers and other scholars, more generally, are strongly encouraged to submit book projects that seriously address race and the process of racialization as a deeply embodied, existential, political, social, and historical phenomenon. The series is open to examine monographs, edited collections, and revised dissertations that critically engage the concept of race from multiple perspectives: sociopolitical, feminist, existential, phenomenological, theological, and historical.

RECENT TITLES

Hip-Hop as Philosophical Text and Testimony: Can I Get a Witness?, by Lissa Skitolsky
The Blackness of Black: Key Concepts in Critical Discourse, by William David Hart
Self Definition: A Philosophical Inquiry from the Global South and Global North, by Teodros Kiros
A Phenomenological Hermeneutic of Antiblack Racism in The Autobiography of Malcolm X, by David Polizzi
Buddhism and Whiteness: Critical Reflections, edited by George Yancy and Emily McRae
Black Christology and the Quest for Authenticity: A Philosophical Appraisal, by John H. McClendon III
For Equals Only: Race, Equality, and the Equal Protection Clause, by Tina Fernandes Botts
Politics and Affect in Black Women's Fiction, by Kathy Glass
The Habits of Racism: A Phenomenology of Racism and Racialized Embodiment, by Helen Ngo
Philosophy and the Mixed Race Experience, edited by Tina Fernandes Botts D. Hill
The Post-Racial Limits of Memorialization: Toward a Political Sense of Mourning, by Alfred Frankowski
White Self-Criticality beyond Anti-racism: How Does It Feel to Be a White Problem?, edited by George Yancy

Hip-Hop as Philosophical Text and Testimony

Can I Get a Witness?

Lissa Skitolsky

LEXINGTON BOOKS
Lanham • Boulder • New York • London

Published by Lexington Books
An imprint of The Rowman & Littlefield Publishing Group, Inc.
4501 Forbes Boulevard, Suite 200, Lanham, Maryland 20706
www.rowman.com

6 Tinworth Street, London SE11 5AL, United Kingdom

Copyright © 2020 The Rowman & Littlefield Publishing Group, Inc.

All rights reserved. No part of this book may be reproduced in any form or by any electronic or mechanical means, including information storage and retrieval systems, without written permission from the publisher, except by a reviewer who may quote passages in a review.

British Library Cataloguing in Publication Information Available

Library of Congress Cataloging-in-Publication Data

Names: Skitolsky, Lissa, 1974- author.
Title: Hip-hop as philosophical text and testimony : can I get a witness? / Lissa Skitolsky.
Description: Lanham : Lexington Books, [2020] | Series: Philosophy of race | Includes bibliographical references and index. | Summary: "The author defends the philosophical value of underground hip-hop through illustrating how the culture significantly contributes to debates in multiple academic fields. She also examines the exclusion of hip-hop from discourses on knowledge, racism, genocide and trauma as a reflection of the neoliberal sensibility that hip-hop exposes and opposes"— Provided by publisher.
Identifiers: LCCN 2020040567 (print) | LCCN 2020040568 (ebook) | ISBN 9781498566704 (cloth) | ISBN 9781498566711 (epub) ISBN 9781498566728 (pbk)
Subjects: LCSH: Hip hop—Social aspects—United States. | Culture conflict—United States. | African Americans—Social conditions. | Racism—United States. | Violence—United States. | Hip-hop—Philosophy.
Classification: LCC HN90.S62 S595 2020 (print) | LCC HN90.S62 (ebook) | DDC 306.089/96073—dc23
LC record available at https://lccn.loc.gov/2020040567
LC ebook record available at https://lccn.loc.gov/2020040568

To my son Lev,

For always keepin it real. I wrote this book to explain why this is so important and so difficult—a lifelong task that is its own reward, one that should inspire and humble us.

Contents

Acknowledgments	ix
Introduction: It's Bigger Than Hip-Hop	1
1 Know What I'm Sayin?	31
2 Can I Get a Witness?	53
3 Claimin' I'm a Criminal	77
4 But You Don't Hear Me Tho	113
5 You Feel Me?	135
6 Fuck Tha Police	147
Conclusion: The Aesthetic Politics of Underground Hip-Hop	159
Playlists by Chapter	173
Discography	177
Bibliography	181
Index	185
About the Author	189

Acknowledgments

As I write these acknowledgments to thank those who made this text possible, we are living through and dying from a global pandemic, weaponized by the United States as another occasion to inflict atrocities on black communities in accord with the white supremacist political economy whereby the protection of white life depends upon the destruction and exclusion of black life from moral consideration and the protection of the law. The apparent indifference of the administration to the obscene death toll that has disproportionately affected African Americans had already provoked renewed civil unrest when the gruesome police murder of George Floyd evoked collective public anguish that transformed this unrest into a global movement of citizens demanding that their nations bear witness to and dismantle the system of anti-black violence upon which their capitalist economy depends. At this long-overdue moment of global reckoning, it is more imperative than ever for white people to examine how our failure to see and feel the moral horror of systemic racism is essential to its reproduction, and the way in which we do perceive and "make sense" of the world allows us to defer the fact of this system *as the condition of our ability to be white.* White people who are newly devoted to anti-racist action cannot become 'woke' through liking a meme or participating in a protest, but I am hopeful that the current climate may lead many white people to take hip-hop *more seriously* as a form of art that can interrupt and expose patterns of sense-making in the dominant discourse as "non-sense" that serve to obfuscate and perpetuate anti-black genocide.

For the past year I have been teaching Jewish studies in the philosophy department at Dalhousie University in Halifax, Nova Scotia, and I am preparing to apply for permanent residency in Canada. Now that it is unclear if or when I will return to the United States, I feel an even greater need to express my appreciation for those who have supported me and my work during the turbulent and horrifying events that have transpired since the 2016 U.S. presidential election.

First and foremost, I am grateful to my parents, Stacy and Robert Skitol, for their infinite patience in raising and supporting a daughter who was often contentious, angry, depressed, and pure *Davka*. I hope that this book helps to explain—in part—how my mood was affected by what I was learning from hip-hop; or rather, how hip-hop started a process of reckoning with the reality of my country that was founded on and organized by a system of exploiting and destroying black communities, and reckoning with how I benefited from this system. I am so grateful for your unconditional support and love even (and especially) when it was hard to understand me.

The idea for this book first occurred when I was talking about my love of hip-hop to my friend Martin Shuster, and he said, "So when is the book coming out?" I laughed and said, "Yeah that'd be cool." A couple of months later he texted me: "Yo how's the book on hip-hop going?" Martin's expectation that I would write this book, and his view that it had to be written for the sake of our field, was the stimulus for the entire project. For he is both a brilliant scholar and my close friend, and I didn't want to disappoint him or continue to defer his question with lame excuses. Martin's faith in me and the philosophical importance of this project gave me the initial confidence to write up a proposal, and I could not have finished the text without his constant support and friendship. Love ya, man.

Further, I would not have been in a position to write this book, able to draw on my experiences with hip-hop culture, without the wisdom, friendship, support, and love from my crew who often accompany me to presentations about my work at universities and conferences. I don't know who I would be right now without the love and wisdom of BL Shirelle, DonChristian Jones, J. Remedy, Bates, Kourtney Harris, and Kelo. I am equally indebted to the women I was honored to meet when I taught classes at the State Correctional Institution for women in Muncy, Pennsylvania, especially Cynthia Alvarado and Heather Thomas. I am a better person because of my friendship with these beautiful, brilliant women; the fact that they are serving life sentences (or have been sentenced to die-in-prison) ought to provoke moral horror and the will to dismantle the prison industrial complex. The fact that they are but two of the millions of victims of our penal system indicates the extent to which our criminal justice system produces and re-produces profane travesties of justice.

I am also indebted to my colleagues and close friends Al Frankowski and Michael Thomas, for their help in framing and thinking-through my ideas about the philosophical value of hip-hop. My argument in this text draws from their groundbreaking scholarship and our dialogue at conferences and concerts, as well as over email correspondence and long phone conversations about art, racism, and academic philosophy. Al's book on *The Post-Racial Limits of Memorialization: Toward a Political Sense of Mourning* (Lexington, 2015) was particularly essential in providing the aesthetic conception of sensibility and its limits that frames my argument about the existential value of underground hip-hop. While I was writing this book, Michael was also writing a book chapter about the singular genius of Kendrick Lamar ("Sensibility in Section 80: Kendrick Lamar's Poetics of Problems"), and our long conversations about hip-hop provided me with a constant source of inspiration and motivation to finish this text. Thank you, Al and Michael, for your enduring support and commitment to our philosophical work together. You have helped me become the academic I have always wanted to be.

I am also so grateful to the students who I taught in my course on "Philosophy and Hip-Hop" at Susquehanna University, who showed me the power and promise of rap music in a course devoted to exploring the philosophy of race and political theory through a study of the aesthetic form and content of underground hip-hop. Every single class was transformative for us as we listened to and discussed specific songs that helped us *become better* at having difficult conversations about race and racism in a largely white, Christian, conservative town in rural PA. Their enthusiasm, intellectual curiosity, and openness to new—sometimes disconcerting—ideas in the history of hip-hop culture helped me feel a sense of purpose at the university and enhanced my insights about the pedagogical and moral importance of engaging underground hip-hop as a source of *philosophical* text and testimony. Further, this class always gave rise to a new controversy every time that it was taught, and my students went to great lengths to keep the class on the curriculum and push back against administrators who feared the white backlash of honoring the right to say Fuck tha Police more than they desired to understand the political and philosophical importance of honoring our right to say it.

I received important feedback about this project even before I drafted a proposal for a book from a wonderful workshop on "Trauma, Memory and Representation" organized by María del Rosario Acosta López at DePaul University on November 12–13, 2015, sponsored by Universidad de Los Andes, Department of Philosophy, and the Vincentian Endowment Fund at DePaul University. María was very generous to invite me to present my early work on trauma and hip-hop in an intimate workshop with esteemed scholars, and it proved pivotal to the trajectory of my research. At this workshop I was also fortunate to reunite with Cathy Caruth, who introduced me to trauma theory twenty years ago when I was a graduate student in her course on "Trauma and the Death Drive" at Emory University. This class certainly changed the course of my life, and I will be forever grateful to Cathy for her patience and even joy with my often contentious behavior in her class as I resisted the difficult truths she presented in a last-ditch effort to resist the loss of my comforting philosophical pretensions about reason and freedom. When I tried to apologize twenty years later at this conference on trauma, she replied, "Oh no I loved it! You took the class *seriously*." Thank you, Cathy, for seeing and hearing and guiding me.

The analysis of underground hip-hop is a curious project for mainstream academic philosophy, and I was concerned that I would not be able to find a publisher. From the very start I knew that I wanted George Yancy to be my editor, but when I submitted my proposal to Lexington Books, I had not yet met him. I did have occasion to meet him before the proposal was accepted, and his kindness only reinforced my hope that I could work with him and my fear that I wouldn't. George is the only prominent academic philosopher and public scholar I know who is unabashedly in love with hip-hop, and his early work on the theoretical and therapeutic value of hip-hop paved the way for this project. I did not have to convince him of the value of this book or defend this project as adequately philosophical. I am so, so grateful for George's unflagging support and encouragement and enthusiasm for this book, after a career in which I have consistently provoked controversy simply by drawing on testimony and texts from hip-hop culture. Thank you George, for your feedback and dialogue, support, and friendship.

I am also grateful for the support and friendship of Lewis R. Gordon, Paul C. Taylor, and Chike Jeffers, who I met while I was actively reading their groundbreaking work on race, racism, and black aesthetics as research for this project. Their enthusiasm for dialogue and patience with all of my questions, as well as their interest in hip-hop culture, provided me with all of the professional recognition that I needed to feel confident about writing this book. The field of philosophy is much better for their work, service, and scholarship, though in my view, it does not deserve or adequately appreciate them.

The term "Hip-Hop Nation" refers to those who identify with and gain strength from underground hip-hop culture and strive to live in accord with hip-hop ethics and politics. It also refers to our status as a nation within our nation that brings people together in an aesthetic space to live through and examine and resist the crisis of the present. I'm grateful to my friends in Hip-Hop Nation who text me all the new tracks and albums that I must listen to, who provide me with opportunities to talk and write about hip-hop, who call me on my shit and help me to keep it real, and who respect my love and admiration for Kanye West. I'm thinking of my hip-hop heads Jay Ijams, Matt Strohl, Alvin Santos, Dorota Glowacka, Elisa von Joeden-Forgey, and Jared Minori—some of my happiest moments in life have been spent listening to hip-hop with you.

This book was also made possible by the feedback I received from colleagues and students at academic conferences and universities where I was afforded opportunities to present my early research on philosophy and hip-hop. I am especially grateful to Jürgen Manemann for inviting me to give my first presentation on hip-hop at the exceptional and radical conference he organized in June 2015—"Stimmen der Stadt—HipHop-Botschaften"—at the Forschungsinstituts für Philosophie in Hannover, Germany. His early support and feedback on my presentation on "American Rap as Testimony to Genocidal Wounds" was essential to my ability to take myself and this project *seriously*.

I am grateful for all of the subsequent opportunities to share earlier versions of the chapters in this book: "Hip-Hop and Philosophy" (*Bucknell University Philosophy Symposia*, October 2015), "Hip-Hop as Philosophical Text and Testimony" (Dalhousie University, November 2016), "The Relation between Hip-Hop Studies and Hip-Hop Nation" (*Stay Woke: Using Hip Hop as a Tool for Consciousness Raising*, Stockton University, December 2017), "Hip-Hop and Holocaust Studies" (Goucher College, November 2017), "Can I Get a Witness? Hip-Hop as Philosophical Text and Testimony" (*Annual Meeting of the Canadian Philosophical Association*, Ryerson University, May 2017), "Philosophy and Hip-Hop" (*Philosophy Colloquium Series*, Vanderbilt University, October 2018), "Hip-Hop and the Apocalypse" (*Annual Meeting of the American Academy of Religion*, November 2019), "Reflections on Hip-Hop and Jewish Culture" (Dalhousie University, March 2020).

I am filled with gratitude for my new community in Halifax and the activists, scholars, artists, and hip-hop heads who welcomed me with open arms and hearts. They have also been essential to my ability to keep it together as a single mom in a new country so that I could complete and promote this book. I am especially grateful to the incomparable El Jones who—like a rap god—is the very model of activist-artist, hero, and sage who inspires me to become better and do more than I am doing for those who need it the most. I am thankful that Jim Spatz created the position of the Simon and Riva Spatz Visiting Chair of Jewish Studies at Dalhousie University that enabled me to move to Halifax, and for his support and friendship. I also need to give a shout-out to Harry Critchley, Asha Jeffers, Tiffany Gordon, Duncan MacIntosh, Taylor MacLeod-Warren, Clarisse Paron, Emily Pickett, Victoria Snow, Ryan Veltmeyer, Sobaz Benjamin, Gayle Quigley-Smith, Cory Bowles, Michale Earle, and Thai Bear for their support, friendship, and enthusiasm for working with me. Having a community here that wants me to succeed is not a small thing but everything—so thank you for being my new crew.

Introduction

It's Bigger Than Hip-Hop

As research for this book, I have interviewed hundreds of underground, unsigned rappers about their love of hip-hop, and at some point almost every rapper has stated—in an effort to help me understand what hip-hop *means*— "Hip-hop saved my life." And they almost always add: "No, literally. It literally saved my life." The power of hip-hop as a *culture* that supports a community that refers to itself as Hip-Hop Nation is also evident in two other iconic phrases of devotion and gratitude: "I am hip-hop" and "I do it for hip-hop."

All three of these phrases ("Hip-hop saved my life," "I am hip-hop," "I do it for hip-hop") have also served as the name of specific tracks in some of the thousands of hip-hop songs that are written *about* hip-hop, often personified as a rapper's lover or savior who he betrays at the cost of his freedom and redemption. As Nas puts it, "You say you want to rap, to this bitch you must commit."[1] Though it may appear derogatory to refer to hip-hop as a "bitch," here Nas suggests that rappers regard hip-hop as a "bitch" only because—like many strong women—her love is given only to those who honor specific moral and political commitments. This sub-genre of hip-hop about hip-hop has also served to situate the birth and history of Hip-Hop Nation in the context of the post-civil rights struggle for black liberation, and these tracks remind the fans that ultimately hip-hop is not "about" hip-hop, but instead about bearing witness to and resisting the infliction of anti-black violence in every social and political institution in the United States. Bearing witness to anti-black violence is the sacred duty of Hip-Hop Nation because the *systemic* nature of this violence is obfuscated, normalized, and disavowed in the media, political discourse, and educational system. As Dead Prez chants over and over again in their acclaimed song "Hip-Hop": "It's Bigger Than Hip-Hop."[2]

My aim in writing this book is to illustrate that hip-hop culture serves as a source of philosophical wisdom about the nature, politics, and consequences of anti-black violence in the United States, as well as a source of resistance against anti-black violence in the city and the cell. As one Latina woman explains in a letter to me from a state prison in PA where she is currently serving a life term, "Hip-hop is a gateway drug to freedom. An expression of heart. It releases the rage of disparities, the fear of failure, and the love that no one can break. It appears through rain, sleet or snow. It is everything that should have been. It makes a poor man feel rich, a jailed man feel free. It is everything that we need. Hip-hop is the epitome of everything, and anything you are. I love hip-hop. From da bricks to da sticks."

Although hip-hop studies is now an established, interdisciplinary field that explores the political, ethical, aesthetic, linguistic, religious, cultural, historical, and global dimensions of hip-hop as music and culture, it is still difficult—if not impossible—for most academics to take hip-hop seriously as a source of evidence to support or critique philosophical, epistemological, and political theories about the nature and logic of anti-black violence in the United States. However, if our aim is to create theory that can inform revolutionary praxis, then the refusal to grant hip-hop any value as a source of wisdom or resistance against anti-black racism is a grave and lethal mistake. While American academics debate the possibility of agency and resistance in a structurally racist society that is discursively and aesthetically represented as a "post-racial" democracy that guarantees the same freedoms to all citizens, they ignore the political importance of underground hip-hop that already serves as a vital source of resistance against the harms inflicted by institutional practices of violence in the U.S. criminal punishment and educational systems that target entire black communities *as such*. In accord with the argument presented by Adam Burgos in his text *Political Philosophy and Political Action: Imperatives of Resistance* (2016), political theory should take its cue from already existing political practices of popular resistance rather than consider the abstract possibility of agency "as such."[3] The women I have met in prison and the underground rappers I have spoken with testify to the power of hip-hop to provide a psychic space of resistance against the logic of anti-black destruction operative in our social, economic, and political institutions.

For many people, hip-hop has also served to expose and disturb the willful ignorance and moral indifference to black suffering that are defining features of white sensibility or how we are conditioned to think, feel, imagine, and see black people in America. The revolutionary potential of hip-hop helps explain the public and political outcry that it provoked in the 1980s and that continues today through the demonization of rappers in the media and legal efforts to criminalize the production and dissemination of hip-hop.[4] Hip-hop artists have never been protected by the First Amendment because rap music does not "appear" to be a form of art to many politicians, judges, activists, and law enforcement officers who "hear" the lyrics of black artists that testify to their un-natural vulnerability to state violence *as* a series of confessions of criminal intent against police officers that incite and contribute to this violence. This was the reasoning provided by the Federal Bureau of Investigation when they sent a letter in 1989 expressing their disapproval of the song "Fuck Tha Police" by the group N.W.A. to Priority Records, the company that distributed their music.[5] The letter, authored by Milt Ahlerich, then the Assistant Director of the Bureau's Office of Public Affairs, marked the first time that the F.B.I. had ever taken a position on a work of art. Shortly after the letter was sent, the F.B.I arrested the members of N.W.A. on obscenity charges after they performed "Fuck Tha Police" at the Joe Louis Arena in Detroit.

Since the 1989 letter and arrest of N.W.A., the legal system has found a variety of ways to criminalize the production of hip-hop music, most notably in criminal cases involving the prosecutorial use of rap lyrics as evidence in trials to prosecute and convict black men. These cases depend on the mis-representation of rap lyrics that testify to the violent, anti-black consequences of our social and legal practices *as* true confessions of the intent to commit crime and as a directive to others to commit the crime. This gross mis-perception indicates that the inability to hear rap music is closely related to the inability to see black men as artists, which illustrates how the limits of white sensibility produce cognitive distortions that perpetually reinforce those limits.

This legal practice that sends black men to prison for making art rests on a collective or shared distortion of sensibility *about* these men that also depends upon a refusal to hear the music and testimony that contests this very sensibility. However it also testifies to the enduring threat of hip-hop culture to the white establishment. In a perverse and ironic example, while I was completing the first draft of this book in the Spring of 2019, the Supreme Court declined to review a case from 2014 in which the Pittsburgh rapper Jamal Knox ("Mayhem Mal") was convicted and sentenced to two to six years in prison on "terroristic threats" over his song "Fuck the Police"—written with explicit reference to the N.W.A. song.[6] In a concerted effort to persuade the court to review the case, a group of prominent hip-hop artists submitted a legal brief to the Supreme Court in March 2019 and a "primer on rap music and hip-hop" to try to persuade the court to hear the appeal, in which they state that Knox's song is "a work of poetry . . . not intended to be taken literally, something that a reasonable listener with even a casual knowledge of rap would understand."[7]

Though Knox has repeatedly appealed the 2014 conviction by invoking his right to free speech protected by the First Amendment, the Pennsylvania

Supreme Court stated that it ultimately found the song's lyrics to be a "true threat"—a category of speech not protected by the Constitution—and the Supreme Court appeared to agree. In this book, I will attempt to explain this threat in terms of the power of hip-hop as a form of aesthetic practice and political resistance and explain how the criminalization of hip-hop indicates just how much is at stake in excluding and not-hearing the distinct form of poetic testimony offered in the intricate and multi-layered verse of underground rap songs. From the start, the production of hip-hop is judged to be a criminal act because it exposes the criminal enterprise of our racial democracy and the lethal operation of white sensibility through poetic testimony that affects the emotions rather than simply appeals to the intellect.

In 1988 Public Enemy released its widely acclaimed album *It Takes a Nation of Millions to Hold Us Back*, with a track titled "Caught, Can We Get a Witness?"[8] The song co-opts this question, and the method of call and response, from the African American church, which then provides the cultural context in which the question is asked. Since the release of this track the phrase "Can I get a witness?" has appeared in countless rap songs and was also the title of a song released in 1993 by Run-D.M.C.[9] Why did this phrase gain so much currency in rap music? Why is it a question that rappers feel must be asked again and again in relation to the testimony they offer? What type of testimony is offered in hip-hop, and what does it mean to "bear witness" to rap music? I will address these questions in the effort to argue that hip-hop culture has always served as an important source of text and testimony about anti-black racism in the United States, despite the relative neglect of hip-hop by scholars in the field of philosophy. As text and testimony, as testimony and art, hip-hop can affect our sensibility rather than simply our understanding of the everyday varieties of anti-black violence inflicted through the social, economic, educational, and political institutions in the United States.

When underground rappers ask, "Can I get a witness?" they are asking that those who listen to their songs do more than simply enjoy them. Like the preacher, the rapper demands that his audience hears and responds to his testimony, and aims to *agitate* and *stimulate* his audience to action.[10] This is in accord with the tradition of black aesthetics that, as explained by Paul C. Taylor in his book *Black Is Beautiful: A Philosophy of Black Aesthetics*, has not usually been a matter of "art for art's sake," for "it could not afford to be."[11] Instead the tradition of black aesthetics "exists as a cultural phenomenon and as a subject of philosophical study because of political conditions."[12] The question "Can I get a witness?" is both a political demand that we *see* the systemic and brutal infliction of anti-black violence as the counter-part and underbelly of our American democracy and a moral demand that we give a shit about eradicating the predictable and entirely preventable forms of state violence that undermine the wellbeing of entire black communities. Until white Americans can feel the moral horror of systemic racism, even and especially at the cost of their certainty and complacency, rappers will not get a witness.

However their love of hip-hop is based, in part, on its power to disrupt our sensibility and our presumption to understand the American present so that we can better feel moral horror at the everyday, state-sanctioned infliction of lethal violence against black communities *as such*. Against the popular view that racism is a problem of ignorance that can be overcome with greater knowledge and better education, Tupac Shakur explained that the problem of systemic anti-black violence is that "They don't give a fuck about us." Shakur is right, insofar as the problem regards a fundamental lack of empathy and respect for black citizens.[13] And yet in the form and content of his song titled, "They Don't Give a Fuck About Us," it is possible to feel the disjunction between what we already know—or the everyday police and civilian violence against black citizens *as* black citizens—and what we ought to *feel* in relation to this knowledge. In the last hook of the song, Shakur sings: "They wanna see us die/They kick us every time we try/'Cause they don't give a fuck about us,'" and then implores his audience to "Rise, rise."[14] From its birth, hip-hop has provided a space and the means to feel anger and sorrow about the systemic destruction of black lives, and so a space that acts as the emotional register for the horror of the present, able to affect our sensibility about the American past, present, and future.

What do I mean by "our sensibility about the American past, present, and future?" When I refer to our sensibility, I am referring to the general framework by which we see, feel, and remember our experiences, as well as our general orientation toward and perception of the society in which we live. As black existentialist philosophers such as W. E. B. Du Bois, Franz Fanon, and James Baldwin have illustrated, our perception, memory, and imagination are not somehow "neutral" capacities for the representation of our experiences but instead operate in accord with our racialization so that "white sensibility" serves to reinforce the ideological assumptions and feelings necessary to sustain, affirm, or ignore the subordination and systemic violence inflicted against black citizens. The point is *not* that all white people are proudly racist or consciously hate black people; rather as Du Bois explains in his acclaimed work *The Souls of Black Folk*, white citizens see black citizens only through a veil that inevitably reinforces their own perception of current events in order to assure themselves of their own innocence and moral integrity.[15] Du Bois explains that in order for white people to sustain this sort of moral certainty and emotional indifference toward the violence inflicted on black bodies for the sake of their own economic and political supremacy, they perceive black people as *a problem* that is unrelated to their own being-in-the-world. Du

Bois does not suggest that we can lift the veil, but the power of his writing indicates that it is possible to pierce the moral apathy that is so often a degenerating symptom of white sensibility.

Again, when I refer to our "sensibility," I am not only referring to what we consciously sense but to the general framework that makes sensing and interpreting the world around us possible in the way that we do. In the field of aesthetics, many critical race theorists identify the contours of white, neoliberal sensibility as sustaining an in-sensitivity to black suffering or the *absence* of moral dread and horror about anti-black state violence.[16] When I refer to our "neoliberal sensibility," I am not referring to the support of any particular economic policy but the general *stance* toward the problem of anti-black violence as one that can be solved through legal and economic reforms, understood as an occasional and tragic by-product of a more racist era that we haven't fully overcome. The neoliberal support for civil rights is incompatible with the neoliberal support for our structurally racist capitalist economy, but it is reconciled by the refusal to see or think of anti-black violence as a *system* that is inflicted in the everyday exercise of the law rather than through the imperfect application of the law. The neoliberal sensibility that defers the reality of *systemic* anti-black violence in order to remain complacent about the racist distribution of power and capital is closely related to our *post-racial sensibility* that historicizes the political oppression of African Americans as a problem of our distant past, overcome in the present. The neoliberal and post-racial stances toward our social reality provide part of the framework for a white sensibility that "reads" and "interprets" the facts in a way that minimizes the harm and extent of anti-black violence and obfuscates its structural importance to American politics in the past and present.

In this sense, the philosophical discussion of white sensibility and anti-black racism is not a discussion about whether certain individuals or texts are racist, nor is it a discussion about the political leanings or activism of any particular scholar or politician. Critical race theorists are often misinterpreted as claiming that every white person is willfully racist or a white supremacist in his heart or mind.[17] These misunderstandings are suspect because they allow critics to defer the larger problem of how our racialization creates limits as to what can be seen or imagined that is central to the economy of anti-black violence. The discussion about the limits of our sensibility also assumes the post-modern perspective that we lack an Archimedean point for any sort of "objective" sensibility that is not already informed by the specificity of our gender, race, class, sexuality, and abilities.[18]

My use of the term "white sensibility" refers to the *product* of the dominant discursive and epistemological practices that undergird and justify the racist organization of power and capital so that it *appears* to make sense. Charles Mills refers to this discursive system as "the epistemology of ignorance," which he identifies as a feature of "the racial contract"—the moral, political, and epistemological agreement between whites that undergirds the social contract and gives rise to global white supremacy.[19] Mills explains that the "epistemology of ignorance" refers to a "pattern of localized and global cognitive dysfunctions (which are psychologically and socially functional)" that collectively comprise a "cognitive model that precludes self-transparency and genuine understanding of social realities," and undergird the "cognitive and moral economy psychically required for conquest, colonization, and enslavement."[20] His account reveals that ignorance is not simply the absence of knowledge but a shared practice between white people, sustained by a self-perpetuating system of assumptions, ideas, logics, and beliefs that are also the terms in which we perceive, remember, and imagine our experience.

The patterns of thought that produce "cognitive dysfunctions" that are functional-for being-white also rest on the exclusion of other accounts and beliefs that throw them into question, and so white sensibility is also sustained by the *refusal* to ask specific kinds of questions or analyze taken-for-granted assumptions and, at a group level, more active attempts to rewrite commonly held histories.[21] For example, in the academic field of genocide studies—based on the comparative analysis of different genocidal systems—scholars have never considered the genocidal logic of chattel slavery or included a discussion about the institution of American slavery in any historical genealogy of genocide in western politics.

With my co-author Alfred Frankowski, I have presented and published work in this field that illustrates how this default exclusion of American slavery from the concern of genocide scholars is rationally indefensible and yet never *appears as an exclusion* to be defended.[22] And our personal experiences sharing this work with our white, male colleagues in the field have indicated just how determined certain genocide scholars are to sanction their *refusal* to think about anti-black violence by regarding it as a sort of moral imperative, conveyed by their *ad hominem* attacks on our work. For example, I have personally been told that the very *idea* we are proposing—or the need to consider how the exclusion of anti-black violence from our conception of genocide serves the epistemology of white ignorance—indicates that I do not respect "professional standards" of research and that I lack in "moral integrity." I am also regularly accused of "trashing" the reputations of scholars who have always been devoted to civil rights and whose work has been essential to raising awareness about the global problem of genocide. Indeed these experiences have only reinforced my view that it is not possible to question or expose the limits of white sensibility in the terms of the dominant discourse, and requires, instead, an aesthetic stimulus for the interruption of sense-making that momentarily disrupts the totalizing hold of this discourse on sensibility.

When I refer to the "dominant discourse" I am not just referring to a set of false beliefs that are essential to white sensibility, but the norms that govern discourse as a whole in public, private, and professional spaces of our racial democracy. The norms that govern discourse between white people play an essential role in defining them as the group that they are, in shaping their self-awareness, in directing group members' interactions with other in- and out-group members, and in sustaining their dominance over and against other social groups. On Mills's account, according to Linda Martín Alcoff, white racism functions as "a type of subjectivity that forms patterns of perceptual attentiveness and supplies belief-influencing premises that result in a distorted or faulty account of reality."[23]

The epistemology of ignorance that produces the white sensibility of our American social reality such that it makes "sense" as a functional democracy also rests on presumptions regarding the credibility of other epistemic agents, so that those who are not-white are not viewed as credible or trustworthy, and their discursive objections to patterns of white ignorance can be ignored and excluded from the dominant discourse. The operation of the epistemology of ignorance and the role it plays in the production of white sensibility and the economy of anti-black violence indicate that discursive practices will continue to serve as the central means by which white people propose, communicate, evaluate, and legitimize claims and perceptions to perpetuate larger patterns of what Kristie Dotson refers to as "pernicious ignorance"; social (mis) understandings that perpetually defer awareness of the moral cost of their whiteness, or the genocidal violence against black communities that sustains the material conditions for white economic and political supremacy.[24]

If we can't lift the racist veil through which we perceive, remember, recall, and imagine our experiences, we can nevertheless acknowledge that what Du Bois referred to as the "color line" creates real limits as to what white people can understand about being-black in the United States. As a hip-hop head this is not confusing or controversial to me, but as a white, academic woman raised in a bourgeois Jewish family, I am also aware of how difficult it is to act and speak and think in the light of this truth, mindful of the real limits to my sensibility and knowledge—no matter how much I study critical race theory or how much I love hip-hop.

However in my classes and at academic conferences, I am also privileged to be able to bear witness to the power of underground hip-hop to disrupt the calm certainty of white sensibility and create a space in which to *feel* the moral horror of the racist present; in my experience white people can feel empathy for racialized "others" only when they can admit and feel the limits of their own knowledge and perspective about race and society. Indeed, the frequent refusal of white people to suspend any self-certainty regarding their understanding and perspective of anti-black racism—repeatedly reinforced by their refusal to take seriously black testimony or works by black scholars and artists—supports the uncritical performance of anti-black racism that George Yancy refers to as being "ambushed" by the unexplored layers of one's whiteness.[25]

The white refusal to acknowledge the limits of white sensibility is especially acute in academia, and in particular in the field of philosophy that is still largely informed by a cannon of dead white men who claimed to profess universal truths about the mind, soul, Justice, and the Good, taught in universities in which these "truths" still serve to obfuscate and perpetuate systems of oppression that serve to benefit white, straight, able-bodied rich men at the expense of everyone else. And I have found that in the academic world, hip-hop can serve as an aesthetic intervention against the totalizing claims of white sensibility. For example, when I present my research on the ethics and politics of hip-hop at academic conferences, there is almost always a white man present who will proclaim before I begin to speak: "This talk should be interesting as I've never listened to hip-hop. I just don't like hip-hop." In response, I ask him: "Does it make sense for someone to say 'I've never listened to rock-and-roll, I just don't like rock-and-roll?'" He will admit that he can't imagine someone hating the entire genre of music. I will then say something like, "In my view, your refusal to listen to hip-hop indicates a refusal to take seriously the testimony of young black men and women describing the varieties of their everyday un-natural vulnerability to torture and death."

In these frequent exchanges my aim is to draw attention to the general sensibility that supports the refusal to listen to hip-hop, a sensibility informed by un-natural limits as to what can be perceived or heard as music *worth listening to*. Similarly, when I cite the testimony of prisoners and rappers as evidence to defend the need for a more expansive understanding of genocide and genocidal violence, I am often told by a white man that their testimony "doesn't matter" as it does not pertain to the *academic* discussion about the nature of genocide and does not "count" as evidence. In response there is very little I can say, as the absolute refusal to grant any value or relevance to the testimonies and experiences of black men and women in a discussion about the genocidal harms inflicted by state violence against racialized groups as such is not a rational decision but a refusal central to white ignorance and moral indifference—a refusal produced and re-produced by the frame and limits of white sensibility.

When I was told by a cousin of mine at Passover—the Jewish holiday that celebrates liberation from slavery and systemic state oppression—"I just don't like hip-hop, and I don't want to listen to a bunch of thugs talking about being thugs," I heard another iteration of this refusal that serves to reinforce his in-sensitivity and indifference to the testimony and plight of black citizens in his own country. And this refusal reinforces the perception of black citizens *as a problem* in an otherwise free and just society—a problem unrelated to his own white way of being-in-the-world.

And yet, just as frequently as I hear this refusal, I also witness the power of hip-hop to make this refusal uncomfortable and disrupt the complacency with which it is stated and performed. For those white academic men who were at first so comfortable declaring their general dislike of all hip-hop are also those folks who are usually the most affected by listening to a few tracks in the course of my presentation and afterward will usually approach me to ask for a few playlists of underground hip-hop they can use in the classroom. Experiences like these have convinced me that hip-hop culture can affect white sensibility toward the state system of anti-black violence and the victims of this violence far better than an academic book or newspaper article about the racist nature of the criminal justice system. Even more, hip-hop is far more effective than the typical "dialogue on race" often sponsored by universities and the media in which the participants more often than not simply double-down on their ideological assumptions and defensive posture characteristic of so many white citizens ("I'm not racist!") that serves to reinforce a *post-racial sensibility* about the United States, which consigns administrative, systemic anti-black racism to a problem of the past, overcome in the present.[26]

This post-racial sensibility supports the cognitive and moral blindness to the pervasiveness of anti-black violence that allows for its normalization in the legal and judicial systems and, in fact, every major institution and industry in the United States. This is the theme of so many underground rap songs, which as a whole testify to the fact that the American pursuit of Justice has always been organized to support white supremacy through the systemic infliction of anti-black violence. Even more, rappers illustrate that the historical repetition of this violence is made possible, in part, by our refusal to hear the testimony of the traumas suffered from a system of anti-black genocide. Indeed, the persistent mis-representation of *traumatic violence* inflicted against black communities as isolated episodes of *tragic violence* suffered by individuals indicates that it is not possible to testify to anti-black genocide in a discourse that has always been post-racial or has always served to consign systemic racism to a problem of the American past. Hip-hop acts as a traumatic rupture in the language that can "make sense of" the reality of American anti-black genocide only through its dis-articulation in the dominant or "professional" discourse. I use the term "dis-articulation" to indicate that these misinterpretations of the nature and cause of anti-black violence are not random or innocuous misstatements but instead emerge from and support the contours of post-racial sensibility and white complacency about state violence against black communities. In its cultural genesis, hip-hop emerged as a new form with which to expose and resist this discursive violence that perpetuates and obfuscates the systemic, lethal harms inflicted by American institutions and policies that undermine the social vitality of black communities and their intergenerational bonds.

Hip-hop burst onto the music scene in the 1980s, just as our politicians lay the groundwork for the prison-industrial complex through the guise of a new "War on Drugs" that targeted black men. This "war" received greater funding and public support after the white house and media incited panic about the use of crack-cocaine in low-income, inner-city neighborhoods. At the same time, Ronald Reagan identified "welfare queens" and "criminals" as largely responsible for the ills of black communities. Rap music was born as a form of counter-testimony about the nature and source of the suffering of African Americans and drew on African traditions of music as well as earlier genres of African American music in creating the novel genre of hip-hop that is based on the skills of the DJ (sampling and scratching) and the MC (who spits pre-written bars or freestyles his poetry-in-motion). Though hip-hop is now a global phenomenon, in this text, I will focus on the nature and history of the underground scene in the United States—with which I'm most familiar—in order to heed the hip-hop injunction to "know where I'm from" and "represent" for my community. For this reason, my focus on hip-hop as a source of wisdom about specifically anti-black violence emerges from the roots of American underground hip-hop in black culture and black communities as a form of testimony and empowerment.

Rap music is only one aesthetic expression of hip-hop culture, which also incorporates distinct forms of visual art (graffiti and fashion), as well as dance (breakdancing), a language (referred to as "Hip-Hop Nation Language" by the sociolinguist H. Samy Alim[27]), ethics, and political theory. This text draws on "underground" as opposed to "commercial" hip-hop, even though these have always been contested terms in the culture and in hip-hop studies. In my view these should remain contested terms, as part of hip-hop culture is the ongoing collective examination and debate about what it means "to be" hip-hop or "keep it real" rather than "sell out" and abandon the tenets of hip-hop for the sake of commercial success. In fact, this perpetual reassessment of what it means to honor hip-hop culture is also the force behind so many "beefs" between rappers and the "diss tracks" they produce to explain and defend "real" hip-hop from commercially successful rap music that departs from the tradition of the underground.

The ongoing collective conversation about the past, present, and future of hip-hop is essential to hip-hop culture itself, and while we cannot perfectly define what it means to be "underground," we can agree that those who identify as underground believe that hip-hop carries and furthers a moral and political mission beyond itself, so that what provokes and inspires the production and dissemination of hip-hop is always "bigger than hip-hop." From its origins, hip-hop has served as an interruptive force that aims to make new sounds from the ceaseless interruption and disruption of soothing melodies; the "scratch" is incomprehensible in itself and instead represents the sound of interruption, the sound of the indecipherable. In this text I argue that in both form and content, underground hip-hop in the United States presents aesthetic depictions of the *traumatic* violence suffered from American anti-black genocide in order to counter the *tragic* depiction of black life central to the post-racial sensibility that supports white ignorance and indifference to the suffering of black communities.

Underground hip-hop is identified, in part, by a certain attitude toward the United States (embodied in Ice Cube's oft-repeated term *AmeriKKKa*), that is at once a protest and a politics of anxiety, and this sensibility produces specific commitments (critical analyses of American race and racism, prisoner advocacy, revolution).[28] There are three iconic phrases in underground hip-hop that, when taken together, inform the main argument of this text: "Can I Get a Witness?," "Claimin' I'm a Criminal," and "(But) You Don't Hear Me Tho." Taken together, these phrases signify that (1) the normalization of systemic racism is made possible by the discursive criminalization of black life (2) hip-hop is politically significant as a form of testimony about anti-black violence and (3) *the refusal to hear rap music as testimony* is complicit in the repetition of this violence. Underground rappers testify to the traumas of anti-black genocide that elude our discursive practices that *are informed by and reinforce a post-racial sensibility* that whitewashes the harm, continuity and severity of carceral torture, police brutality and our racist economy.

Underground hip-hop has always served to contest the standard, romanticized narrative of American democracy and progress with phenomenological accounts of the varieties of anti-black violence on which our system depends and the distinctly genocidal harms they inflict. Underground rappers testify to the racist state violence that still supports the hegemonic order of white male supremacy that requires the gratuitous suffering of black citizens to preserve itself, and it is this *systemic, lethal, and entirely preventable* suffering of black communities that our politicians would rather not confront or address. Instead of acknowledging the trauma of being-black in America, targeted for destruction, our politicians characterize every police murder of a black citizen as a singular tragedy, an exception to the norm of a Just Justice system.

As both text and testimony about systemic anti-black violence, hip-hop identifies itself as a form of resistance against the dominant discursive practices that both obfuscate and rationalize this violence. As put in the song "Conspiracy" by Gang Starr: "They want to send us to war and they want to ban rap/What they really want to do is get rid of us blacks."[29] Hip-hop interrupts those narratives and discursive practices that allow us to disavow the excessive state violence against black Americans as the "exception" to the rule of an otherwise free and democratic system. As Gang Starr puts it in the next bar of the song: "Genocide is for real and I hope that you're hearing me/you must be aware to combat the conspiracy." For this reason, I argue that hip-hop—in both content and form—can act as an aesthetic intervention to disrupt *post-racial sensibility* and then interrupt the *sense* of post-racial discursive practices.

Although the American media has judged the sub-genre of "gangsta rap" to glorify the grisly conditions of life in the urban ghetto and American prisons, one of its earliest and most celebrated writers is the rapper-turned movie star and producer Ice Cube, who first conceived of his work as "reality rap" rather than "gangsta rap." As portrayed in the movie *Straight Outta Compton*—produced by Ice Cube and Dr. Dre—early rap about the negative conditions in inner cities and their existential toll on African Americans was the first form of popular culture to insist that Black Lives Matter.[30] This genre represented a new call to arms against the status quo of racist oppression through, first, *aesthetic resistance* against the invisibility of systemic, anti-black violence in the media and dominant discourse.

Departing from a concern that has always been expressed by politicians and judges, I do not think that all so-called gangsta rap glorifies "criminal" behavior or black victimization, but I do think this term has been wielded as one type of weapon with which to attack and undermine the sacred mission of underground hip-hop to confront the underbelly of American democracy as the infliction of anti-black genocide—that upon which it depends, normalized through discursive practices that criminalize and demonize black bodies, as well as represent racist oppression as a problem of the distant past. For over thirty years, underground rappers have exposed and analyzed and coopted these discursive practices, and many have done so, in part, for the sake of political resistance against white ignorance and moral indifference to American anti-black genocide.

There is already a significant amount of scholarly work in hip-hop studies about the relation between hip-hop and black culture, hip-hop and the post-civil rights struggle for black liberation, and the therapeutic importance of hip-hop for black citizens and communities in the United States.[31] In the introduction to a volume of interdisciplinary essays about hip-hop as therapeutic practice (edited by Susan Hadley and George Yancy), George Yancy writes: "Rap music's valorization and encouragement of oral facility and storytelling provide a powerful impetus for finding one's voice, making sense of one's own narrative."[32] From my own perspective and experience of how hip-hop can affect white sensibility, I argue that the form and content of hip-hop can serve to disrupt the ability to "make sense" of the American present through tragic narratives that reinforce moral apathy and indifference to the suffering of black communities.

For those who suffer from the infliction of systemic anti-black violence, hip-hop is the only form of popular culture that testifies to the traumas suffered from being-black in America, thus—as Yancy explains—can help them to make sense of their experiences in a culture that otherwise obfuscates and disavows their reality. However for those who can make sense of their experience only through the post-racial narratives about the United States that reduce racism to a problem with specific, racist individuals in an otherwise free country, hip-hop can disrupt the totalizing hold of these narratives and the general sensibility that supports and produces them. In other words, hip-hop can act as a disruption in the ability of white citizens to reconcile themselves to the narratives that have always allowed them to "make sense" of their experience at the cost of moral apathy and willful ignorance about the suffering of black communities. This argument also rests on my larger claim that the form of hip-hop—based on the interruption, distortion, and co-option of beats, melodies, and lyrics—mirrors or evokes the form of post-traumatic stress disorder (PTSD), characterized by a set of symptoms (such as flashbacks of an earlier trauma) that signify the interruption of the present by the violence in the un-mastered past. The traumatic flashback recurs to the extent that the violence it bears witness to cannot be "understood" with our categories or reconciled with our narratives, and so returns to the extent that traumatic violence is excluded from discourse and memory. Before I provide an outline of my argument, it is important to clarify my view of hip-hop, as well as its connection to trauma and our sensibility of anti-black racism.

ON HIP-HOP AND THE EROTIC

In my effort to illustrate the relation between the form and content of underground hip-hop and the form and dynamic of traumatic violence, I am not claiming that traumatic experience is the source or "essence" of hip-hop as a genre of music with roots in African American culture.[33] Hip-hop, like every genre of music, is an expression of our erotic power, understood by Audre Lorde in her seminal essay on "Uses of the Erotic: The Erotic as Power," as "a resource within each of us that lies in a deeply female and spiritual plane, firmly rooted in the power of our unexpressed or unrecognized feeling. In order to perpetuate itself, every oppression must corrupt or distort those various sources of power within the culture of the oppressed that can provide energy for change."[34] For Lorde, the erotic is our deepest source of knowledge and feeling connected to the capacity for joy, integrity, and community, both productive and threatened by distortion and corruption.

In her essay Lorde inverts the traditional hierarchy between the mind and the body, thought and feeling in western philosophical thought by identifying the erotic as "the nurturer or nursemaid of all of our deepest knowledge."[35] Indeed the traditional hierarchy in western ethics that denies the moral worth of our feelings serves the patriarchal distortion and exploitation of the erotic as the pornographic and denigrates the source of that wisdom as "mere" body. For this reason, the expression and affirmation of the erotic are both personal and political, visceral, and cultural. Lorde explains:

> The erotic functions for me in several ways, and the first is in providing the power which comes from sharing deeply any pursuit with another person. The sharing of joy, whether physical, emotional, psychic, or intellectual, forms a bridge between the sharers which can be the basis for understanding much of what is not shared between them, and lessens the threat of their difference. Another important way in which the erotic connection functions is the open and fearless underlining of my capacity for joy. In the way my body stretches to music and opens into response, hearkening to its deepest rhythms, so every level upon which I sense also opens to the erotically satisfying experience, whether it is dancing, building a bookcase, writing a poem, examining an idea.[36]

Underground hip-hop culture is loved as a conduit for the erotic wisdom felt and expressed by those who flourish and feel joy despite their oppression, who can share something of their psychic and emotional state through spitting bars against the break-beat. Indeed one sense in which rappers mean that "hip-hop saved my life" is that it provides a form for the aesthetic expression of certain emotions that can then *find* expression and be shared and felt with-others. There is something distinct about the form and content of underground hip-hop that allows it to act as an emotional register of-and-against the present. The field of hip-hop studies testifies to the variety of ways in which we can appreciate the socio-political, religious, economic, and aesthetic value of hip-hop culture, which cannot in itself be reduced to one or another lens through which we assess its cultural importance.

In this text, my aim is to focus on just one way that the form and content of hip-hop emerge from and convey the emotional and aesthetic terrain of being-black in the United States, by focusing on hip-hop as the *aesthetic expression of traumas* that are mis-represented and dis-articulated in the popular discourse for the sake of sustaining our post-racial sensibility of anti-black violence as occasional, accidental, and tragic. With this focus on hip-hop and trauma, I mean to draw attention to one important aspect of hip-hop that accounts, in part, for its cultural and political role and the threat it poses to the white establishment. I argue that viewing hip-hop through the lens of traumatic experience (and its dis-articulation in tragic narratives) also helps explain the relation between hip-hop, sensibility, and resistance against anti-black racism.

ON HIP-HOP AND TRAUMA

The term "trauma" refers to both the distinctive type of physical and psychological violence that is inflicted against entire communities as such and the nature of the distinctive harm often suffered from being subject-to this violence or a set of symptoms that act as mis-placed reactions to the traumatic past and often preclude the ability to form healthy relationships in the present. These symptoms of PTSD include flashbacks to past episodes of traumatic violence, rage, hyper-vigilance, and patterns of self-destructive behavior.

As someone who studies and suffers from trauma, I have learned far more about how and why trauma recurs from my immersion in underground hip-hop culture than from trauma theory or counseling. Although the clinical practice of Eye Movement Desensitization and Reprocessing (EMDR)—a process of recollecting emotionally disturbing memories while simultaneously focusing on an external stimulus such as light or vibration or sound—was essential to my ability to find lasting relief from my symptoms, I will explain how this process was far easier and more intuitive for me to adopt as a hip-hop head. EMDR is currently the only clinical practice proved to help alleviate the symptoms of PTSD, but research also suggests that EMDR is helpful for the treatment of panic attacks, grief, dissociative disorders, disturbing memories, phobias, pain disorders, performance anxiety, stress, addictions, and personality disorders.[37]

In my experience with the final, "processing" stage of EMDR through which new insights help one to fundamentally re-orient oneself toward one's past, my self-reflection produced specific ideas about how hip-hop wisdom departed from and challenged the dominant scholarly and professional discourse about trauma. Further, my ability to heal actually depended upon questioning and displacing these dominant narratives which portray PTSD as an *individual* pathology suffered after an experience of excessive violence—a pathology that exposes our *inability* to adequately adapt to overwhelming circumstances. Departing from this view, underground rappers consistently portray trauma as a social pathology or a symptom of a pathological *system* that is produced by a contingent set of conditions that sustain a white supremacist organization of political and economic power. Through the form and lyrics of underground hip-hop, rappers illustrate that trauma is not simply a medical but a political problem and the symptoms of PTSD do not indicate an individual's weakness but rather serve as an indictment of our structurally racist society and the institutions that regularly inflict forms of violence to which no one should be subject and no one should adapt.

These insights also helped me to better understand another idea consistently conveyed by underground rappers, namely, that the mis-representation of trauma in media and discourse exacerbates the symptoms of PTSD and plays a role in its historical repetition. For this reason, the aesthetic depiction of trauma in hip-hop acts as an essential form of resistance against its invisibility and repetition. My love of hip-hop is connected to the role it has played in my ability to cope with and heal from past traumas, and this experience has provided me with a distinct vantage point from which to convey the distinctly post-traumatic wisdom that it offers; wisdom that is essential both to those who do and do not suffer from moral violations produced and re-produced by systemic forms of violence inflicted against racialized and gendered communities.

As previously cited, the edited volume on the *Therapeutic Uses of Rap and Hip-Hop* presents a wealth of empirical evidence to support the important therapeutic role that hip-hop can serve for youth from marginalized communities, unnaturally vulnerable to traumas inflicted by the very institutions tasked with their support and protection. This book is meant as a contribution to this discussion by focusing on how the aesthetic parallel between hip-hop and trauma also helps explain the therapeutic value of hip-hop and the distinct way it can affect our sensibility. Specifically, I will illustrate that underground hip-hop can act as a form of EMDR, modeled on the recollection of painful memories with sensory stimuli that allow us to re-orient ourselves toward the past and present. The ability of hip-hop to act as a form of EMDR also explains another sense in which we can understand the claim that "hip-hop (literally) saved my life," for suffering from PTSD often feels like one's life has been hijacked by patterns of behavior that one did not choose or sanction. Finding relief from the symptoms corresponds with the ability to break these patterns and carve out a life for oneself in the present that is not hijacked by fears produced by traumas suffered in the past. Lastly, I claim that the parallel between hip-hop and trauma also helps explain the political power of hip-hop and the consequent criminalization of rappers that supports the white refusal to hear them.

ON HIP-HOP AND WHITE SENSIBILITY

Though hip-hop can provide therapeutic value to those who suffer from trauma, it can also affect the sensibility of those who are conditioned to ignore, misinterpret and minimize the harms of systemic anti-black violence in order to protect their status as "white" by deferring their awareness of what this means in a structurally racist society. Thus the problem of "white sensibility" is not primarily a problem of false ideas but a problem of how white people learn to see and feel and read the world around them—how they *encounter* the world—to perpetually defer any "sense" of being-white in a white supremacist state. Thus our "sense" of ourselves is protected and reinforced by our aesthetic rather than rational encounter with the facts of the world.

When I use the term "white sensibility," I mean to draw attention to the larger aesthetic framework in accord with which we can "sense" and make sense of the world through which we interpret the facts of the world. Though we tend to regard the visual field as neutral or somehow the same for all, we know from the history of police brutality and police murders in the United States that this simply isn't true. In fact, part of the problem is that we deny that the visual field is racialized, so that when police officers claim they felt "threatened" by the black men and women who they murdered, this is somehow taken as evidence that their victims did pose a threat and so exonerates murderers and vilifies victims of state violence.

The terms of the dominant discourse often serve to hide the presence of our sensibility as a larger framework through which we "read" what we "see," and aesthetic works—which appeal to our emotions—are often successful in helping us detect it through provoking a certain dis-orientation of sense where we can't "understand" what we are hearing or seeing in accord with our conditioned sensibility-of-the-world. In addition to providing therapeutic value to those who suffer from the traumas of anti-black violence, I argue that the form of hip-hop—based on sampling, distortion, and re-signification—acts as a disruption of the dominant discourse and a site for the creation of subversive discursive practices that contest the white sensibility of our experience, or the ability to "make sense" of senseless violence. Drawing on work in cognitive psychology and music theory, I argue that this aesthetic disruption of white sensibility—through which we can feel or detect its presence—is connected to the capacity for enhanced empathy for black people and enhanced discomfort with the material and social terms of one's whiteness.

Underground rappers demand a "witness" to that which we cannot think or see past the limits of white sensibility that also determine the conditions of thought and perception and discourse that re-produce our emotional indifference and willful ignorance about anti-black violence. So how can we bear witness to that which we can't know, master, or see? For white people it means that we can bear witness to and admit the limits of our sensibility that is neither neutral nor universal. This type of witnessing occurs when hip-hop interrupts our "sense" of the American past and present and so disrupts our ability to "make sense" of the present; this disruption in our sense-making abilities also exposes the limits of our sensibility and often provokes some unease or horror about what these limits exclude, condone, and perpetuate. This is no small feat, as the disruption of white certainty and complacency can also check the refusal to grant any epistemic or moral value to the testimonies and experiences of racialized others. This, in itself, interrupts the totalizing hold of the dominant, anti-black discourse on the conditions of sensibility and thought.

So why is it so hard for hip-hop artists to get a witness? As underground rappers know, most people don't want to hear the testimony of the traumatized, and we come up with all kinds of "reasons" to refuse to listen. In the first part of this book, I draw on hip-hop as text to examine specific discursive practices common to white sensibility that serve to allow white people to perpetually defer awareness of their whiteness and thus the moral and human cost of their own privileges and opportunities. In the second part of this book, I draw on hip-hop as a testimony of traumatic violence to illustrate the political significance of hip-hop as a form of resistance against the genocidal logic of American racism.

In my own experiences in academia and in therapy, I have also encountered opposition to my efforts to incorporate testimonies of trauma into my work. For example, I have been told by therapists during sessions that some of my claims about my traumatic experiences were "too academic" or "too philosophical," at the same time that my academic career has suffered because it is not "philosophical" or "academic" to draw on hip-hop as evidence for my claims about state violence or cite the testimony of women in prison as a source of authority. Against this opposition, this book examines the philosophical significance of underground hip-hop culture as text and testimony about the traumas suffered from our system of anti-black racism. Already, this sentence doesn't "make sense" to philosophers who regard the study of trauma to be a psychoanalytic endeavor rather than a properly philosophical concern and/or do not regard an aesthetic practice to be a form of philosophy. I hope this text illustrates how these views—and the conception of "philosophy" on which they are based—emerge from and reinforce the dominant discourse that is organized around the exclusion, dis-articulation, and obfuscation of traumatic violence for the sake of sustaining the authority of white sensibility.

CHAPTER DESCRIPTIONS

Drawing from and adding to the literature on hip-hop as a form of political resistance against anti-black oppression, I argue in the first three chapters of this text that the form and content of hip-hop indicate its vital importance as a source of philosophical wisdom about the nature and logic of anti-black oppression:

Chapter 1: Know What I'm Sayin?

In the first chapter, I examine the relation between the dominant discourse and white sensibility, and how they operate in a way to impair the capacity for empathy for those who are not-white. Then I introduce the terms necessary to provide a preliminary analysis of how underground hip-hop operates as a form of discursive resistance and a vital source of phenomenology able to contest and disrupt the dominant post-racial and neoliberal narratives that are produced by and reinforce white sensibility.

I also draw attention to how the epistemic value of Hip-Hop Nation Language has been ignored by contemporary analytic philosophers who work on the problem of "epistemic injustice," a term coined by Miranda Fricker to describe the habit of viewing certain gendered and racialized individuals as "untrustworthy" or lacking in full epistemic integrity. These scholars also ignore the work of black existentialists who describe the psychological and existential dynamics of this form of social violence in their phenomenological essays on white sensibility and the white gaze. In their efforts to examine the habit of epistemic injustice in isolation of those texts written by black philosophers and artists who describe and suffer from this violence, analytic philosophers perform the same type of epistemic injustice that they aim to examine and rectify. Lastly, I argue that the academic refusal to hear hip-hop as a source of wisdom about the nature and logic of anti-black racism is a similar form of epistemic injustice that serves to support a white, neoliberal, and post-racial sensibility about the American present.

Chapter 2: Can I Get a Witness?

In the second chapter, I argue that the form and content of hip-hop evoke the form and symptoms of PTSD so that underground hip-hop—based on the co-option, distortion, and re-signification of beats, melodies, lyrics, and words—can be heard as an aesthetic depiction of the distinctly traumatic form of anti-black violence in the United States. The aesthetic depiction of the systemic and traumatic nature of anti-black violence in underground hip-hop conflicts with the discursive mis-representation of anti-black violence in the media and popular culture as the result of a series of individual, tragic accidents. In underground hip-hop, the masterful flows, novel rhyming schemes, ever-changing slang, and art of freestyling all work to supersede the white dis-articulation of anti-black violence through aesthetic creation. Finally, in this chapter I draw attention to how rappers depict the dis-articulation of black suffering in the dominant discourse as another form of social violence central to its repetition.

Chapter 3: Claimin' I'm a Criminal

In the third chapter, I argue that the form and content of hip-hop illustrate the distinctly genocidal character of anti-black racism in the United States, and illustrate that it depends upon the discursive and visual criminalization of black men. The consistent use of the term "genocide" in underground hip-hop lyrics to describe the system of anti-black violence in the United States can be understood as an effort to take up the mission of the now-defunct Civil Rights Congress (CRC), who presented a petition to the United Nations in 1951 that appealed to the (then recent) United Nations Convention on the Prevention and Punishment of the Crime of Genocide (ratified in 1948), in order to formally accuse the United States of genocide against black Americans.

At the time the CRC petition, titled *We Charge Genocide: The Crime of the American Government against the Negro People*, was ignored by the world community and has been largely ignored by Holocaust and genocide scholars. In this chapter I draw on earlier work with my colleague and co-author Alfred Frankowski to argue that the effort to sweep this potent historical event into the dustbin of history indicates the moral and political power of the term "genocide" as well as the anti-black *sensibility of genocide* that informs both academic and popular discussions about the history of genocide in western politics. In this context, the use of the term genocide in underground hip-hop both co-opts and re-signifies the term outside of the limits of white sensibility.

The distinct form of hip-hop music and culture accounts for its political importance as a form of resistance, and the subsequent chapters in this book examine the value of hip-hop as survivor testimony from the "underground," or as a testimony to the visceral, corporeal, and distinctly genocidal wounds suffered from our racial democracy. The testimony in hip-hop serves a therapeutic and a political role as an aesthetic practice that combines intellectual with sensory stimuli for the sake of recollecting individual and collective traumas in the past in order to re-enact and re-signify them from the subject position in the *present* as someone who survived-them. This practice aligns with the therapeutic practice of EMDR that also works through the combination of intellectual and sensory stimuli to create a form of recollection that leads to an entirely new orientation about how and why one suffered from the violence that allows for greater control over one's symptoms in the present.

PTSD is the only mental disorder caused by experience, rather than genetic inheritance, and its symptoms can be understood as reflecting the psychic wounds suffered from forms of social violence to which no one should be subject. As such, it is not really an individual pathology but a pathology of human society or the product of a pathological arrangement of social relations whereby the wellbeing of some depends upon the subordination and destruction of "others," through institutional practices and norms that leave entire communities marked by race and gender in a position of un-natural vulnerability to death and devastation. The clinical approach to PTSD that regards it as an individual pathology that reflects the failure of individuals to adapt to life-threatening situations treats the contingent conditions of racial and heterosexist oppression as "natural" or inevitable forms of violence and in this way de-politicizes and dis-articulates the cause, nature, and treatment of the disorder.

My view that underground hip-hop provides essential text and testimony about the traumatic experience that counters the clinical and theoretical approach to PTSD is the product of what I've learned from my own experiences as someone with this disorder, as a scholar who writes about genocide and trauma theory, and as a hip-hop head who can't get through the day without listening to some Pac and Wu and Lauryn Hill. I have struggled with the symptoms of PTSD in both the clinical and academic environments, and finally found some relief when I practiced EMDR for three years. This process coincided with greater awareness about the power and importance that hip-hop has always played in my ability to cope with my past, and a sharper understanding of how hip-hop—as practice, as theory—is able to testify to the systemic traumas excluded from our narratives and the media, as well as provide a path to better confront and recover from them. In fact, I didn't understand the deeper meaning of so many hip-hop songs that I had loved for 20 years until I was well into the process of EMDR. My point is not that hip-hop can cure PTSD, but that it presents a distinct form of traumatic testimony that disrupts those placid and professional and academic discourses about trauma and violence that actually misrepresent trauma and preclude our recovery as individuals and a nation. Thus in the last three chapters I examine the political and therapeutic value of hip-hop as a form of testimony:

Chapter 4: But You Don't Hear Me Tho

In the fourth chapter, I argue that since the form and content of hip-hop evoke the structure and symptoms of PTSD, it can function as a form of therapeutic practice and political resistance against the totalizing hold of white sensibility. The clinical treatment of PTSD makes use of a psychotherapy treatment called EMDR, in which the client initiates a process of recollecting emotionally disturbing memories while simultaneously focusing on an external stimulus. In this chapter I argue that underground hip-hop culture has also served as a form of EMDR, or an essential means with which to confront, recall, reinterpret and process past traumas suffered from our system of anti-black violence in order to better cope with and resist the ruthless repetition of traumatic violence still inflicted by the pathological conditions that sustain our racial democracy.

Further, the affinities between hip-hop and PTSD, rap music and EMDR, help explain why rappers depict the American system of anti-black violence as the return of the repressed trauma of anti-black *genocide* that recurs to the extent that it is rendered invisible by the discursive representation of

American history and democracy. Lastly, underground hip-hop illustrates that the refusal and/or inability to *hear* (as opposed to consume) the testimony of underground rappers is a symptom of our pathological attachment to black suffering.

Chapter 5: You Feel Me?

In the fifth chapter I draw on the psychological notion of "emotional contagion" to argue that as a form of poetic testimony, underground hip-hop can produce an aesthetic rupture in white sensibility that disrupts the ability to "make sense" of anti-black violence in post-racial or neoliberal terms that historicize and minimize the systemic, genocidal nature of this violence. This aesthetic rupture of sense-making opens a space in which to feel moral dread about anti-black state violence and the limits of one's own sensibility.

Chapter 6: Fuck Tha Police

There has always been a social and aesthetic interrelation between hip-hop culture and penal culture that informs the moral and political commitments of Hip-Hop Nation. In this final chapter I examine this interrelation in order to argue for the distinctly *philosophical* value of underground hip-hop as critical theory and anti-racist practice, based on its subversive production of "subjugated knowledges" that expose the *contingent* and *genocidal state of affairs* masked by our discourse and media in order to incite local ruptures in the power relations that sustain the systemic infliction of anti-black violence.

Although common themes are explored across chapters, my analysis of underground hip-hop as "text" in the first part of the book is more concerned with an analysis of specific insights from the culture that could significantly contribute to and/or change the current direction of scholarship in multiple fields, with particular emphasis on the disciplines of philosophy of race, trauma theory, and genocide studies. My analysis of hip-hop as "testimony" in the second part of the book is more concerned with the political value of American hip-hop as a means of resistance against neoliberal discursive practices that normalize state-driven, anti-black violence and so produce and reinforce white indifference or *in-sensitivity* toward the suffering of black people. This problem is particularly acute in academic discourse that is still modeled on a Kantian distrust of the emotional life, and so tends to deaden the senses and our capacity to *feel* moral horror about the regularity and brutality of state violence against black people *as such, even and especially* when the mainstream media covers a particular instance of police brutality or a recent police murder of an unarmed, young black man or woman as an isolated, tragic event.

As testimony, underground hip-hop can affect white sensibility or disturb the post-racial and neoliberal sensibility that cannot *see* or *feel* moral dread about American genocide in the past and present. At the same time, hip-hop serves as a vital source of "life-force" or provides the means to assess, critique, and oppose the routine, administrative infliction of anti-black violence in American culture (in the educational system, the health care system, the real estate industry, the government, the police force, the financial industry, the labor market, the criminal justice system), that together create a system of anti-black genocide that must be navigated, even if it cannot be escaped. Hip-hop artists also illustrate that the ability to navigate and survive a system that is organized around one"s destruction is a profound form of resistance against anti-black genocidal violence. In doing the research for this book, I came to understand more and more that hip-hop is a culture and a way of life, one that sustains and inspires the critical capacity and creative will to oppose a system designed for one's self-loathing, alienation, and destruction. This is another way to make sense of the frequent claim "hip-hop (literally) saved my life."

This book is primarily informed by my effort to illustrate the continued importance of the philosophical insights about race and racism that hip-hop artists have been conveying for three decades and that—if taken seriously as philosophical text—can open up new lines of inquiry in the fields of critical race theory, genocide studies, trauma theory, and political theory. To this end I examine how we as scholars can better bear witness to the testimony offered by underground rappers. However, I am equally concerned with our failure to bear witness to this testimony, so this book is also informed by the effort to examine how our own discursive practices, epistemic assumptions and neoliberal commitments have precluded our ability to hear (as opposed to enjoy or consume) the testimony of underground rappers. Through the analysis of specific underground rap songs and specific contributions of hip-hop culture, I argue that the failure of underground rappers to get a witness is related to the political threat posed by underground hip-hop as a form of resistance against the status quo, able to expose and disrupt the post-racial sensibility that undergirds the logic and repetition of anti-black genocidal violence in the present.

In the latter part of the book, I argue that the academic propensity to view hip-hop as *either* text *or* testimony has served the neoliberal co-option of hip-hop culture which pushes the focus of underground hip-hop—the material and political and social conditions that perpetuate American anti-black genocide—to the margins of thought. The ability to hear underground hip-hop as both text and testimony is necessary for its political function—or its ability to provoke the aesthetic dis-orientation in our thought and perception of the United States so necessary to pierce the colonizing force of our post-racial sensibility. In the Conclusion, "The Aesthetic Politics of Underground

Hip-Hop," I review the specific insights from underground hip-hop that depart from academic and popular discourses on racism, history, and trauma and review the distinct properties of hip-hop music, in order to more fully explain the political value of hip-hop or the threat that it poses to our white supremacist state that has always criminalized rappers in order to sanction the white refusal to hear them. Lastly, I detail some of my own "hip-hop interventions" in the academy and provide a selection of playlists of underground rap songs that illustrate the central themes of this text.

The importance of the aesthetic domain for political action should be all the more apparent in the political crisis of the American present when we are (mis)led by the reckless and temperamental desires of a petulant white man who flaunts his disrespect for truth and facts in order to promote the racist and heterosexist commitments responsible for his own political and economic success. Akin to life in an authoritarian regime, it is no longer possible to appeal to facts or ideals in the political domain in order to shape and critique public policy; instead, "The word of the Führer is Law."[38] For this reason political resistance also requires aesthetic interventions to shock our "common sense" and interrupt the ways that we "make sense" of the senseless horror unleashed by this dysfunctional, fascist administration. I am convinced that underground hip-hop serves as an essential aesthetic intervention against the lethal non-sense of the dominant political discourse, and it's my hope that more professors and policymakers take it more seriously as a source of wisdom and praxis.

METHODOLOGY

My work is informed by the testimonies of hip-hop artists and many of the women who I have met in prison. Many of these women are hip-hop heads, and I have also been fortunate to develop friendships with two talented MCs who I first met when they took my course on philosophy at the State Correctional Institution for Women in Muncy, Pennsylvania. Indeed, the idea for this book was made possible by my discussions with women in this prison, as they allowed me to see the connection between my life-long passion for hip-hop and my academic work on the logic and rhetoric of contemporary genocidal practices. These women also connected me to underground rappers in Philadelphia, central Pennsylvania and New York City who graciously spoke with me at length about their love of hip-hop and agreed to read and critique drafts of this manuscript.

As a hip-hop head who is also a white, Jewish, academic woman, I understand the importance of grounding my interpretation of hip-hop in the testimony of black artists who produce underground hip-hop as a means of resistance and survival. For this reason my analysis draws on testimonies and texts, and each chapter title is a phrase from Hip-Hop Nation Language relevant to the theme of the chapter. I often describe my contribution to hip-hop studies as "a work of translation," for the ideas that I examine originate in the underground, but my academic training allows me to translate the terms of Hip-Hop Nation Language in which they are expressed (and affect our sensibility) into a discourse that is more readily accessible for many professors with a personal and/or professional interest in hip-hop who lack any background in or familiarity with the music and culture. Hip-hop does not need or benefit from this process of translation, but I am appealing to an academic vocabulary in an effort to better get the attention and interest of scholars who have previously ignored and refused to listen to hip-hop. At times I have wondered if this project of translation is really all that valuable, for the point of my work is not to encourage people to read about hip-hop but instead to *hear it* and gain a greater appreciation for the aesthetic genius and political importance of the genre. However, I have been told by so many rappers and prisoners who have read my work that this act of translation is also meaningful for them, and they appreciate and enjoy the effort to bring these two worlds together.

My methodology departs from the approach taken by Jim Vernon in his recent text *Hip Hop, Hegel, and the Art of Emancipation: Let's Get Free* (2019), which describes the historical significance of hip-hop in terms of George Wilhem Hegel's philosophy of art and his meta-narrative of aesthetic creation and its essential relation to human emancipation. He explains that his aim "is to use Hip Hop to isolate and defend the core and enduring thesis of Hegel's theory of art, precisely in order to use that thesis to articulate, amplify, and philosophically comprehend the voices of Hip Hop's pioneers in their (there really is, in my view, no other phrase for it) heroic struggle to emancipate themselves and their community through collective forms of aesthetic creation."

My own approach to the philosophy of hip-hop differs in key ways from Vernon's, as I am preoccupied with how underground hip-hop exposes the obstacles to black emancipation in an aesthetic form that can affect the white sensibility marked by a refusal to see or care about them. Vernon is clear that he is "using" hip-hop to detect what is "right" about Hegel's aesthetics and reject what is so very wrong. On the contrary, my aim is to draw on insights that emerge from within hip-hop culture to better account for the racist sensibility of white philosophers; or how, for example, Hegel could sanction antiblack violence in his *Essays on the Philosophy of World History* even while espousing the emancipatory potential of aesthetic creation. Further, my aim is not to draw attention to the aesthetics of hip-hop for the sake of aesthetic theory but, instead—in the spirit of hip-hop—to draw attention to how the form and content of underground hip-hop expose the discursive conditions that continue to dis-articulate the harms of anti-black racism and the genocidal conditions of American society that are minimized and obfuscated by this discourse.

As a hip-hop head, I also understand the importance of creating opportunities for the underground artists who lend me their time and wisdom, and so I have a "crew" of underground rappers and DJs who receive funding to speak with me about hip-hop and perform at colleges and universities [shout out to B. L. Shirelle, J. Remedy, Bates, Kourtney Harris, Kelo, DonChristian Jones, and Dynasty]. These experiences have also enhanced my understanding of hip-hop culture and the philosophical and political importance of underground rap music.

My own efforts to "keep it real" and honor the values and commitments of Hip-Hop Nation even while working within the system of higher education that is structured around a neoliberal and post-racial sensibility have met with mixed—often quite controversial—results. This book is born from my desire to better represent for Hip-Hop Nation. One Love.

NOTES

1. DJ Khaled, "Hip-Hop," Produced By J.U.S.T.I.C.E. League, Written By LL Cool J, Rick Rubin, J.U.S.T.I.C.E. League, Scarface, Nas and DJ Khaled, Release Date: August 21, 2012.

2. Dead Prez, "Hip-Hop," Produced By Hedrush & Dead Prez, Written By Dead Prez, Release Date: March 30, 1999.

3. Adam Burgos, *Political Philosophy and Political Action: Imperatives of Resistance* (London: Rowman & Littlefield International, 2016).

4. Here are three recent examples of artists or fans suffering legal consequences for producing or sharing rap music: 1) Jessica McKinney, "Dallas Rapper Sentenced to 12 Years in Prison over Violent Lyrics in Cocaine Case," *Vibe*, July 23, 2018. McKinney reports that Dallas-based rapper NaNa was sentenced to 12 years in prison based on his "violent" lyrics. However, NaNa was charged for a nonviolent crime with a maximum of 6 years. (https://www.vibe.com/2018/07/dallas-rapper-sentenced-to-prison-over-violent-lyrics/) 2) Sarah Jasmine Montgomery, "Teen Faces 10 Years in Prison For Graphic Rap Song Uploaded to SoundCloud," *Complex.com*, June 12, 2018. Montgomery reports that Michael Schmitt, an 18 year old high school student from New Jersey, is currently facing up to 10 years in prison for creating a "false public alarm" after he shared a rap song he uploaded to SoundCloud on social media 10 days after the Parkland shooting. Schmitt is currently on house arrest, waiting for his potential trial. (https://www.complex.com/life/2018/06/teen-faces-10-years-in-prison-for-graphic-rap-song-uploaded-to-soundcloud) 3) Desmond Metcalf (as told to Maurice Chammah), "I Made a Rap Video in Prison: And It Got a Million Clicks," *The Marshall Project*, June 23, 2016. Metcalf reports that after he and six other men incarcerated at Kershaw Correctional Institution performed two songs they had written, captured on a phone smuggled into the prison, the video was uploaded to

WorldStarHipHop in March 2014 and received over a million views. He reports that the men were subsequently sentenced to a combined 20 years in solitary confinement, along with the loss of visitation, commissary, and phone privileges. (https://www.themarshallproject.org/staff/maurice-chammahhttps://www.themarshallproject.org/staff/maurice-chammah)

5. N.W.A. "Fuck Tha Police," Produced by DJ Yella and Dr. Dre, Written by The D.O.C., Ice Cube and MC Ren, Release Date: August 9, 1988.

6. Mayhem Mal, "Fuck The Police," Produced by Ghetto Superstar Committee, Written by Soulja Beaz & Mayhem Mal, Release Date: December 2, 2012.

7. Adam Liptak, "Hip-Hop Artists Give the Supreme Court a Primer on Rap Music," *The New York Times*, March 6, 2019, https://www.nytimes.com/2019/03/06/us/politics/supreme-court-rap-music.html?smid=nytcore-ios-shareq.

8. Public Enemy, "Caught, Can We Get a Witness?," Produced by Bomb Squad, Written by Chuck D., Hank Shocklee and Eric Sadler, Release Date: June 28, 1988.

9. Run-D.M.C. "Can I Get a Witness," Produced by Jermaine Dupri, Written by Jam Master Jay, D.M.C. and Rev Run, Profile Records, Release Date: May 3, 1993.

10. There is a significant body of scholarly literature on the relation between hip-hop and African American religious traditions, as well as a growing body of scholarship on the current sub-genre of gospel rap. See especially: *The Hip Hop and Religion Reader*, ed. Monica R. Miller and Anthony B. Pinn (New York: Routledge, 2015) and *In Search of Soul: Hip-Hop, Literature, and Religion*, ed. Alejandro Nava (Oakland: University of California Press, 2017). My book is indebted to these studies, though I will focus on the specifically philosophical importance of underground hip-hop in the United States for critical race theory, ethics, political theory, and resistance against post-racial and neoliberal discursive practices that have always normalized American anti-black genocide and serve to produce the white sensibility that can neither see nor hear the moral horror of anti-black racism in the United States.

11. Paul Taylor, *Black Is Beautiful: A Philosophy of Black Aesthetics* (Hoboken, NJ: Wiley-Blackwell, 2016), 10.

12. Ibid., 76.

13. In chapter 1, I will draw on Janine Jones' essay on "The Impairment of Empathy in Goodwill Whites for African-Americans," where she provides a strong argument for understanding racism and the performance of whiteness in terms of a fundamental lack of empathy for black people and black suffering (*What White Looks Like: African-American Philosophers on the Whiteness Question*, ed. George Yancy (New York: Routledge, 2004), 65–86).

14. 2Pac and Outlawz, "They Don't Give a Fuck about Us," Produced by Johnny J., Written by Young Noble, Napoleon (Outlawz), Kastro, E. D. I. Mean, Johnny J., Yaki Kadafi and 2Pac, Release Date: November 26, 2002.

15. W. E. B. Du Bois, *The Souls of Black Folk* (1903) (New York: Dover Books, 1994).

16. See especially: Franz Fanon, *Skin White Masks* (1952) (New York: Grove Books, 2008); James Baldwin, *Going to Meet the Man*, in *Going to Meet the Man:*

Stories (New York: Vintage, 1995); George Yancy, *Black Bodies, White Gazes* (Lanham, MD: Rowman & Littlefield, 2008).

17. For a vivid and particularly unnerving example of this hysterical reaction and claim about the discussion of white sensibility, see the collection of racist responses to Dr. George Yancy's essay "Dear White America" (published in *The New York Times*, December 24, 2015) presented in Yancy's book *Backlash: What Happens When We Honestly Talk about Racism in America* (Lanham, MD: Rowman & Littlefield, 2018).

18. See especially Kimberle Crenshaw's pivotal article, "Mapping the Margins: Intersectionality, Identity Politics, and Violence against Women of Color," *Stanford Law Review* 43, no. 6 (1991): 1241–1299.

19. Charles Mills, *The Racial Contract* (New York: Cornell University Press, 1997), 18.

20. Ibid., 18–19.

21. Ibid., 95.

22. Alfred Frankowski and Lissa Skitolsky, "Lang's Defense and the Morbid Sensibility of Genocide Studies," *Journal of Genocide Research* 20, no. 3 (2018): 423–428, and "The Event of Morbid Sensibility: Anti-Blackness, Genocide Discourse, and the Aesthetic Limits of the Critical," *Patterns of Prejudice* (forthcoming); Lissa Skitolsky, "Slavery, the New Jim Crow and Genocide," in *Rethinking Genocide in Africa and the African Diaspora*, Routledge Studies in Genocide and Crimes against Humanity, ed. Adam Jones, Alfred Frankowski, and Jeanine Ntihirageza (London: Routledge, forthcoming).

23. Linda Martín Alcoff, "Epistemologies of Ignorance: Three Types," Chapter 2, *Race and Epistemologies* of *Ignorance*, ed. Shannon Sullivan and Nancy Tuana (New York: SUNY Press, 2006), 48.

24. Kristie Dotson, "Tracking Epistemic Violence, Tracking Practices of Silencing," *Hypatia: A Journal of Feminist Philosophy* 26, no. 2 (Spring 2011): 233–251. https://doi.org/10.1111/j.1527-2001.2011.01177.x

25. George Yancy, *Black Bodies, White Gazes* (Lanham, MD: Rowman & Littlefield, 2008), 23.

26. My understanding of the *post-racial sensibility* that always already consigns structural anti-black violence to a problem of the American past and the importance of the aesthetic domain as a site of political resistance is indebted to the recent book by Alfred Frankowski, *The Post-Racial Limits of Memorialization: Toward a Political Sense of Mourning* (Lanham, MD: Lexington Books, 2017), as well as the review essays in the symposia about this text in *Syndicate Philosophy*, edited and with an introduction by Lissa Skitolsky (Eugene, OR: Cascade Books, June 2017). https://syndicate.network/symposia/philosophy/the-post-racial-limits-of-memorialization/.

27. H. Samy Alim, "'Bring It to the Cypher': Hip Hop Nation Language," in *That's the Joint!: The Hip-Hop Studies Reader*, ed. Murray Forman and Mark Anthony Neal (New York: Routledge, 2011).

28. Ice Cube, *Amerikkka's Most Wanted*, Produced by the Bomb Squad, Released May 16, 1990.

29. Gang Starr, "Conspiracy," Produced by Guru & DJ Premier, Written by DJ Premier & Guru, Release Date: May 5, 1992.

30. *Straight Outta Compton,* Universal Pictures, Directed by F. Gary Gray, Screenplay by Jonathan Herman and Andrea Berloff, Release Date: August 14, 2015 (USA).

31. See especially: Tricia Rose, *Black Noise: Rap Music and Black Culture in Contemporary America* (Middletown, CT: Wesleyan, 1994) and *The Hip Hop Wars: What We Talk about When We Talk about Hip-Hop—and Why It Matters* (New York: Civitas: Books, 2008); Imani Perry, *Prophets of the Hood: Politics and Poetics in Hip Hop* (Durham, NC: Duke University Press, 2004); James Braxton Peterson, *The Hip-Hop Underground and African American Culture: Beneath the Surface* (Basingstoke, UK: Palgrave Macmillan, 2014); Fernando Orejuela, *Rap and Hip Hop Culture* (Oxford: Oxford University Press, 2014); Paul Butler, *Let's Get Free: A Hip-Hop Theory of Justice* (New York: The New Press, 2009); Susan Hadley and George Yancy, Editors, *Therapeutic Uses of Rap and Hip-Hop* (London: Routledge, 2012); Murray Forman and Mark Anthony Neal, Editors, *That's the Joint!: The Hip-Hop Studies Reader* (London: Routledge, 2012).

32. Susan Hadley and George Yancy, *Therapeutic Uses of Rap and Hip-Hop* (London: Routledge, 2011), Xxvi.

33. I am grateful to George Yancy for helping me understand the importance of distinguishing the existential source of hip-hop from the experience of trauma, as well as for recommending Audre Lorde's essay on the erotic to illustrate this difference.

34. Audre Lorde, *Sister Outsider: Essays and Speeches*, "Uses of the Erotic: The Erotic as Power" (Berkeley, CA: Crossing Press, 1984), 53.

35. Ibid., 56.

36. Ibid.

37. *EMDR Canada,* https://emdrcanada.org/emdr-defined/ (accessed December 27, 2019).

38. Giorgio Agamben, *Homo Sacer: Sovereign Power and Bare Life,* translated by Daniel Heller-Roazen (Stanford, CA: Stanford University Press, 1998), 98.

Chapter 1

Know What I'm Sayin?

WHITE SENSIBILITY, EMPATHY, AND THE TRAP OF THE DOMINANT DISCOURSE

The late artist Tupac Shakur occupies a singular position in the history of hip-hop as the voice and conscience of the underground. In a taped interview on MTV in 1994, two years before he was murdered, journalist Tabitha Soren (hidden from view) asks Shakur if he can account for the sharp shift in tone in rap music from the early 1980s to the present.[1] As an example, she cites the early song "The Message" by Grandmaster Flash & The Furious Five (released in 1982), quotes its famous verse—"It's like a jungle sometimes/ It makes me wonder how I keep from going under"—and then claims "The whole root of what that song was, was basically saying look these are the problems here." Then she contrasts this early message with the present mood of hip-hop culture: "And here we are 10 years or plus later, these problems are still there, and the intensity of the music has built, to the 'no- hope,' the 'I- don't- give- a. . . .' attitude."

Shakur answers Soren's question by offering an analogy between the evolution of hip-hop and the evolution of someone's efforts to get inside a hotel room where people are stuffing themselves with food in order to get something to eat. In the course of developing his analogy, Shakur gives voice to many themes briefly mentioned in the Introduction about the relation between hip-hop and black aesthetics, hip-hop and trauma, and hip-hop and political resistance:

> Again, you have to be logical. You know. If I know, that in this hotel room, they have food every day. And I'm knocking on the door, everyday, to eat, and they open the door, let me see the party, let me see like them throwing salami

all over, I mean just like *throwing* food around, but they are telling me that there is no food in there.

You know what I'm sayin *everyday,* I'm standing outside trying to *sing* my way in—you know what I'm sayin [*he sings*], "we are hungry, please let us in, we are hungry, please let us in." After about a week, that song is going to change to [*he chants*], "we hungry, we need some food." After two, three weeks, it's like [*he raps*] "give me all the food or I'm breaking down the door"! After a year, it's just like you know what I'm sayin [*he raps again, in a more deliberate flow, with gestures that depict the act described*], "I'm picking the lock, coming through the door blastin!"

Shakur's direct appeal to logic to explain the evolution of hip-hop conceals that his answer also includes an appeal to Soren's empathy, as he invites her to imagine herself as starving, locked out of a room where there is more than enough for everyone to eat, trying to "sing" her way in. Tupac assumes that if she can imagine this scenario, she may be able to feel something that helps convey the natural course of hip-hop from "The Message" to "Fuck the Police" in terms of the emotional anxiety, anger and desperation provoked by the broken promises of the civil rights generation and the mass incarceration of black men as a *political priority* of the "War Against Drugs."

And yet whenever I listen to the interview, I always wonder if Soren ever thought, "Yes but why sing? Why not just knock really loudly?" For the way in which Soren forms her question and the way in which she characterizes hip-hop—as concerned with vague "problems" that are "still here"—indicates that she has missed something fundamental about hip-hop culture or has failed to feel something with regard to the brutality of anti-black violence in the present.

In her essay on "The Impairment of Empathy in Goodwill Whites for African Americans," Janine Jones draws on the definition of empathy developed by Paul Thagard and Allison Barnes as "the attempt to comprehend either positive or negative [mental] states of another," to postulate that "goodwill" white people are impaired in their ability to feel empathy for black people (despite their ideals) because they cannot *comprehend themselves as white,* as benefiting from a racial caste system, without damaging their comfortable beliefs about themselves as "good" people and champions of liberty. The group of "goodwill whites" to which Jones refers is also characterized by their attempts to avoid discussions about racism and tend to understand racism simply as racial prejudice. She explains that "by not understanding racism as a system of advantage based on race, the goodwill white avoids the considerable pain, guilt, and shame that might be elicited by a definition of racism that clarifies how she benefits from racism and perhaps serves as an active, intentional, though unconscious participant in it."[2] In her effort to sustain psychic homeostasis, the goodwill white perpetually defers comprehension of herself as white.

The moral and psychological problem with this refusal or this limit of white sensibility to understand itself as white is that it precludes the ability of goodwill whites to feel empathy for black victims of systemic racism. As explained by Jones, "Whites' inability to form the belief that they are white skews the nature of relationships that exist between whites and blacks. It affects their ability to empathize because they are unable to import an ingredient essential to empathy: an appreciation of their own situation."[3] Ideally, we can feel empathy for an individual who is in a predicament that is foreign to us through an *analogy* to a situation in our own life that we can better comprehend; analogies can work to close the emotional divide between people with disparate life histories who (at least) comprehend themselves, if not the racialized other.

However, Jones illustrates that if white people distance themselves from their own whiteness, regard themselves as somehow "outside" of race, then there is no possible framework in which they can attempt to "comprehend" the emotional state of black people who suffer from the *system* of white supremacy that they cannot see or imagine as pertaining to themselves. More often than not they will judge the feelings of black people to be *illegitimate* rather than try to find a way to "map" the experiences of black people onto their own when this requires some comprehension of the system of white privilege and their role within this system. If someone racialized as white perpetually defers the fact *that there is a system* organized around and responsible for her racialization, then it is not possible for her to imagine the continuity of this system over time or the regular, systemic infliction of state-sanctioned violence against black citizens *as such* to sustain the racist distribution of power and capital in our racial democracy.

As a feeling, empathy is not the comprehension of another's mental pain but instead marked by the *effort* or emotional inclination to better comprehend and attend to the other, in the same way that one can comprehend and attend to oneself. However when goodwill whites refuse to comprehend themselves *as white*, and view themselves *as unrelated to racism,* they perpetually defer the presence of the actual framework that could support the effort to better comprehend and attend to black people; for the understanding of *being-white* in contrast to *being-black* allows white people to grasp that they are in a fundamentally different and more privileged position, in need of a better understanding of the plight of black people in a white supremacist state from which they, themselves, benefit. Only if citizens racialized as white admit their whiteness can they *feel* the moral obligation to *make a better effort* to hear and learn from black people. For this reason Jones concludes that the real problem is not the possibility of white empathy for black suffering, but instead the problem of the goodwill white's motivation to empathize at all, or interrupt the deferral of her whiteness to better comprehend the condition of being-black at the cost of her own moral and epistemic confidence.

Goodwill whites cannot imagine an actual system of anti-black racism that inflicts physical, psychological, and social violence everyday (as Shakur kept insisting, "*everyday*") and undermines the social vitality and wellbeing of entire communities and their intergenerational bonds. Their inability to imagine a system of anti-black racism due to their refusal to regard themselves as white often translates into the judgment *that there is no system of anti-black racism*. For this reason, their effort to comprehend the experience of black citizens *as a group* will always lead to a *dis-articulation* of anti-black violence as tragic, accidental, or deserved.

The use of analogies cannot help bridge the emotional divide between white and black sensibility when they are thought in isolation of the conditions of one's own racialization, stripped from the context that accounts for *why* white people need to try better to understand the visceral conditions of being-black in a white supremacist state, the only context that could promote empathy. Thus I imagine that Shakur's analogy did not allow Soren to comprehend the emotional despair and devastation that followed from the mass incarceration and harsh punitive policies developed for the "War on Drugs" throughout the 1980s and 1990s, that help to explain the "turn" in hip-hop music from diagnosis ("here are the problems") to despair ("no-hope") and rage ("the I-don't-give-a—"). Soren can't bring herself to say "black people" or "racism" in her discussion about hip-hop with Shakur, presumably because she would then *become aware* of her own whiteness and perhaps her own limitations in understanding hip-hop culture. Instead her assessment of hip-hop also functions as a dis-articulation of anti-black violence in the past and present (the "problems" it describes are still "somehow" around), so it's hard for me to imagine that she could empathize with the need to "sing" one's way into the hotel room—much less comprehend the relation between black aesthetics and politics—or imagine why the door would be closed in the first place.

To continue the analogy, Soren would only be able to feel empathy if she could comprehend herself as *inside* the hotel room, with too much to eat, refusing to see or hear or talk about black people. As Jones illustrates, the white refusal to see oneself as white precludes the possibility of empathy for black people, and in this sense we can understand the common hip-hop phrase "Know what I'm sayin?"—always asked again and again in the course of a conversation—as a response to this refusal that also calls out the impossibility of being heard. Indeed Shakur makes use of this phrase again and again in his interview with Soren, and after he tries to offer an analogy to explain the evolution of hip-hop, he tries again to explain the importance of anger in contemporary hip-hop as an emotional register of the horror of anti-black violence in the present:

> You know what I'm sayin it's like you're hungry, you've reached your level, you don't want to ask anymore. We asked 10 years ago, we was asking with The Panthers, we was asking with them. The Civil Rights movement, we was asking. You know now that those people that were asking, they are dead or in jail. So now what do you think we're going to do? And we shouldn't be angry? And my raps that I'm rapping to my community shouldn't be filled with rage? You know what I'm sayin they shouldn't be filled with the same atrocities that they gave to me? And the media they don't talk about it, so in my raps I have to talk about it, and it just seems foreign because there's no one else talking about it.

Here Shakur situates hip-hop music as a political response to the failure of the civil rights movement, made evident by U.S. government's assassination or incarceration of all of its principal leaders (Shakur's mother, Afeni Shakur, was one of the few leaders to successfully defend herself in prison [while pregnant with Tupac] and survive the assassinations ordered by the FBI directive COINTELPRO). Then Shakur associates the horror of these deaths and the continuity of anti-black violence with the tone of his music: "And we shouldn't be angry? And my raps that I'm rappin to my community shouldn't be filled with rage? You know what I'm sayin they shouldn't be filled with the same atrocities that they gave to me?" Here, again, Tupac appeals to Soren's sense of empathy; doesn't it make sense to be filled with rage about the atrocities still inflicted on black communities? But then he provides the reason why Soren is unlikely to empathize or the fact that the content of so much underground hip-hop—descriptions of the everyday varieties of racist violence suffered by black men and women—is absent from the popular media and dominant discourse ("there's no one else talking about it"). And again Shakur repeatedly asks, "You know what I'm sayin?" to both mark and respond to what Du Bois referred to as the "Veil" that separates white sensibility from black sensibility about the United States and makes these discussions about race and racism so necessary and yet so seemingly impossible.

A more recent example of the white refusal to *see oneself in a system of anti-black racism* occurred when CNN correspondent Michael Smerconish interviewed hip-hop artist Meek Mill after his release from a state penitentiary, where he was sentenced after he was found guilty for a violation of his parole. Mill recently wrote a powerful op-ed for *The New York Times* on the need for radical prison reform, and Smerconish begins by asking Mill to explain the meaning of a statement he made in a separate interview he gave to the NYT: "The plantation and the prison are actually no different. The past is the present. It ain't no coincidence. This was the plan since abolition, to keep us subjugated by creating this system." Mill situates the prison system in the continuous history of anti-black oppression in the United States, and Smerconish frames his response in the following way:

> I think we can reach general agreement among people of all different political persuasions today that the criminal justice system needs to be reformed but what's the basis for saying that today it's all part of a plan to keep people subjugated?[4]

The question itself betrays Smerconish's refusal to see a system of white supremacy that is the context for understanding why Mill was targeted for arrest and framed by police officers and the context for understanding his own position as a white man who benefits from this system. His question is made possible by the Veil that separates white and black sensibility and illustrates Jones' insights on the emotional impairment of goodwill whites.

Mill responds to Smerconish's question by providing specific examples of how the criminal justice system routinely works to inflict injustice on black communities:

> Just going as far back as parle and probation. A lot of people who go back in and out of prison are being stuck by a parole system or probation system where not even committing crimes puts you back in prison. I learned from personal experience. I actually spent time with men that had 28 months in prison for $100 bail. They weren't even found guilty for their crimes and $100 kept them in prison and we had to—tax payers even myself had to pay money to keep guys like this in prison. It was for like a petty crime. Things like that never made sense to me even being on probation. I've been on probation since I was 19 years old; I'm 31 years old. Growing up in the system, I always thought this was normal and I didn't value myself the way I value myself now.

Though Mill provides poignant testimony that describes the illogical, devastating and yet routine administration of bail and probation as examples of how black men get caught in the prison system that targets them from birth, Smerconish is still not convinced, as he responds: "But in the video you say this is part of the plan, that it's all about subjugation of African-Americans and I'm not understanding where's the evidence for that. That we have an unfair system, I get it, but that it's all part of a grand design, I'm not seeing." Of course, Smerconish's original question about the existence of systemic racism is impossible to "prove" through providing specific examples of racist policies, but that is the point. The question itself is a trap; it only makes sense in accord with the limits of white sensibility or a framework of interpretation made possible by being-white, in a position to benefit rather than suffer from our racial democracy, and so capable of deferring and distorting and denying the existence of the system itself. The white question about the existence of racism is also an active refusal to see or care about black suffering, and it is part of the web of discursive practices that shape and reinforce white sensibility and the persistent dis-articulation of systemic anti-black violence as so many individual, isolated, tragic events.

As he states himself, Smerconish cannot "see" the system of anti-black racism, but he also cannot "see" that this system provides the context for understanding Mill's experience as a victim of the criminal justice system and the larger implications of his plight, as well as a context for empathy for Mill's suffering. And indeed Smerconish proceeds to question whether Mill is the "right" person to advocate for criminal justice reform and objects to the notion of a racist "system" with reference to the fact that the judge who recently sentenced Mill to prison is an African American woman. Smerconish's refusal to grant that Mill's experience has anything to do with being-black is not rational, but follows from his own refusal to see himself as white. This white refusal of one's whiteness produces the dis-articulation of the systemic as the particular and accidental, that is also essential to the post-racial and neoliberal sensibilities that historicize systemic anti-black racism as well as minimize its harm in the present through the belief in our continuing historical progress toward social, economic, and political equality between white and black Americans.

This white refusal of one's whiteness that produces the judgment that a system of anti-black racism does not exist, is essential to the image that white people have of themselves as "good people," and so when someone who is not-white questions their right to this refusal, white people often lash out with anger and violence in an effort to harm and discredit this person and protect their right to moral and epistemic blindness about white racism and black suffering. This was recently illustrated in a very public and traumatic way following the publication of George Yancy's editorial "Dear White America" in *The New York Times* on December 24, 2015, when his humble plea for white citizens to think about their whiteness angered thousands of white Americans who lashed out against Yancy through verbally abusive, overtly racist hate mail, phone calls, and emails that threatened to torture and kill him—often in graphic and pornographic terms.[5]

Yancy recounts his harrowing experience in his book *Backlash: What Happens When We Talk Honestly about Race in America*, in which he provides an analysis of the white, racist backlash against his editorial and many of the actual messages he received, to observe patterns of anti-black hate speech (even and especially from goodwill whites) that indicate patterns of white sensibility or how white people prevent themselves from knowing themselves as white.[6] He explains that "to be Black in America is to be always already *known*, and white people assume that they know *everything* about me."⁷ Yancy explains the white refusal of whiteness in terms of a refusal to be vulnerable, or acknowledge that we are fallible, that there are limits to what we can understand *as white people,* and a refusal to be vulnerable to our shame, or acknowledge how we benefit from the political and economic subordination of black people.

Yancy's experience of the backlash and his narrative of his experience also painfully illustrate how this white refusal of whiteness is bound up with the white right to harm and kill black people with impunity. When "we talk honestly about race," white people feel a desire to harm black people as a way to "deny" that we should talk about race at all, motivated by the view that black people who talk about race are the problem who needs to be destroyed. Here white people perform their right as white people to harm, ignore, subordinate, and kill black people in the course of their discursive denial of white racism; in Yancy's terms, white people are "ambushed" by their own performance of whiteness when they refuse to explore their own psychic and social and emotional investment in being-white. So an honest discussion about race in the dominant media often becomes a collective event of white ambush against black scholars, artists, and activists who initiate these discussions.

One of the principal aims of underground hip-hop is to illustrate the systemic and unrelenting infliction of violence against black communities in the United States, its predictable and yet entirely preventable repetition against every generation in socio-political practices and institutions that change but do not entirely replace each other over time (slavery, Jim Crow, police violence, mass incarceration). Rather, as rappers illustrate, each historically distinct system for the legal infliction of anti-black violence perpetuates logics and specific tactics inherited from previous systems. Further, the form and content of underground rap music often aim to illustrate what it *feels like* to be born into a system in which one is un-naturally vulnerable to being killed by the same police force we depend on for our safety. This is illustrated in one of the most iconic songs of underground hip-hop, *Sound of Da Police*, released by KRS-One in 1993.⁸ The hook opens with the sound of the police siren "Whoop, Whoop," followed by "That's the sound of da police!," another "Whoop, Whoop," followed by "That's da sound of da beast!" The imitation of the sound of the police siren that opens the song, the sound of "da beast," doubles as the sound of a common psychological trigger of symptoms of post-traumatic stress disorder for black people who have been profiled, harassed, arrested, and/or beaten by police officers for *being*-black. And that's just the hook.

The lyrics present a sonic and analytic comparison of the American slave *overseer* and the American police *officer*, after KRS-One raps: "Take the word 'overseer,' like a sample/Repeat it very quickly in a crew, for example/

Overseer, overseer, overseer, overseer/Officer, officer, officer, officer/Yeah, officer from overseer/You need a little clarity, check the similarity." Here he lyrically introduces his historical comparison of these socio-political roles in American society by exposing the phonetic similarity of the terms "overseer" and "officer," through rapping the words in a distinct "flow" or rhythm. In so doing, KRS-One draws attention to the continuity of racist discourse that we uncritically inherit and that informs our "modern" sensibility even to the extent that our euphemisms for state-sanctioned perpetrators ("overseer," "officer") *sound* the same. This is powerful precisely because this insight is delivered in a novel rhythm, so that we can *hear it* in a distinct register, with which we are unfamiliar, even (and especially) because we cannot immediately comprehend it in the post-racial or neoliberal register of meaning about American history.

After his sonic introduction to the historical transformation of the slave overseer into the police officer, KRS-One raps a point-to-point comparison of the two socio-political roles that includes the bars: "The overseer had the right to get ill/And if you fought back, the overseer had the right to kill/The officer has the right to arrest/And if you fight back they put a hole in your chest." The lyrics deftly illustrate the continuity of state violence against black communities in the United States in terms of the powers exercised by the slave overseer and the police officer that—both then and now—allow white people to kill black people with impunity. In this way KRS-One illustrates this larger structure of systemic anti-black racism as the only context in which his experience *can be conveyed* and the only context in which we can "hear" the sound of the police siren as both an instrument of anti-black violence and a psychic trigger of trauma. Throughout the song KRS-One draws attention to the generational repetition and inheritance of the traumas inflicted by American anti-black racism: "My grandfather had to deal with the cops/ My great-grandfather dealt with the cops/ My great-great-grandfather had to deal with the cops/ And then my great, great, great, great—when it's gonna stop?!"

Following his analytic comparison of the overseer and the officer accomplished through poetic verse delivered in a distinct rhythm, KRS-One raps: "Your laws are minimal/Cause you won't even think about lookin' at the real criminal/This has got to cease/Cause we be getting hyped to the sound of da police." Here KRS-One conveys that the discursive, visual, and imaginative criminalization of black men—the victims of state violence—perpetuates the administrative, everyday infliction of violence against black men that is notseen as criminal or violent but instead dis-articulated as necessary, deserved, inevitable, or accidental. Then he alludes to the psychic wounds suffered as *a target* of the police force by protesting: "We be getting hyped to the sound of da police!" also alluding to how the police siren (imitated in the hook of the song) acts as a trigger for symptoms of fear, anxiety, rage, depression, and shock that undermine the wellbeing of entire black communities targeted for police surveillance and brutality.

As a whole, *Sound of Da Police* illustrates that the psychic wounds left by historical traumas cannot heal when there is always a new violation and a new source of psychic pain in the everyday socio-political and economic practices that enforce the color line. The song itself is composed of novel phrases and rhythms that present an aesthetic depiction of the systemic and traumatic nature of the violence inflicted against black communities in American history that contests the white sensibility of the accidental and occasional nature of this violence, "understood" by goodwill whites as a product of racist individuals who represent an exception to the norm of a Just Justice system.

As a final example of the type of discursive practice that emerges from the white sensibility that separates itself from (and so remains blind to) a system of anti-black racism, I will cite the moment during the last vice-presidential debate when Mike Pence chided Tim Kaine for Hilary Clinton's use of the terms "implicit bias" and "systemic racism" which, he claimed, serve to politicize tragedies and denigrate our police officers. Here Pence dis-articulates the systemic and traumatic infliction of anti-black violence as accidental, tragic, and sporadic in order to reinforce the courageous and heroic character of white police officers. The problem with the dominant discourse is that it reinforces the limits of white sensibility and serves to make those limits *invisible* in the form of questions and assumptions that only "make sense" to someone racialized as white, or conditioned to make sense of a world in which they benefit at the expense of those racialized as black.

In his seminal work on the phenomenology of racialization and the psychodynamics of anti-black racism *Black Skin, White Masks*, Franz Fanon also wrote about the "trap" of discourse as a means with which those racialized as black can contest racist assumptions that are also the very terms in which they seen, judged, heard, and imagined by white people who perpetually defer the fact of their own whiteness. In a striking example of this trap, Fanon explains: "When they like me, they tell me my color has nothing to do with it. When they hate me, they add that it's not because of my color. Either way, I am a prisoner of the vicious circle."[9] The "vicious cycle" of discourse is that one is recognizable and so seen and treated *as a black or white person,* at the same time that white people discursively distance themselves from the racial terms of recognition even and especially when acting in an overtly racist manner.

In *Black Skin, White Masks*, Fanon makes use of the term "overdetermined" to describe the experience of the white gaze that perceives him *as black,* and so can only perceive him through the racist associations and assumptions that inform the category of "black," and which—at the level of sensibility—inform the white perception of black skin. As Fanon explains:

"But in my case everything takes on a new guise. I am given no chance. I am overdetermined from without. I am the slave not of the "idea" that others have of me but of my own appearance."[10] Fanon describes the problem of the overdetermination of black men as a problem of sensibility that exposes the relation between the epistemic and the aesthetic, insofar as he is trapped by the way he necessarily *appears* to citizens racialized as "white," who see him as someone who is not-white, and thus trap him within the confines of "blackness" from which he cannot escape as he cannot appeal to a false *idea* they have of him, or appeal to their reason to recognize their error.

Fanon's work helps explain why the problem of anti-black racism is not a problem of individuals who are "ignorant" or "irrational," in need of more knowledge, but instead a problem of white sensibility as the framework in which people appear as white or black, who can only be "read" in terms of the racist categories that allow them to be visible at all. In white sensibility of black skin, the aesthetic appearance and epistemic understanding of black people mutually reinforce each other through the dominant discursive practices that dis-articulate the nature of racism and black suffering and enforce the limits of white sensibility.

In his essay on "Fanon, Philosophy, and Racism," Lewis R. Gordon succinctly describes Fanon's argument about why the dominant discourse has served as a trap for those who aim to "become white" through its mastery:

> Here is Fanon's argument: Blacks have attempted to escape the historic reality of blackness through language, which offers semiotic resources for self-deluding performances of emancipation. If blacks can speak the European language well enough and even use it against the European with the ferocity of Shakespeare's Caliban, perhaps they will "become" European and consequently "become" white. Value-neutral semiotic resources do not exist, however, in an antiblack world. Signifiers that overtly deny color are governed by a colonized life-world . . . from the perspective of many blacks, a black who speaks the national language well is someone who "speaks like a white person" . . . In other words, the semiotic turn only leads to phony whiteness and pitiful blackness . . . The black discovers, however, that he or she is always already negatively signified by the system of signs that constitute antiblack racism.[11]

The belief that discourse exists separate and apart from our sensibility, that words can be used in a value-neutral way for the sake of communication and knowledge acquisition, supports the white belief that a white person can exist separate and apart from whiteness, free from the limitations in sensibility and understanding that hinder "other," racist white people from respecting and understanding black people. So the trap of discourse is also sustained by a false view of discourse as a medium for truth rather than an instrument for the production of truths, inseparable from the worldview that informs our general sensibility as white or black citizens.

Underground hip-hop is consciously created as a form of discursive or epistemic resistance against the dominant or "professional" discourse that obfuscates and normalizes the genocidal violence inflicted against black communities. As rapped by Lord Jamar, in lyrics from the song *Claimin I'm a Criminal* (1994) by the group Brand Nubian: "But still I won't bite my tongue/I just write tight shit to incite the young, to fight the one/Who keeps them on a level that's minimum/That's the number one reason."[12] Hip-hop culture created a distinct *language* based on the co-option and distortion and re-signification of terms in the dominant discourse in order to convey the system of anti-black genocide perpetually deferred by white sensibility and rendered invisible in the dominant discourse. Underground rappers resist their epistemic overdetermination as black men and women through aesthetic works that contest and dis-rupt the aesthetic sensibility of white people or the post-racial and neoliberal framework for understanding the American past and present.

HIP-HOP NATION LANGUAGE AND EPISTEMIC RESISTANCE

Although Ludwig Wittgenstein introduced the notion of "language-games" in order to reconceive of language from a medium for truth to a tool (or a series of tools) to communicate in accord with rules connected to actions and an entire worldview, he did not explicitly connect the language games of specific cultures to specific socio-political and economic arrangements of power relations that achieve specific forms of oppression and domination. This is one way to approach Foucault's notion of the *episteme* or those rules that inform the production of the dominant discourse that is viewed as the only logical, rational, professional way in which to communicate and "make sense" of one's ideas to others. For example, though many of us would feel comfortable cursing in professional environments, this will always be perceived as a "vulgar" and "unprofessional" form of communication. There is no objective reason why this must be the case; instead this rule is silently accepted and more rigorously enforced with regard to groups already marginalized by the racist, heterosexist, and ableist terms of the dominant discourse and more vulnerable to discipline and sanctions in educational and professional environments. Indeed despite the adolescent and crude form of political discourse under the current regime in which lies are circulated in order to insult, shame, and harm one's political opponents, politicians still deride rap music as "vulgar" due to the regular use of profanity in the lyrics. Here it is a matter of who is sanctioned to be "vulgar" and use profanity, and for what end. Underground rappers have always used profanity as a way to register their emotional pain and anger about the status quo, as well as reject the "polite" discourse that "makes sense" of anti-black violence only through its dis-articulation.

Foucault's notion of the *episteme* reinforces Wittgenstein's insight that language games are not value-neutral but also situates them within the social field that is organized around relations of power in order to illustrate their political function in relation to preserving systems of oppression. In interviews and texts Foucault describes the *episteme* as the system of assumptions that allows us to separate those statements that we regard as "making sense" or as epistemically valuable, from those that we regard as "senseless" or without epistemic value.[13] Foucault limits his analysis of the *episteme* as referring to that web of assumptions that informs thought and the production of the dominant—or authoritative—discursive practices in every field and sector of society. This interconnected web of assumptions and rules that is "the" *episteme* predetermines what does and does not make "sense" in public discourse in order to exclude those discourses that oppose the *episteme* and expose the arbitrary and oppressive organization of power relations in any given institution or social structure. For example, the dominant discourse and standard assignments in academia that are considered "professional" and as indicative of knowledgeable subjects, exclude alternative discourses from marginalized communities as "real" or "important" sources of knowledge, and this serves to reinforce the sexist and racist structure of the academy.

In her essay about the Rodney King verdict, *Endangered/Endangering: Schematic Racism and White Paranoia*, Judith Butler expands Foucault's notion as she argues that the racist, classist, and heterosexist structure of the *episteme* also informs our visual and imaginative fields.[14] She illustrates that in order to make sense of the jury's verdict that the police officers who assaulted and tortured Mr. King were found not-guilty of any wrongdoing, we must consider the racist saturation of the visual field and the problems this raises for any appeal to white perception as evidence for our judgments. The epidemic of police murders of unarmed black men and women depends upon the criminalization of black citizens *as a group*, who are always already "seen" as a threat to the social order. For example, in his statement to a grand jury about why he murdered Michael Brown—a black, unarmed teenager—officer Darren Wilson testified about his perception of this young man right before he started shooting: "The only way I can describe it, it looks like a demon, that's how angry he looked."[15] On the basis of his testimony—including his racist overdetermination of Brown *in the act of perceiving him*, Wilson was not charged with any crimes.

In his *Lectures at the College de France* titled "Society Must Be Defended" (1975–1976), Foucault refers to the existence of "subjugated knowledges" in every society that serve to contest the *episteme* and are generally regarded as naïve or crude forms of knowledge:

> When I say "subjugated knowledges" I mean two things. On the one hand, I am referring to historical contents that have been buried or masked in functional coherences or formal systemizations . . . Second, when I say "subjugated knowledges" I am also referring to a whole series of knowledges that have been disqualified as . . . insufficiently elaborated knowledges: naive knowledges, hierarchically inferior knowledges, knowledges that are below the required level of erudition or scientificity.[16]

Insofar as underground hip-hop culture in the United States has always served to contest neoliberal and post-racial narratives about American anti-black racism through its form and content, or through the disruption and co-option of melodies, beats, and lyrics as well as through phenomenological accounts of the lived experience of black Americans in the past and the present, it has always served as one of these "subjugated knowledges" that critique and disrupt the totalizing hold of the *episteme* on our sensibility and thought.[17] This is one reason why hip-hop artists—including DJs, rappers, and breakdancers—have been demonized in the media as "gangsters" and "thugs" since the 1980s, and why academics still view the sophisticated construction and multilayered meaning of hip-hop verse—referred to as "Hip-Hop Nation Language" by the sociolinguist H. Samy Alim—as outside the parameters of professional and scientific interest, as a naïve and philosophically inferior form of discourse.[18]

In his ground-breaking text *Roc the Mic Right: The Language of Hip-Hop Culture*, Alim establishes the parameters for a study of Hip-Hop linguistics (HHLx) as a variant of the recently codified field of black linguistics, for it shares the mission—as explained by Ngugi wa Thiongo—of "decolonizing Black language and thought," or granting black culture the authority and value as a source of excellence and knowledge that is precluded by white sensibility about black culture, and aims to contest the authority and value *of* white sensibility.[19]

In his text Alim draws on the fields of sociolinguistics and cultural theory, anthropology, education and literary studies, English and literary analysis, hip-hop studies, as well as interviews with rappers to depict and explain the role of HHNL as a form of discursive politics and political action against white racism that is consciously produced to oppose the "linguistic supremacy" of the dominant discourse. He explains that "the central focus of HHLx is language and language use within Hip Hop communities. Since language ain't neva neutral, HHLx interrogates the development of unequal power relations between and within groups . . . There is a reason why Hip

Hop communities resist others' attempts to control their language varieties (you can slap on all the "explicit lyrics" stickers you want). [Hip-Hop] Heads know that policing language is a form of social control that amounts to nothing less than policing people."[20] Hip-hop is animated by the need to oppose the discursive violence of the dominant discourse in order to oppose the oppressive relations of power that it sanctions and obfuscates.

Alim refers to hip-hop culture as a "black language space," and explains that "Black American tonal semantics can be thought of as the creative force that drives Hip Hop lyrics," that are formed in accord with grammatical and syntactic rules that allow for both structure and spontaneity in the co-option, distortion, and creation of words and phrases. He quotes John Wideman to explain how Black American Speech provides the discursive structure for Hip-Hop Nation Language (HHNL): "What's fascinating to me about African American speech is its spontaneity, the requirement that you not only have a repertoire of vocabulary or syntactic devices/constructions, but you come prepared to do something in an attempt to meet the person on a level that both uses the language, mocks the language, and recreates the language."[21] Alim's research about the socio-linguistic significance and syntactic, poetic, and phonic complexity of HHNL confirms that hip-hop culture is significant as a type of subjugated knowledge made possible by and emerging from the language of Black American Speech—also formed as a response and rejection of the dominant discourse, as a subjugated knowledge that contests the racist *episteme* that informs the limits of white sensibility. In its political function, HHNL serves as a creative means with which black Americans escape the "trap" of assimilating to the dominant episteme for a recognition that they will never receive. As Wa Thiongo explains to Alim, "By making up your own words, you are freeing yourself of linguistic colonization."[22]

However if HHNL is a form of discursive resistance to white sensibility, how can it move or affect the sensibility of goodwill whites who can only make sense of the world by deflecting the fact of their own whiteness? Given the overt racism and misogyny of mainstream political discourse and the apparent impotence of critical thought against our susceptibility to false beliefs and manipulation by presidential tweet, journalists and scholars are re-examining the nature of empathy and in particular our ability to lose our empathy for different groups we regard as different from ourselves. In his *New York Times* article "The Kernel of Human (or Rodent) Kindness: What we can learn from lab rats that don't show empathy for other rats," Henry James Garrett draws on research by scientists at the University of Chicago about patterns of empathy in rats to draw conclusions about how we can lose empathy for whole groups of human beings.[23]

According to Garrett, these scientists "found that a white rat raised among only white rats will do nothing to save a black rat from a trap. Rats, like humans, can be biased in how they act on, or don't act on, their empathy. In a variant of the experiment, a white rat raised among only black rats would save a black rat from a trap—but would fail to save other white rats. And a white rat raised among black and white rats rescued rats of both colors. The researchers found that it is not the rat's color that determines which type of rat it will show empathy for, but the social context in which it was raised." Garrett draws an analogy between the rat's and human's capacity for empathy:

> Likewise, when human empathy can be partial, it is because the experiences of people from some groups are hidden from our view, which limits our empathy toward them. It's vital to recognize that prejudice is not baked-in: It is the result of our ignorance. A failure to learn about people (or rats) of different kinds can mean that we fail to recognize their pain as genuine pain. Empathy can be switched off. Empathy by itself is not enough. It becomes an accurate guide for moral action only when combined with knowledge of people of all different backgrounds—knowledge that can be attained only if you are willing to actively listen to people whose voices have been silenced.

Although both rats and white people are impaired in their ability to feel empathy for groups they do not know or understand, goodwill whites (unlike rats) believe they understand what it means to be-black (to quote Yancy again, "white people assume that they know *everything* about me"). Further—to refer back to Jones—goodwill whites are not generally motivated to question their false beliefs about racism to better empathize with black citizens when their beliefs reassure themselves of their own moral integrity. For this reason their capacity for empathy for black people *depends on their ability to acknowledge the limits of their sensibility* rather than positive knowledge about being-black in America; only if goodwill whites can sense these limits is it possible for them to hear and respect the authority and epistemic value of black testimonies and texts. Yet as we have seen, white sensibility is largely characterized by patterns of discourse that serve to reinforce its limits and render them invisible. For this reason *aesthetic interventions* are necessary to disrupt our "sense" of reality and oppose the discursive frame of white sensibility with images and narratives that it cannot understand; the aesthetic dis-orientation of white sensibility can expose its limits in making-sense of being-black and provoke discomfort and concern about those limits.

We can see this difference between goodwill whites who sense the limits of their sensibility and those who do not as animating the historical "beef" between white rappers in hip-hop culture who frequently accuse each other of co-opting and disrespecting black culture in order to become commercially successful. These beefs lead to judgments passed by Hip-Hop Nation about which white rappers are "real" hip-hop versus "wack" rappers. Recently Eminem—the source of constant controversy over the apparent misogyny and homophobia in his lyrics—has taken it upon himself to diss those white rappers who co-opt and disrespect black culture in a series of tracks that emerged from his beef with the white rapper Machine Gun Kelley (MGK).[24] Hip-Hop nation has collectively judged the white rapper Iggy Azalea to be wack and offensive, and has collectively judged Eminem to be a rap god. How did Eminem achieve this status, and how does he have the authority to condemn specific white rappers as "wack?"

In hip-hop culture, the ethical injunction to "keep it real" also provides a standard by which white rappers are judged as either respecting the culture—and the limits of their own participation—or co-opting and "leeching off" the culture for the sake of their own material success, in ways that are decidedly opposed to hip-hop. Examples of the former include the Beastie Boys and Eminem, who immersed themselves in hip-hop culture and wrote songs from their own experiences that contributed something new to both the form and content of rap music and shared the political and moral commitments of hip-hop culture to oppose anti-black violence and racist ideology.

When Toure Neblett interviewed Eminem in 2004 for *Rolling Stone* and asked him why he wouldn't use the term "nigga" in his lyrics when it is often used by both black and white kids as a term of love, Eminem replied: "Yeah, it's just a word I don't feel comfortable with. It wouldn't sound right coming out of my mouth . . . Some white kids feel comfortable throwing the word around all day. I don't . . . It doesn't feel right to come out of my mouth." When he was then asked: "Does it bother you when a black man says, "Eminem is my nigga?," he replied "No. If a white kid came up to me and said it, I probably would look at him funny. And if given the time to sit down with him I'd say, 'Look, just don't say the word. It's not meant to be used by us. 'Specially if you want something to do with hip-hop.'"

Eminem explains his refusal to follow other successful rappers and use the n-word in his music in terms of his *discomfort as a white man*, concerned with crossing or denying the limits of his sensibility to feel or "be" black; this concern leads to his discomfort about co-opting a racial epithet whose harm he cannot feel or understand. Further, he associates the ability to be aware of and respect these limits with his love of hip-hop culture and, indeed, *insists that one cannot hear or be associated with hip-hop* unless one already accepts these limits to white sensibility. In contrast, when Iggy Azalea—a white woman from Australia—released her chart-topping rap song "Fancy," she was criticized for cultural appropriation for imitating the accent and cadence of black rappers (derided as "verbal blackface" by her critics), as well as including insensitive lyrics in her songs ("When the relay starts I'm a runaway slave-master"), and appearing largely indifferent to anti-black violence in the United States. As a result, Azalea was "called out" by numerous underground rappers on Twitter and then largely rejected by the hip-hop community (despite having been mentored by T.I., a successful black rapper, who also ended his collaboration with her after she insulted some of the rappers who had criticized her).[25]

At the height of the controversy Azalea was quick to shed the persona of a hip-hop artist, as she stated in an interview with *Vanity Fair*: "People have said I'm not real rap or real hip-hop. But I don't care if people think I'm pop or rap. Everyone interprets music differently."[26] Azalea was rejected from hip-hop nation because she lacked any sensibility of her limits as a white woman that would have allowed her to "keep it real," or rap from her own experiences, rather than imitate and mock the sensibility of black artists, which is decidedly opposed to hip-hop culture. The injunction to "keep it real" also serves to assess the extent to which someone who has listened to hip-hop has actually heard it, or been affected to the extent that one is able to adopt a critical stance toward discursive practices and perceptions that serve to evade, defer, or dis-articulate the extremity and regularity of state-sanctioned, anti-black violence in the United States. This is not to claim that it is possible to "lift" the Veil that separates those on either side of the color line, but it is possible for hip-hop to disrupt its totalizing hold on our thought and imagination so that goodwill whites are in a better position to empathize with the plight of black Americans or feel some of the discomfort and moral horror of *being-white* that is perpetually deferred by the sense-making of white sensibility. Aesthetic works affect the emotions rather than simply the intellect and temper the discomfort that attends our dis-orientation with awe at the beauty and poetic excellence of the work itself.

THE WHITE SENSIBILITY OF EPISTEMIC INJUSTICE

Recently analytic philosophers have started a discussion about "epistemic injustice," a term coined by Miranda Fricker to name a specific type of harm that we regularly inflict on gendered and racialized others, whereby we doubt their epistemic and moral integrity or their ability to discover and honor the truth. According to Fricker, this epistemic harm becomes habit due to our inability to *imagine* or *perceive* certain individuals as trustworthy, as capable of honoring the truth. She recommends that the "virtuous learner" now aspire to greater epistemic justice through, in part, honing our "virtuous perceptual capacity,"[27] even though the root of this harm regards the *limits* of our sensibility rather than our penchant for morally sluggish perception.

The academic discussion of epistemic injustice in Anglophone philosophy has largely excluded the work of black philosophers who write about the specific harm designated by the term "epistemic injustice" from the perspective of suffering from this harm under the white gaze that overdetermines their appearance and undermines their ability to be seen or heard as knowledgeable or rational or trustworthy. In her essay on "Decolonial Praxis and Epistemic Injustice," Andrea J. Pitts points out that the analytic analyzes of epistemic injustice in Anglophone academic philosophy have also largely ignored the work of Latin American, U.S. Latina, and Caribbean philosophers who address the habit of epistemic injustice in the historical contexts of colonialization, capitalism, race-thinking, and the academic discourses in epistemology that position themselves as outside and unrelated to these historical phenomena.[28]

And perhaps it goes without saying that they have not turned to hip-hop as a source of knowledge about the relation between epistemic injustice and systemic racism. However one way to understand the philosophical and political importance of Shakur's work is that nearly every single song he wrote is devoted to exposing and overturning epistemic injustices and illustrating the connection between false ideas about the United States and young black men and the (political) atrocities that follow. He consistently illustrates that black communities suffer from atrocities produced by the racist disparity of wealth and privilege, and that these atrocities are mis-represented as inborn pathologies—another epistemic injustice. ("You claimin' I'm a criminal and you the one that made me").[29] In framing their discussion about the harm of epistemic injustice in isolation of those texts and testimonies about suffering from this harm in a racial democracy, Anglophone philosophers perform the epistemic injustice that they strive to describe; for they exclude the testimony of racialized others from the dominant discourse about how and why we exclude certain individuals from our community of possible knowers, in order to reassure themselves of their own moral and epistemic integrity.

Fricker's recourse to sensibility as the practical solution to the problem of epistemic injustice is based on her assumption that we can make a "perceptual judgment" about the visual field, that is "non-inferential," "spontaneous," and "unreflective," through honing our sensitivity "to morally salient features of the situation confronting" us. There are no grounds for this assumption or the possibility of "non-inferential judgment" grounded in our sensibility. Indeed, Du Bois coined the notion of the "Veil" to refer to the irreducible difference between the sensibilities of those on either side of "the color line." In the field of critical philosophy of race, the notion of the Veil is necessary to expose the limits of white sensibility that reinforce our moral indifference to black suffering.

Likewise, academic philosophers have largely excluded the testimony of underground hip-hop artists from their analyses of race and anti-black racism in the United States. This text argues that hip-hop culture provides an essential source for understanding the *systemic* infliction of epistemic injustice as a feature of white sensibility and a source for confronting this habit of *undermining the epistemic agency of racialized others* through exposing and critiquing the conditioned limits of white sensibility. If we heed the wisdom of hip-hop and the work of critical race theorists who emphasize that white sensibility is characterized by a profound lack of empathy for black communities, then it becomes clear that instead of a call to better "know" or "perceive" the racialized "other," we should recommend a greater effort to accept the limits of white sensibility and examine how the sheer *acknowledgement* of these limits acts to counter the willful refusal to grant the testimony of racialized others any epistemic value.

NOTES

1. YouTube, 1994 2PAC MTV interview, Full interview posted on August 2, 2008 by Girl Outlaw: https://youtu.be/pNSRx14s7B4.
2. Jones, "The Impairment of Empathy in Goodwill Whites for African-Americans," 69.
3. Ibid., 70.
4. CNN News, "Rapper Meek Mill on his New Album and Criminal Justice Reform," posted on YouTube Dec. 1, 2018, CNN (https://youtu.be/fRm7cpDSKHI).
5. Yancy, "Dear White America."
6. Yancy, *Backlash: What Happens When We Talk Honestly About Race in America*.
7. Ibid., 11.
8. KRS-One, "Sound of da Police," Produced by Show, Written by KRS-One, Release Date: December 6, 1993.
9. Franz Fanon, *Black Skin, White Masks* (1952) (New York: Grove Books, 2008), 96.
10. Ibid., 116.
11. Lewis R. Gordon, "Fanon, Philosophy, and Racism," in *Racism and Philosophy*, ed. Susan E. Babbitt and Sue Campbell (Ithaca, NY: Cornell University Press, 2018), 32–49.
12. Brand Nubian, "Claimin I'm a Criminal," Produced and Written by: Lord Jamar & Sadat X, Release Date: 1994.
13. See especially an Interview with Michel Foucault, "The Confession of the Flesh," in *Power/Knowledge: Selected Interviews and Other Writings, 1972–1977*, ed. Colin Gordon (New York: Pantheon Books, 1980), 194–228.
14. Judith Butler, "Endangered/Endangering: Schematic Racism and White Paranoia," in *Reading Rodney King, Reading Urban Uprising*, ed. Robert Goodings Williams (New York: Routledge, 1993).
15. "Darren Wilson Explains Why He Killed Michael Brown," by Terrence McCoy, *The Washington Post*, November 25, 2014.

16. Michel Foucault, *"Society Must Be Defended": Lectures at the College de France (1975–76)*, Translated by David Macey (New York: Picador, 2003), 7.

17. It is important to note that rap music is only one aesthetic expression of hip-hop culture, which also incorporates distinct forms of visual art (graffiti and fashion), as well as dance (breakdancing), a language (referred to as "Hip-hop Nation Language" by the sociolinguist H. Samy Alim), an ethics, and a political theory.

18. Alim, "'Bring It to the Cypher'."

19. H. Samy Alim, *Roc the Mic Right: The Language of Hip Hop Culture* (London: Routledge, 2006), 7.

20. Ibid., 9.

21. Ibid., 532.

22. Ibid., 73.

23. Henry James Garrett, "The Kernel of Human (or Rodent) Kindness: What We Can Learn from Lab Rats that Don't Show Empathy for Other Rats," *Opinion, The New York Times*, December 28, 2018.

24. Eminem's recent diss tracks follow his recent album *Kamikaze* (2018), which is in-itself a series of diss tracks against a group of new young rappers that have been condemned as "mumble rappers" by the older generation of hip-hop artists. See: Killshot (https://youtu.be/FxQTY-W6GIo); Pac Man (https://youtu.be/tnCqBifyZIQ); Stan I'm Not Done (https://youtu.be/QpWRDS_yDyo).

25. Jeff Guo, "How Iggy Azalea Mastered Her 'Blaccent'," *Economic Policy, The Washington Post*, January 4, 2016, https://www.washingtonpost.com/news/wonk/wp/2016/01/04/how-a-white-australian-rapper-mastered-her-blaccent/?utm_term=.2691ac373d6c.

26. Lisa Robinson, "Hot Tracks: Iggy Azalea," *Vanity Fair*, vanityfair.com. January 7, 2015, https://www.vanityfair.com/hollywood/2015/01/iggy-azalea-fancy-fame.

27. Miranda Fricker, *Epistemic Injustice: Power and the Ethics of Knowing* (New York: Oxford University Press, 2009).

28. Andrea J. Pitts, "Decolonial Praxis and Epistemic Injustice," in *The Routledge Handbook of Epistemic Injustice*, ed. Ian James Kidd, José Medina, and Gaile Pohlhaus, Jr. (New York: Routledge, 2017), 150.

29. 2Pac, "Po Nigga Blues," Produced by DJ Daryl, Written by 2Pac, Remixed by Scott Storch, Release Date: December 12, 2004.

Chapter 2

Can I Get a Witness?

HIP-HOP AS TRAUMATIC TEXT

As mentioned in the Introduction, underground rappers frequently write songs about hip-hop culture in order to express their gratitude and their concern with the ways in which it is coopted by rappers who produce "commercial" hip-hop for the sake of greater material success; the commercial version that is produced by the music industry and played on the radio circulates images and ideas that are decidedly anti-hip-hop, or disrespect the values and political commitments of Hip-Hop Nation. This problem is exacerbated by the fact that people who are unfamiliar with the culture tend to confuse commercial with underground hip-hop; this perpetuates the refusal to take hip-hop culture seriously as a source of wisdom and beauty, as well as perpetuates negative stereotypes about hip-hop artists. Thus the concern for those in the underground to "keep it real" against the forces of the music industry and the lure of commercial success is felt as a moral and political imperative.

At times the struggle has seemed so doomed that hip-hop heads have declared "Hip-Hop is Dead" to mourn the loss of "conscious" hip-hop as a discursive, political weapon with which to oppose the dominant discourse of white sensibility organized around the *exclusion* of systemic anti-black violence from perception and thought. This concern that "Hip-Hop is Dead" was especially acute in the aftermath of the murders of Tupac Shakur (1996) and Christopher Wallace (a.k.a. Biggie Smalls, 1997), and this concern helped provoke a new wave of "conscious" hip-hop initiated by the brilliant work of Nas, Lauryn Hill, JAY-Z, Mos Def (now Yassin Bey), and Talib Kweli.

In his acclaimed 1999 album *Black on Both Sides*, Yassin Bey (as Mos Def) reiterates the mission of underground hip-hop in the first bar of the track "Hip-Hop": "Speech is my hammer, Bang the world into shape, Now let it

Fall! (Huh!)."[1] Here Bey associates speech with a tool with which to "bang the world into shape" as well as to tear it apart and "let it fall," highlighting the political imperative of underground hip-hop to resist systemic racism through the aesthetic disruption of discursive practices that allow us to evade, defer, and normalize its brutality and regularity in the everyday administration of public policy.

Nas co-opts the frequent phrase "Hip-Hop is Dead" for the title of his acclaimed 2006 track, so that the phrase itself becomes the basis for the song that proves it wrong. In the song he addresses the critics of hip-hop: "Kidnappings, project buildings, drug dealings/Criticize that, why's that?/'Cause Nas rap is compared to legitimized crap."[2] Here Nas indicates that "real" hip-hop describes the conditions of black life in Amerikkka, whereas commercial rap, "legitimized crap," exists to undermine this effort. Both Nas and Mos Def also associate the history and future of hip-hop as an aesthetic form with the conditions and fate of being-black in America. Mos Def explicitly associates the state of hip-hop with the socio-political vitality of black communities in the preamble to the first song on *Black on Both Sides*, "Fear Not of Man," when he addresses those concerned with the fate of hip-hop who ask him:

"Yo Mos, what's gettin' ready to happen with hip-hop?"
("Where do you think hip-hop is goin'?")
In order to counsel and assure them:

I tell em, "You know what's gonna happen with hip-hop?
Whatever's happening with us."[3]

His words reflect the common refrain in hip-hop culture "I am hip-hop," which conveys the idea that hip-hop emerges from and reflects the perils and promise of black culture in the United States. Mos Def continues to express this sentiment throughout the preamble by linking the vitality of black communities with the vitality of hip-hop:

If we smoked out, hip-hop is gonna be smoked out
If we doin' alright, hip-hop is gonna be doin' alright

He counsels the hip-hop head to turn the concern around to examine oneself in order to examine and attend to hip-hop culture:

So the next time you ask yourself where hip-hop is going
Ask yourself: where am I going? How am I doing?

The new group of rap gods that emerged from the self-aware "conscious" phase of hip-hop history in the late 1990s and first decade of the 2000s associate "real" hip-hop as respecting its roots in black life and culture, and respecting its political mission as the effort to protect both through the aesthetic intervention of rap music and Hip-Hop Nation Language.

If conscious hip-hop is motivated by the need to bear witness to what is deferred and obfuscated by the dominant discourse that "makes sense" of the senseless amounts of state violence against black communities through its dis-articulation as individual, tragic, and accidental incidents, then the form and content of hip-hop discourse must subvert the "sense" of this discourse rather than aim to re-present the trauma of black life. For as opposed to suffering from a tragic occurrence such as heartbreak, a traumatic experience cannot be re-presented and mediated through categories of the understanding that could allow for it to be grasped *as* a meaningful event in the life of the person who suffered from the assault. Since trauma violates every expectation we can have for what could or should happen to us, we cannot describe traumatic suffering with the categories of the understanding that convey what is meaningful and significant and ideal in human life.

The invisibility of the distinctly traumatic (systemic, un-natural, and preventable) nature of anti-black violence in the dominant discourse ensures the dis-articulation of anti-black violence in the present and weakens the possibility for white empathy for black suffering. As explained in chapter 1 with reference to the work of H. Samy Alim on the linguistics of Hip-Hop Nation Language, rappers are keenly aware of the role language plays in obfuscating the severity and regularity of anti-black violence that also allows for its normalization and repetition. Alim explains that Hip-Hop Nation Language (HHNL) is a language "with its own grammar, lexicon, and phonology as well as unique communicative style and discursive modes."[4] He emphasizes that HHNL "includes ideologies of language and language use," and is best viewed as "the synergistic combination of speech, music, and literature."[5]

As a sociolinguist, Alim is particularly fascinated with the use of HHNL as a conscious tactic with which to oppose the sense of the dominant discourse: "Hip Hop artists assert their linguistic acts of identity in order to 'represent' the streets. This may be viewed as a conscious, linguistic maneuver to connect with the streets as a space of culture, creativity, cognition and consciousness."[6] Alim also explains that this linguistic maneuver to shift the source of our sensibility from popular culture to the streets occurs through "*street-conscious copula variation*—the conscious variation of copula absence in order for the artist to 'stay street,' or to stay connected to the streets."[7] In chapter 1, I drew attention to the political significance of HHNL through drawing on Wittgenstein and Foucault to explain the role that discourse plays in perpetuating relations of power that sustain a racial democracy; language does not re-present the world but instead creates a world-of-meaning within which we see, understand, interpret, and imagine our relations and responsibilities to others. The dominant discourse establishes un-natural limits as to what can be "understood" or "imagined" that facilitate the political project of white supremacy.

Mos Def draws attention to hip-hop as a *rejection* of the dominant (white) discourse in his track "Hip-Hop" from *Black on Both Sides* when he raps:

> Used to speak the King's En-ga-lish/
> But caught a rash on my lips, so now my chat just like dis

In the use of slang and poetic verse delivered in a distinct rhyming scheme, Mos Def situates HHNL as the rejection of "the Kings En-ga-lish" that spreads a "rash on the lips" or a disease that perpetuates our decay. He continues:

> It is a back water remedy/Bitter and tender memory, a class E felony/
> Facing the death penalty (huh!).

In opposition hip-hop serves as a "back water remedy," one made necessary by the "backwater" conditions inflicted on black communities that serve to remove and exclude them from the "current" of American democratic freedoms. Emerging from traumatic conditions of socio-political and economic subordination, hip-hop as-remedy is a "bitter and tender memory," at the same time that it's "a class E felony," or viewed as a "criminal" form of activity, waged by those "facing the death penalty." Through the album, Bey illustrates a keen understanding of the role language plays in sustaining the conditions of white supremacy through the way it affects and informs white sensibility of black citizens and black suffering.

As mentioned in the Introduction, the popular media, our politicians, and the courts have always sought to criminalize the production and dissemination of hip-hop as a "vulgar" form of music that incites violence. Rappers co-opt the historical criminalization of hip-hop as a sign of its political power against the dominant discourse and the white desire to erase and defer the fact that white citizens benefit from a system of anti-black violence. The most famous example of this co-option is the phrase "T.H.U.G. Life," coined by Shakur as an acronym that stands for "The Hate U Give Little Infants Fucks Everyone." Shakur made use of "T.H.U.G. Life" to refer to the status of those marginalized by the white supremacist organization of American politics, dismissed as "thugs" or "criminals" so that they are never seen or heard as the victims of this system, exploited, and targeted for police brutality and incarceration. The literal meaning of the acronym refers to the genocidal logic of the system that targets black citizens on the basis of race, rather than their individual actions, from the moment they are born.

Shakur always speaks to and for the "outlaw" or those always already excluded from the protection of the law. In other words, he speaks to and for those who have been silenced, ignored, harmed, oppressed, and enslaved by the system of American racial democracy. Though frequently accused of "inciting" a civil war, Shakur exposes the civil war that is already happening, that is both perpetrated and disavowed by the white establishment that benefits from the subordination of black and brown bodies. In this sense to be opposed to this subordination is to be opposed to the status quo and thus TO BE A THUG. In co-opting "thug" as a term of pride, Shakur illustrates that the terms the establishment uses to denigrate and dis-empower black people are actually the signs of their strength and power that threaten this very establishment. Only someone in the position of being seen as a "thug" is vulnerable to traumatic violence inflicted by a system of white supremacy that inflicts and dis-articulates this violence as a form of "national security." White people denigrate racialized communities who threaten the racial caste system they seek to preserve in order to deny the existence of the system itself. This is similar to the way in which a woman's power to create life is turned against her as a disability or as signaling her weakness as opposed to her strength, for she is "merely" a "bitch" who gives birth. And for similar reasons, women often co-opt the term as a source of pride, as a sign of a strong, successful, and loyal woman.

Scholars have drawn attention to the aesthetic brilliance of the form of hip-hop, composed of the art of sampling, the creation of the break-beat (the cutting and looping of drum beats) and the scratch, all of which serve to produce new sounds from the deconstruction and interruption of previous recordings. They have also associated these innovative techniques with the West African cultural predisposition for collage and diverse textures in music. However, scholars have not emphasized the *political* significance of the hip-hop break beat or how it affects our sensibility of the present. In his seminal work, *Breaking Beats: the art of sample-based hip-hop,* Joseph G. Schloss explains that the creation of the break beat in hip-hop reflects an African American aesthetic:

> The looping aesthetic in particular ... Combined a traditional African American approach to composition with new technology to create a radically new way of making music. As breaks are torn from their original context and repeated, they are reconciled—by performer and listener alike—as circular, even if their original harmonic or melodic purposes were linear. In other words, melodies become riffs. The end of a phrase is juxtaposed with the beginning in such a way that the listener begins to anticipate the return of the beginning as the end approaches. Theme and variation, rather than progressive development, become the order of the day. And, although it would be easy to overstate this aspect, there is clearly

a political valence to the act of taking a record that was created according to European musical standards and, through the act of deejaying, physically forcing it to conform to an African American compositional aesthetic.[8]

Given his detailed explanation of the genesis of hip-hop from African and African American aesthetic sensibilities in his text, it is not clear why Schloss mentions the political significance of the *form* of hip-hop only to claim that "it would be easy to overstate this [political] aspect." In fact his text repeatedly suggests that the aesthetic forms of hip-hop—looping, the break-beat, signifyin' and flipping—are also political strategies insofar as they affect sensibility of time, space, and meaning. This is made more explicit at the end of his text:

> While looping may not change the *sound* of the music—its rhythm, melody, harmony, or timbre—it changes the entire sensibility within which this sound is interpreted . . . In the best beats, in fact, a virtual call-and-response develops in which a break actually answers *itself*—the end of the break establishes a tension that is resolved by the return of its own beginning. Looping—creating a cycle out of linearly conceived melody—imparts a new compositional logic to preexisting material and once-random juxtapositions. Moreover, in cases where the original recording was not in an African-influenced genre, it serves to "Africanize" musical material by reorganizing melodic material in accordance with specific African preferences such as cyclic motion, call and response, repetition and variation, and "groove."

MCs tear breaks from their original context in order to produce a circular, repetitive beat based on variation rather than progression, and in this way change "the entire sensibility within which this sound is interpreted." If we focus on the form of hip-hop then we can recognize hip-hop as *the political activity* of interrupting, co-opting, distorting, and repeating sounds to rupture our sensibility or produce sounds, images, and melodies that shatter our linear, teleological framework for making-sense of reality.

The teleological view of American history as linear and progressive is central to both our post-racial sensibility that views systemic racism as a problem of the distant past overcome in the present, as well as to our neoliberal sensibility that promotes piecemeal legal reforms and a fair market as the "solution" to the racist distribution of capital and power. If we think about this aesthetic disruption of linear form with the aforementioned relation between hip-hop culture and the socio-political conditions of being-black, then we can better grasp how the form distinct to hip-hop could serve to depict the type of collective suffering that "breaks" black communities and "breaks" the sense of popular narratives that reinforce moral and epistemic blindness to this suffering.

In his book on black aesthetics, *Black is Beautiful*, Paul Taylor draws on evolutionary psychology to help explain the role that rhythm plays in human culture as an essential means of sociality. Adding to this perspective, I think the capacity for rhythmic musicking is also an essential means with which humans cope with trauma, as we cannot, like a deer in the woods, dispel trauma by trembling when faced with a mortal threat. Instead we often dissociate and so lock the trauma in place, excluded from memory and history, and then suffer the repetition of the traumatic violation in flashbacks and patterns of behavior that emerge from the deferred pain of the original assault. In my view, the ability of underground hip-hop to move its listeners or affect their sensibility is due to its form—sampling and scratching—that evoke the form of PTSD, as well as its content or language that consistently illustrates the difference between tragic and traumatic suffering. Together the form and content of underground hip-hop convey—*at the level of sensibility*—how the trauma of systemic anti-black violence is a pathology of American history that recurs to the extent that it is repressed and dis-articulated in our discourse, historical narratives, and sensibility of the present.

In his track "Hip-Hop" Mos Def describes the existential impact of hip-hop in one bar: "The break beats you get broken with on time and inappropriate." This poetic phrase alludes to the existential impact of hip-hop that produces break-beats that "break" us "on time and inappropriate," or dis-rupt our sensibility by breaking the sense and predictability of "appropriate" melodies and lyrics that obfuscate anti-black violence in the present. The creation of break-beats was an aesthetic intervention in popular sensibility that interrupted conventional ways-of-knowing and hearing, created by black artists who were subject to violence that cannot be re-presented in the discursive terms produced by post-racial and neoliberal sensibility. As an aesthetic intervention based on the interruption of linear melodies to create a cyclic loop that arrests our senses, the form of hip-hop evokes the structure of post-traumatic stress disorder as a psycho-social and historical pathology, and this correlation helps explains the existential impact of hip-hop on our sensibility of the present.

Traumatic violence is distinguished by our inability to *imagine* it, or imagine a type of violence that exceeds everything we believe can or should occur in the course of our lives; traumatic violence is neither inevitable nor predictable, but instead shatters our frame of reference for understanding it *as it occurs*. An incident becomes traumatic to the extent that it overwhelms our conscious powers of mediating the world through symbolic forms that present a coherent and meaningful representation of human experience. Unlike images in a dream, the traumatic flashback does not alter the relation between sign and meaning (such that, e.g., the sign signifies something "other" than what it normally means), because the "sign" or the image of violence suffered in the past does not "mean" anything beyond its literal appearance. And the repetitive appearance of the traumatic flashback is paradoxically linked to the impossibility of its comprehension, so that consciousness is forced to perceive an image that it cannot endow with symbolic meaning.

Individuals who suffer from traumatic flashbacks can re-live and witness the violence they suffered in the past but they cannot adequately describe the violation; in this way trauma cannot be known or forgotten. Similarly, the break-beats and scratching in hip-hop can be heard but they cannot be integrated into a linear melody because they are based on the perpetual interruption of these melodies; break-beats do not "mean" anything beyond how they sound and affect our sensibility. Traumatic flashbacks disrupt our ability to discursively represent and know the atrocities from which we still suffer, and the art of sampling, break-beats, and the scratch disrupt our ability to discursively represent and "understand" what is heard *as the perpetual interruption of meaning.*

In her studies on trauma, Cathy Caruth emphasizes the essential paradox of the traumatic event as something whose sheer literality prevents it from being known, and thus *because* it was never originally mediated into the narrative memory of experience, re-presents itself in the same literal form that originally overwhelmed the conscious power of mediation. She explains: "It is this literality and its insistent return which thus constitutes trauma and points towards its enigmatic core: the delay or incompletion of knowing, or even in seeing, an overwhelming occurrence that then remains, in its insistent return, absolutely true to the event."[9] Caruth's work initiated the field of trauma theory, but academics and clinical practitioners tend to view any experience of extreme loss and pain as potentially traumatic, and are hesitant to associate our vulnerability to PTSD with the contingent social and political conditions to which we are subject. However, the lyrics of underground rappers consistently illustrate the difference between tragedy and trauma, or a form of suffering which is meaningful in the narrative of a human life and a form of suffering which is not "meaningful" to the extent that it cannot be reconciled with a life that is chosen and willed; that is, a form of suffering that disrupts the possibility of narrative itself. Trauma represents an un-mastered past that invades the present despite—or rather because of—all efforts to repress and/or master it as something known, meaningful, and *past.*

In Caruth's book *Unclaimed Experience: Trauma, Narrative, and History,* she emphasizes that the painful repetition of traumatic flashbacks occurs to the extent that we cannot understand or explain a prior traumatic violation which is then repressed and deferred: "the painful repetition of the flashback can only be understood as the absolute inability of the mind to avoid an unpleasurable event that has not been given psychic meaning in any way. In trauma, that is, the outside has gone inside without any mediation."[10] Caruth refers to trauma as "a pathology of history," for the traumatic flashback represents the invasion of the past into the present *against the will of the person* who originally suffered from the force of its assault, and its reoccurrence depends on (1) its absence in our narrative (2) its incomprehensibility.

If we think about Caruth's insights in relation to Schloss' comments about the form of hip-hop, we can think about trauma as *psycho-social space* occupied by communities who are more vulnerable to PTSD given their un-natural vulnerability to state violence; communities who continue to suffer from trauma precisely because this form of suffering cannot be represented or seen or imagined or explained through popular narratives and white sensibility. Shifting the focus from trauma as an individual pathology to a psycho-social space helps us better understand trauma as a product of contingent and un-natural social conditions to which no one should be subject. Hip-hop culture illustrates that the trauma of systemic anti-black violence represents both a pathology of American history and collective memory that perpetuates its reoccurrence through its dis-appearance in thought, perception, discourse, and understanding about race and American society.

THE FORM OF HIP-HOP AND THE PSYCHO-SOCIAL SPACE OF TRAUMA

The importance of the correspondence between hip-hop and trauma is also reflected in the lyrics of so many underground hip-hop songs that make direct reference to "trauma" and the "traumatized," and this focus seems to be even more explicit in the most recent tracks, such as "Trauma" by Meek Mill (2018) which follows his earlier track "Traumatized" (2012), as well as (at least) twelve additional tracks titled "Traumatized" released by hip-hop artists in 2018 alone, by artists as diverse as YoungBoy Never Broke Again, Chief Keef, Bae Bae Savo, 60jay, Dave East, Asian Doll, Baby Smoove, Lil Playah, BloccoSmurf, Greenline, Chris King, and CMO Marcello. However it is not the literal mention of the term "trauma" in hip-hop lyrics that is significant for understanding how the *form* of hip-hop as a genre is distinctly capable of evoking the disruption and interruption and temporal dislocation that characterize the historical and socio-psychic pathology of PTSD.

As previously mentioned, the form of hip-hop music is based on the arts of sampling, the break beat (produced by cutting and looping drum beats) and the scratch; each of these art forms serve to co-opt and re-signify the popular melodies, familiar rhythms, and narratives that reinforce our ability to "make sense" of the present despite the senseless amount of anti-black violence inflicted by the state against entire communities. In his book *The Hip-Hop Underground and African-American Culture: Beneath the Surface*, James Braxton Peterson explains that in the art of sampling—the use of beats and lyrics from once popular songs to create new recordings—the beats and lyrics are not merely reiterated but instead repeated *with a signifying difference*.[11] When rappers sample beats and lyrics from upbeat, naïve songs that reinforce the narrative of the American Dream, the narrative and melody are interrupted or disrupted and *no longer serve to signify what is being heard*. In other words, the sample is removed from the original context that gave it meaning, to re-signify the *excess* that cannot be seen or witnessed or imagined within this very context. For example, beats and lyrics are often sampled from songs that express tragic events—such as heartbreak—as the basis for rap songs that describe types of suffering from systemic harms such as poverty and incarceration that are not tragic, unusual, or inevitable. Here rap music co-opts tragic narratives for the sake of exposing the traumatic *through their im-perfect repetition.* Two excellent examples include the songs "Changes" by Tupac Shakur[12] and "Hard Knock Life (Ghetto Anthem)" by JAY-Z.[13]

Shakur recorded "Changes" in 1992, a few years before his death at the age of 25 in 1996. The song samples the 1986 hit *The Way It Is* by Bruce Hornsby and the Range.[14] The original version presents a tragic narrative about the racist discrimination of the civil rights era as understood by a white man who laments that unemployment is (still) the central problem faced by black citizens. As the opening lyrics state: "Standing in line marking time. Waiting for the welfare dime,' Cause they can't buy a job." Shakur's song "Changes" samples the melody and recognizable chorus of the song, which is sung by Talent:

That's just the way it is
Some things'll never change

The original song also associates the problem of racism with the failure to respect Title VII of the Civil Rights Act of 1964 that prohibits employment discrimination on the basis of race, color, religion, sex, or national origin: "Well, they passed a law in '64, To give those who ain't got, a little more/But it only goes so far/Cause the law don't change another's mind." The song presupposes the neoliberal view that racial equality can be attained through the free market and piecemeal legal reforms to ensure equality of opportunity and fair competition. At the same time, it also reflects the post-racial view that we have overcome the worst forms of American racism even if some individuals continue to harbor their own biases, for "some things'll never change."

Shakur remixes the song for "Changes" and raps over its familiar melody in order to testify to the brutality of American anti-black violence that far exceeds the lack of employment, and undermines the hope and wellbeing of succeeding generations of black communities. In the third verse he raps: "And still I see no changes; can't a brother get a little peace?," followed by: "It's war on the streets and a war in the Middle East/Instead of war on poverty, They got a war on drugs so the police can bother me." In contrast to the Bruce Hornsby song, Shakur does not associate anti-black violence with the failure to respect the law but instead with the regular enforcement of the law "on the streets." And when the song samples the chorus "That's just the way it is," it does not convey the tragic inevitability of human folly but instead the traumatic repetition of needless, gratuitous state violence against African Americans through state policies such as the War on Drugs that create a mandate for targeting and incarcerating black citizens. The phrase is repeated with a signifying difference in order to problematize and reconfigure its meaning; in order to expose the traumatic in the cracks of the tragic, neoliberal narrative about American racism. My larger point is that this is effective and made possible by the art of sampling itself, in which beats, melodies and lyrics are torn from their original context in order to "flip" them and invert their meaning; in order to appreciate the inversion, one must have a "sense" of the original context in which they appear at the same time that one can "sense" how they are re-signified as riffs that are sampled to convey a very different meaning. The art of sampling is a tactic that allows us to grasp the ubiquity of tragic, neoliberal and post-racial narratives at the same time that we can sense their disruption and complicity in cycles of anti-black violence. For this reason Tricia Rose has referred to the art of sampling as "ideological insubordination."[15]

Similar to the way Shakur samples the song "The Way It Is" for his song "Changes," JAY-Z samples the popular song "It's a Hard-Knock Life" from the musical Annie for his 1998 song "Hard Knock Life (Ghetto Anthem)."[16] Recall that the musical is about how Annie—a young white girl who lives in an orphanage under the mean supervision of Miss Hannigan—eventually finds a stable home with a rich, kind white man—"Daddy Warbucks." JAY-Z samples its melody and familiar chorus—"Instead of treated, we get tricked /Instead of kisses, we get kicked/It's the hard knock life!"—to describe his own rags-to-riches story from the ghetto to fame and material success. However in the course of his testimony he makes clear that his rise was extraordinary due to the collective suffering into which he was born and from which others still suffer. In the third verse he raps: "I flow for those 'dro'ed out/All my niggas locked down in the 10 by four, controllin' the house." Following this image of his brothers "locked down," JAY-Z re-signifies the meaning of 'hard knocks' from the musical: "We live in hard knocks/We don't take over, we borrow blocks."

Here JAY-Z co-opts a tragic narrative with a happy ending for the sake of depicting a distinct type of suffering that evades our narratives and undermines the "pursuit of happiness" for entire communities targeted for being-black in America. In so doing, JAY-Z does not aim to doubt whether an orphan suffers in a state orphanage, but rather co-opt the kitschy melody and lyrics that we all associate with a type of suffering that "makes sense" and finds resolution in order to re-signify it as traumatic, or as representative of systemic and historical patterns of collective suffering that cannot and do not appear in popular musicals. In JAY-Z's narrative the problem is not the loneliness and sadness of living without parents but the radical vulnerability to sudden, senseless poverty, incarceration, and death. Like Shakur, JAY-Z co-opts a tragic narrative in order to expose the traumatic reality that escapes it, *through its im-perfect repetition* in a non-linear melody and with the use of a different grammar, lexicon, and phonology so that it can be *heard* on a different register of meaning.

In addition to the art of sampling that re-signifies the meaning of terms, melodies, and beats through their imperfect repetition, the art of scratching is a different form of hip-hop music that serves as an interruptive force in our sensibility or as a rupture in our ability to know or understand what is being heard. Scratching is a DJ technique first developed by Grand Wizzard Theodore and honed by Grandmaster Flash in the late 1970s and, at its simplest, it involves moving a vinyl record with your hand back and forth to produce a distinct sound from its perpetual interruption, done with the needle intact and in a way that does not damage the record. The process of scratching is usually done with a turntable and vinyl record although there are now digital soundboards that also create the distinct sound *produced by the interruption of a record.* DJs who scratch records in innovative ways are called "turntablists" or scratch DJs. Although there are numerous books on the history of scratching and turntablism as innovative forms of music, I will focus my remarks on the connection between the sound of the scratch and the form of trauma, as the "scratch" is incomprehensible in itself and instead represents the sound of interruption, the sound of the indecipherable.

The art of scratching has evolved beyond the simple back-and-forth scratch, as the use of a crossfader allows for different sound patterns to be achieved by cutting the sound of the scratch in and out at certain times. The lexicon of techniques includes the Hydroplane, the Orbit Scratch, Scribble Scratch, Tear Scratch, Transform Scratch, Tweak Scratch, and Zig-Zag Scratch. As Mark Katz explains in his book *Groove Music: The Art and Culture of the Hip-Hop DJ,* the art of scratching transformed the turntable into a musical instrument that could be played to produce a distinct sound that became universally recognized as the invention and sound of American hip-hop. He also comments on the transgressive nature of turntablism:

In the hands of hip-hop DJs, the turntable could also be appealingly transgressive, both in the way DJs handled the equipment and through the sounds they produced with it. Merely touching the surface of a record was taboo, and DJs touched records in most inappropriate ways. Scratching was the ultimate expression of the DJ's transgression. To scratch a record is to damage it—it is a technique that violates its own medium. (Though scratching does not damage the record nearly as much as a needle being pulled across the grooves). In a sense, scratching is, like its hip-hop cousin graffiti, an art of vandalism. It is a celebration of noise, and no doubt part of the pleasure it brought to DJs came from the knowledge that it annoyed the older generation. Perhaps scratching can also be understood as a celebration of the notoriously noisy city of the Bronx, for it transformed what could be considered sonic blight into music, an accompaniment for raucous, joyous dancing. Just as graffiti artists tagged their city with spray paint, DJs, using phonograph needles, etched their own signatures into the city soundscape.[17]

The transgressive nature of the scratch also lies in the fact that it is produced only through the perpetual interruption and distortion of melodies and songs that convey something meaningful, that are created in order to communicate something specific to those who listen to them. There is a cultural expectation that songs are listened to for what they communicate, rather than distorted in such a way that they fail to communicate anything other than the sound of this distortion or the sound of a-failure-to-communicate the message or mood that inspired them. As Katz suggests, the art of scratching is bold and transgressive as the DJ makes use of a record to produce a sound that prevents the record from being heard, a sound produced through the perpetual interruption and cancellation of what it *means* in order to groove to the sound produced by this interruption, or the sound of its distortion; the scratch is a sound that does not "mean" anything beyond its immediate rupture of music.

Scratching is an art that can appear arrogant as the DJ literally "cancels" the meaning of a record in order to create a distinct sound from its perpetual disruption; it is almost as though scratching—based on the *repetition of interruption*—conveys a certain commitment to suspending, cancelling, and distorting the aesthetic works of others in order to celebrate the sound produced by the failure to hear or understand the meaning of these works (a "celebration of noise"). However, in light of my analysis in Chapter One and the insights provided by Du Bois, Fanon, Foucault, Shakur, Taylor and Alim on the relations between discourse and power, art and sensibility, and hip-hop and politics, it is also possible to view the art of scratching—based on interruption and repetition and distortion—as a form of music conducive to the expression of traumatic suffering; a form of suffering in the *present* from violations first suffered in the past, and a form of suffering that seizes our sensibility and recurs to the extent that we evade and defer the existence of these violations that do not "make sense" through our categories and linear narratives.

As illustrated in chapter 1, our dominant discursive practices serve to defer, deny, and obfuscate the systemic traumas inflicted by state-sanctioned violence against black communities *as such* through their dis-articulation as so many tragic accidents inflicted on "suspect" individuals. Through this lens we can better appreciate the art of scratching as a political technique that interrupts the sense of these discursive practices to expose the "noise" that escapes them and in the process shatters their totalizing claim on sensibility as the means through which we hear, assess, interpret, defer, imagine our experience. The scratch evokes the presence of the senselessness that is evaded by our sense-making apparatus, the excess born from violence we cannot acknowledge, describe, or understand in white discursive norms. On the level of *sonic reality*, the scratch functions like a traumatic flashback that interrupts our sense of the present that is organized around the dis-appearance of what is senseless; the scratch is the sonic register of the traumatic assault that is excluded from memory, history, and sensibility. And akin to the traumatic flashback, we can experience the scratch although we cannot understand it or describe what it "means."

The art of scratching is an essential component of the subversive and political function of hip-hop culture as a form of "subjugated knowledge" that opposes the *episteme* because the scratch acts as an aesthetic rupture of sensibility by suspending our ability to understand what is being heard *as it is meant to be heard*; in that moment of hearing a sound born from the interruption of sound, *we can detect the presence of the sense-making apparatus that here fails to make-sense of the scratch*. In other words, the scratch interrupts our sense-making activity by creating a sound produced from its suspension, and we hear this sound despite—and because of—the fact that we cannot understand it. In this way the scratch testifies to the reality behind and beyond "what makes sense" as a meaningful-experience, through producing a sound born from the preclusion and circumvention of lyrics and the temporal dislocation of linear melodies that—akin to trauma—exposes the limits of our ability to mediate the entirety of experience through categories of the understanding. At the same time, the scratch does not traumatize those who hear it but, instead, provokes awe and aesthetic delight at the quality and novelty of the sound-of-interrupting-a-recording or the sound of the indecipherable.

In my view, part of the reason the sound of the scratch elicits awe is because there is something cathartic about feeling the sense of our sense-making apparatus as an *imperfect* instrument with which to re-present experience rather than a universal and absolute faculty that conveys the "truth" of experience. This sense of the partial and imperfect nature of our sense-making apparatus can be felt as cathartic because the *episteme*—or the dominant discursive practices that inform how we see, understand, and imagine our experience—does not actually serve to re-present any person's experience but instead creates ideal norms that no one can fully realize and from which we all suffer (viz. "man" or "woman"). The *episteme* also serves to re-produce the status quo through deferring our awareness of collective traumas that recur *to the extent that they are perpetually deferred* (see my analysis of Meek Mill's interview on CNN in chapter 1). For this reason the scratch—the sound of interrupting the meaning of a record—acts as an aesthetic register of the violence that does not and cannot "make sense," at the same time that the failure of our sensibility *to understand the scratch* releases us from the burden of defending our sensibility *as* universal and infallible even as it serves to distort our experience and alienate us from ourselves. As Katz suggests, scratching is a powerful way in which DJs choose to etch "their own signatures into the city soundscape," though the interruption of lyrics and distortion of linear melodies to produce a sonic register of the senseless violence from which they suffer that undergirds and belies the effort to make sense of the present. Drawing on trauma theory, we can also view the scratch as a sonic register of the traumas that violate and exceed the discursive terms with which we could re-present them.

Although scratching has always been essential to hip-hop culture—though noticeably absent from certain genres such as Trap and the SoundCloud genre of hip-hop initiated by the group of young, "Lil" rappers—there has been a distinct resurgence of scratching in the underground as a political tactic against the current regime. The track "Solid Wall of Sound" by the iconic group Tribe Called Quest on their final album in 2016, *We Got It from Here . . . Thank you 4 your service,* provides a powerful example of the use of scratching and sampling as political tactics that interrupt and re-signify the *episteme*.[18] The group reunited after 18 years to produce this album during the 2016 election after Phife Dawg was diagnosed with cancer. The album is a response to the toxic politics stoked by "Agent Orange"—so dubbed by Busta Rhymes during the 2016 Grammy Awards soon after Phife Dawg had died—and their performance at the Grammy awards served both to memorialize Phife and to protest the new regime.

In "Solid Wall of Sound" Q-Tip samples a bar from the Elton John track "Bennie and the Jets" that comes from the following verse: "You're gonna hear electric music/Solid Walls of Sound." Here Elton John refers to the new art of electronic music and a new musical production technique called "Wall of Sound" pioneered by Phil Spector in the 1960s that became central to the art; the "wall of sound" is created by having a number of electric and acoustic guitarists perform the same parts in unison, then recording the sound using an echo chamber. Tribe's song "Sound of Silence" opens with complex scratching, then several variations of the chorus, in which Q-Tip loops the verse "Solid Walls of Sound" as sung by Elton John with a simple scratch that accompanies and interrupts the verse, at the same time that other members of the group chant "Solid Wall of Sound," thus transforming the plural "Walls" into the singular "Wall." Further, Elton John wrote and played piano for the outro, which includes the line: "A solid wall of sound is here on tour."

At the time of its production, Agent Orange was rallying his base with racist fantasies of a "huge wall" that would keep out all would-be immigrants to preserve the white supremacy of the United States and "make it great again." The discourse surrounding the Wall, rather than its feasibility or practicality, was far more important to rallying the white base to vote against its own interests; the discourse about the dangerous, racialized "others" threatening to invade our country reinforced and "made sense" to white sensibility that is perpetually threatened by the loss of white privilege *at the same time* that it disavows this privilege. By co-opting the phrase "Solid Walls of Sound" from its original context, the title of the track "Solid Wall of Sound" is able to reference both the "Wall" that dominated the 2016 election and represents the systemic racism that informs American politics, as well as reference the power of hip-hop to oppose this Wall and the civil discord it provokes through the sonic intervention of the DJ. Specifically, the scratching that opens the song and accompanies the hook serves to interrupt the "sense" of this Wall by the sonic register of the trauma that it both produces and disavows, at the same time that this scratching acts as a "solid wall of sound" to oppose and contest the narratives that allow for this Wall to "make sense" as an essential form of "national security." For this reason, the song also acts as a call to arms for Hip-Hop Nation to make use of its tactics to oppose the new regime, as underground hip-hop is based on the co-option, re-signification, interruption and distortion of terms and songs in order to point to and expose the traumatic reality that cannot be said, heard, or acknowledged—what fails to be witnessed—in the dominant discourse and white sensibility.

Another powerful example of the use of scratching to oppose the discourse that normalizes the anti-black violence inflicted by this regime is the song "Talk to Me," produced by the group Run the Jewels as the first release on their third studio album, *Run the Jewels 3* (2016).[19] The song opens as Killer Mike raps: "We return from the depths of the badland . . . Went to war with the Devil and Shaytan/He wore a bad toupee and a spray tan," and so explicitly identifies (and mocks) the incoming president as a new threat that they will resist with the power of their skills as MC and DJ. Later the lyrics are even more explicit about the urgency of their protest: "Born Black, that's dead on arrival/My job is to fight for survival/In spite of these #AllLivesMatter-ass white folk." Here Killer Mike reinforces the un-natural vulnerability of black citizens *as such* to state violence, and identifies the role of the MC to fight for their survival through contesting the discursive practices that evade and normalize this violence, such as the oft-repeated phrase "All Lives Matter" coined to oppose the movement of Black Lives Matter formed to protest police brutality against African Americans. And yet the most powerful part of the song comes at the very end, after the phrase "Talk to Me" is followed by 15 seconds of complex and furious scratching, after which the phrase "Talk to Me" is repeated again as the close of the song. The implication is that the only way to "talk" or effectively communicate given the terms of our toxic political discourse is to interrupt its sense and totalizing presence on American sensibility, and scratching can support this effort through rendering this discourse senseless to register the voices that cannot be heard through the din of nationalist, racist, heterosexist narratives on which the current regime depends. On the track, the fervent scratching *feels like* a concrete experience that pierces through the spectacle of politics that creates a simulacra of order (a solid "Wall") as officials target and destroy racialized and gendered communities *as such*.

We can understand the aesthetics and cathartic effect of the scratch as a sonic experience of "breaking through" the mere simulacra of experience in light of Jacques Lacan's assertion in his seminal text *The Four Fundamental Concepts of Psychoanalysis* that trauma is at the origin of the psychoanalytic experience. This is because trauma confirms the psychoanalytic suspicion of the symbolic universe as a privileged domain of meaning, and reveals the presence of "another locality, another space, another scene," or a more fundamental dimension of reality prior to its mediation through symbolic representation. For Lacan, trauma occurs and can be detected in the immediate space of awareness between perception and consciousness.[20] Since traumatic symptoms recur in the present to the extent that we cannot acknowledge or represent traumatic violations from the past, the sonic experience of "breaking through" the symbolic order to aesthetically depict the "locality" or "scene" that both escapes from and belies this order is cathartic for those who need for their trauma to be witnessed—or at least witness the failure of language to represent their experience—in order to cope with trauma and arrest the return of symptoms of PTSD. This reflects the view of analyst Alison Carper that "Trauma Needs a Witness," the title of an op-ed she wrote for *The New York Times* reflecting on her work with her patients (09/15/15).[21]

In both content and form, underground hip-hop has always served as an aesthetic depiction of the historical repetition of traumas that African Americans can neither master nor forget, and which our country routinely disavows in order to sustain narratives that have never been true and have always served to perpetuate those same traumas. Further, hip-hop testifies to the inseparability of police brutality and mass incarceration from our collective disavowal of American slavery *as* a trauma from which we have not recovered nor overcome in our everyday practices and political institutions. In chapter 1 I described the focus in underground hip-hop on how past forms of racist oppression recur in the American present to the extent that they are deferred and dis-articulated with reference to the song "Sound of Da Police" by KRS-ONE, and I cited the following verse: "The overseer had the right to get ill/And if you fought back, the overseer had the right to kill." This verse about the role of the overseer in the system of slavery in the American past is immediately followed by a verse about the role of the officer today: "The officer has the right to arrest/And if you fight back they put a hole in your chest." Rap songs illustrate that the individual and socio-political space of trauma are inextricable from each other as African Americans *inherit* their increased vulnerability to discrimination and violence that is reinforced by contemporary practices of racist oppression (racial profiling, mass incarceration). In this way the psychic wounds left by historical traumas cannot heal when there is always a new violation and a new source of psychic pain. Through sampling and the scratch, hip-hop artists bear witness for themselves and their communities because the traumatic and entirely preventable violence from which they suffer in the everyday conditions of American life cannot be articulated and represented in the dominant discursive terms.

For these reasons, hip-hop offers important lessons for the field of trauma theory, for one of the most perplexing questions raised by trauma theorists is how—or if—it is possible to communicate or describe traumatic experiences that are distinguished by the impossibility of "knowing" or mediating them through categories and narratives about human experience. Although trauma theorists have identified the historical dimension of trauma such that the more we *refuse* to bear witness to the violence in the past that we cannot explain or affirm, the more we create the conditions for the repetition of pathological symptoms in the present, they have not explicitly associated the historical repetition of trauma with systems of oppression against racialized and gendered minorities. Instead, studies in the field tend to focus on individuals who suffer from trauma due to the racist and heterosexist organization of socio-political and economic relations.

When I had the opportunity to bring this point up with Cathy Caruth at a symposium on trauma at DePaul University in 2016, she explained that trauma theorists were wary of making a direct connection between trauma and systems of oppression due to the fact that it is not the case that *every* person who suffers from racist or sexist violence will develop PTSD. While this is certainly true, it does not take into account the relation between the individual's symptoms of PTSD and the larger environment that causes it, or the relation between the mental wellbeing of individuals and the conditions under which their community lives. In contrast, hip-hop artists draw attention to trauma as a psycho-social space *inflicted and sustained by* patterns of state violence against racialized communities; these patterns of violence are not seen or understood *as violent* by white sensibility.

Rappers ask for a Witness to the harms inflicted on black communities, and illustrate that trauma is inseparable from a larger environment in which everyone experiences the effects of traumatic suffering that is consistently dis-articulated as tragic and accidental by the media and our politicians. Underground rappers illustrate that the historical repetition of trauma does not simply occur on the individual, psychic level, and reveal the economy of historical trauma in the United States: Our consistent refusal to register the trauma of anti-black racism in the past sows the seeds for its repetition and for our current indifference to the state-sanctioned torture and murder of black citizens in the present. In other words, rappers suggest that *American history is itself traumatic*, insofar as the traumas inflicted by systems of anti-black violence in the past, recur to the extent that we continue to deny the genocidal nature of anti-black racism in the present.

In the following chapters, I address both the aesthetic politics of hip-hop and its relation to the politics of genocide studies, as well as delineate the role of hip-hop as a form of testimony that affects our sensibility.

NOTES ON HIP-HOP AND THE DEATH DRIVE

In his final work *Beyond the Pleasure Principle*, Freud explains that the psychic breach effected by trauma is disruptive and destructive—it disrupts the temporal continuity of life (the past invades the present) and it destroys psychic harmony (our libidinal economy). In his efforts to explain why the brain would force someone to re-live a near-death experience, Freud postulates the presence of a "death drive" in the psyche that exists alongside and opposes the aim of the "pleasure principle." Freud also associates the compulsion to repeat with the recurrence of trauma, as both indicate a desire for the quietude of death—the imperative of the death drive. In this way the death drive represents "the expression of the inertia inherent in organic life" and the compulsion to repeat is connected with the instinct towards death—total, eternal quietude.[22] Freud explains the counter-intuitive nature of the death drive by surmising that all of our apparent efforts to defend our lives from danger only represent the unconscious desire to *choose* the manner in which we die.

Freud draws a paradoxical implication from his theory of the death drive: "If we are to take it as a truth that knows no exception that everything living dies for *internal* reasons—becomes inorganic once again—then we shall be compelled to say that '*the aim of all life is death*' and, looking backward, that '*inanimate things existed before living ones.*'"[23] In its devotion to testifying to the historical systems of trauma that have always afflicted black communities in the United States, hip-hop culture illustrates that the "death drive" is not simply a biological instinct to return to an inorganic state but instead also the morbid response to the continuity and predictability of state-sanctioned traumatic suffering. When Tupac Shakur raps "They shoulda shot me when I was born, now I'm trapped in the motherfuckin storm," in his song "How Long Will They Mourn Me?," the phrase is not merely an expression of nihilism.[24] Instead, the despair and pessimism that characterizes the mood of so many underground rap songs, acts as the emotional register of being targeted for death, consigned to living and possibly not-living at the same time. Shakur's insistence that "They should've shot me when I was born," reflects Caruth's insight that trauma reveals that "survival is a crisis" without solution or end, and also reflects the psychic desire to choose the means of one's death, the desire *to achieve a decent death* that characterizes the death drive.

The testimony of underground rappers describes the conditions of being-black in the United States, conditions that conspire—at the same time—to destroy this life that is given a liminal status at the margins of society. As the poet Claudia Rankin explains, "Black life is a condition of mourning," where one is always already vulnerable to death and always already lamenting its loss.[25] In this state of "preemptive mourning" where there is always a reason to mourn for the loss of black lives, life is not opposed to death but instead is felt and experienced in view of it; they co-exist in unbearable proximity. Preemptive mourning is perverse, where the danger-of-being rather than death becomes the sentence one cannot escape or prepare for in any way. The anxiety and precariousness of being-black in the United States can undermine the ability and the will to live, for life requires some degree of predictability lest it degenerate into a state of nature in which one loses the status of citizen and becomes the hunted.

Perhaps most prevalent in the work of Shakur is the notion that for a black man in America, "life" is an impossible task that he did not choose and cannot endure, and that every day he survives the imminent dangers of being-black presents yet another crisis or cause-for-mourning that he cannot control. In "How Long Will They Mourn Me?" Shakur raps: "It's kinda hard to be optimistic/When your homie's lyin' dead on the pavement twisted." Though released in 1994, the lyrics "When your homie's lyin' dead on the pavement twisted" evoke an image that is eerily reminiscent of the circumstances of the murder of 18-year old Michael Brown in Ferguson, MI on August 9, 2014.

Brown was an unarmed, black teenager and *for no apparent reason* he was shot by a white police officer around noon, then left where he fell for four hours in the hot summer sun, face down in the middle of the street, blood streaming from his head. The image of Brown's body left in the street was a visceral reminder of the political status of African Americans as expendable, excluded from the protection of the law and moral consideration, *seen as* human beings who lack the value of white human beings whose deaths are mourned as a loss to the human community. In the aftermath of his murder and the protests that followed, a grand jury decided not to indict Darren Wilson, the police officer who killed Brown, based on his testimony that Brown appeared to present a grave threat, or in his words: "The only way I can describe it, it looks like a demon, that's how angry he looked."[26] The genocidal violence against black men *as black men* in the United States is not perceived *as violence* by white sensibility that is conditioned to criminalize and demonize all black men or the fact-of-being-black in order to affirm the status quo of white supremacy that depends on this violence as well as to perpetually defer the fact of white privilege itself.

Further, this social conditioning that produces the terms and limits of white sensibility—reinforced by the dominant discourse and media—undermines the capacity for white empathy for the black victims of state violence. The refusal to indict Wilson—while predictable—also denied any cause for collective horror about his murder of a black teenager; instead this murder was re-presented as a tragic, singular accident. Freud connects the repetition of psychic trauma with the death drive, and in underground hip-hop the expression of the death drive or a certain will-unto-death serves as the emotional register of traumas inflicted by a system of American genocide against black communities.

The harms inflicted by genocidal violence outstrip the harm of mass murder, as genocide is a process of destroying a community rather than a single act, so that it is more accurate to describe genocide as a system that inflicts conditions that undermine the possibility for a decent life-and-death *for entire communities*. Testimonies from victims of genocides often detail types of suffering that can lead to a sort of death-in-life, a state in which one's life becomes insupportable as one's life, and death itself no longer appears as the greater of evils. Escaped slave Harriet Jacobs is quite clear about this in her 1861 autobiography, *Incidents in the Life of a Slave Girl*, when she states: "Death is better than slavery."[27]

As I will further illustrate in the second part of this text that addresses the role of hip-hop as a form of testimony that affects the sensibility, the form and content of underground hip-hop serve as the emotional register of the moral horror we ought to feel in relation to anti-black violence and—as a form of music—can serve to pierce the white indifference to black suffering that sustains white ignorance and complacency about the status quo. In underground hip-hop, the aesthetic depiction of the death drive is also a political weapon wielded against this apathy and the collective white refusal to mourn for black victims of state violence. In this sense Shakur's question "How Long

Will They Mourn Me?" evokes both the precariousness and expendability of black life as well as serves as an indictment against the white refusal to mourn the deaths of black citizens in a genocidal state organized around their subordination.

NOTES

1. Mos Def, "Hip Hop," Produced by Diamond D and Yasiin Bey, Written by Diamond D and Yasiin Bey, Release Date: October 12, 1999.
2. Nas, "Hip Hop Is Dead," Produced by will.i.am, Written by will.i.am, Doug Ingle, Jerry Lordan and Nas, Release Date: November 5, 2006.
3. Mos Def, "Fear Not of Man," Produced and Written by Yassiin Bey, Release Date: October 12, 1999.
4. Alim, *Roc the Mic Right*, 71.
5. Ibid., 72.
6. Ibid., 124.
7. Ibid., 125.
8. Joseph G. Schloss, *Breaking Beats: The Art of Sample-Based Hip-Hop* (Middletown, CT: Wesleyan University Press, 2014), 33.
9. Cathy Caruth, editor, *Trauma: Explorations in Memory* (Baltimore: Johns Hopkins University Press, 1995), 5.
10. Cathy Caruth, *Unclaimed Experience: Trauma, Narrative, and History* (Baltimore: Johns Hopkins University Press, 1996), 59.
11. Peterson, *The Hip-Hop Underground and African-American Culture: Beneath the Surface* (Basingstoke, UK: Palgrave Macmillan, 2014), 2.
12. 2Pac, "Changes," Produced by Big D the Impossible, Written by Bruce Hornsby, Big D the Impossible and 2Pac Release Date: October 13, 1998.
13. JAY-Z, "Hard-Knock Life (Ghetto Anthem)," Produced by DJ Mark the 45 King, Written by Charles Strouse, Martin Charnin, James H. Billington and JAY-Z, Release Date: September 29, 1998.
14. Bruce Hornsby and the Range, "The Way It Is," Produced by Elliot Scheiner & Bruce Hornsby, Written by Bruce Hornsby, Release Date: April 1, 1986.
15. Rose, *Black Noise*, 28.
16. Aileen Quinn, "It's a Hard-Knock Life," Written By Martin Charnin and Charles Strouse, Arranged and Conducted by Ralph Burns, Release Date: June 18, 1992.
17. Mark Katz, *Groove Music: The Art and Culture of the Hip-Hop DJ* (New York: Oxford University Press, 2012), 66.
18. A Tribe Called Quest, "Solid Wall of Sound," Produced by Blair Wells & Q-Tip, Written by Jack White, Phife Dawg, Busta Rhymes and Q-Tip, Release Date: November 11, 2016.
19. Run the Jewels, "Talk to Me," Produced by El-P, Written by Killer Mike and El-P, Release Date: October 24, 2016.

20. Jacques Lacan, *The Seminar of Jacques Lacan: The Four Fundamental Concepts of Psychoanalysis (Vol. Book XI)* (New York: W. W. Norton & Company, 1998), 56.

21. Alison Carper, "Trauma Needs a Witness," *The New York Times*, September 15, 2015.

22. Sigmund Freud, *Beyond the Pleasure Principle* (New York: W. W. Norton & Company, 1990), 43.

23. Ibid., 46.

24. Thug Life, "How Long Will They Mourn Me?" Produced by Warren G and Nate Dogg, Written by Nate Dogg, 2Pac, Macadoshis, Rated R and Big Syke, Release Date: September 26, 1994.

25. Claudia Rankine, "The Condition of Black Life Is One of Mourning," *The New York Times Magazine*, June 22, 2015.

26. "Darren Wilson Explains Why He Killed Michael Brown," by Terrence McCoy, *The Washington Post*, November 25, 2014.

27. Harriet Jacobs, *Incidents in the Life of a Slave Girl* (New York: Dover, 2000), 68.

Chapter 3

Claimin' I'm a Criminal

THE "CRIMINAL" AND THE CRIME OF AMERICAN GENOCIDE

In a recording that was released only after his death, Tupac Shakur raps:

> Crazy, I gotta work with what'chu gave me
> You claimin I'm a criminal and you the one that made me[1]

In his concise phrase "You claimin I'm a criminal and you the one that made me," Shakur illustrates that black communities suffer from atrocities produced by the racist disparity of wealth and privilege that are mis-represented or dis-articulated as the fault of black people; or atrocities that are "caused" or "made necessary" by their "inborn" pathology toward criminality. Further, the next verse alludes to the moral hypocrisy of blaming black men for "criminal" behavior when they face compromised choices imposed by a criminal, genocidal regime organized around their subordination, exploitation, incarceration, and un-natural, untimely death:

> They got me trapped in this slavery
> Now I'm lost in this holocaust headin for my grave G

In appropriating the term "holocaust" to represent the system of American anti-black racism, Shakur's verse serves as a protest against the singular importance granted to the Nazi genocide and a protest against the exclusion of both American slavery and the American penal system from the popular understanding of genocide. In this chapter I illustrate that this exclusion cannot be rationally defended but instead indicates that our sensibility of genocide plays an important role in our ability to defer, deny, and *refuse* to think about the everyday forms of genocidal violence inflicted through American institutions that target black citizens *as such*. And indeed, the discourse and theory about American slavery taught in our schools and assumed by genocide scholars—and the role it occupies in our political imaginary—portrays the systematic destruction of men and women kidnapped from Africa as the tragic but still pragmatic and so intelligible state policy of a new nation.

The iconic phrase "Claimin I'm a Criminal" in hip-hop culture has always served to draw attention to the role that the notion of the "criminal" plays in our racist sensibility of the present and in our ability to ignore, defer, and deny the systemic infliction of anti-black violence in the everyday administration of the police force and the criminal justice system. Underground rappers draw attention to the fact that the term "criminal" is not morally neutral, as white people who break the law are not for that reason overdetermined as "essentially" criminal, or essentially untrustworthy, incapable of fully respecting moral standards and legal bonds. In this way, they draw attention to the role that the notion of the "criminal" has always played in the economy of American genocide against black communities. Further, in their frequent use of the terms "genocide" and "holocaust," rappers do not minimize the harm of genocide but instead co-opt the term from its context in our anti-black sensibility of genocide in order to testify to the infliction of genocidal violence against black communities in the American past and present. In this sense their co-option also serves to mark the difference between our sensibility and the reality of genocide, as well as the complicity of the former in the perpetuation of the latter.

In their song titled "Claimin I'm a Criminal" on their 1994 album *Everything Is Everything*, the group Brand Nubian repeats this phrase over and over in the chorus of the song. In the first verse Lord Jamar raps:

Tell the devil to his face he can suck my dick
It's the whole black race that they're fuckin with.[2]

Here he draws attention to the genocidal structure of the American criminal justice system that targets the "whole black race" *as such* in order to keep black people "on a level that's minimum," to preserve the racist disparity of power and capital essential to white supremacy. The hip-hop phrase "Claimin I'm a Criminal" serves to expose the historical importance of the category of the "criminal" to the efficient functionality of anti-black genocide in the United States, insofar as the category serves to *criminalize* black people in thought and perception so that white people can rationalize and normalize the infliction of genocidal violence against black communities as the use of "legal force" to prevent and destroy "threats" to public safety. The criminalization of black people in white sensibility is also essential to its ability to defer the fact and social privilege of its own whiteness.

In the United States, the institution of slavery was sustained by the creation of legislation that gave slave owners the right to use corporal punishment against their slaves as well as to kill them. In order to sustain the absolute power of white citizens over their black slaves, a series of laws was passed to effect the legal criminalization of black life through criminalizing basic capacities such as reading and writing and agency and movement until there was always already a provocation for punitive punishment. Thus in its origins the U.S. criminal justice system largely served to legalize a system of white supremacy through the exploitation of Africans and the destruction of their families. Their exploitation was first achieved through chattel slavery and justified with reference to racist ideology; rappers emphasize that it is now achieved through slave labor in the prisons and justified with reference to crime and punishment. The association of black people with criminals serves to efface the irreducible individuality and vulnerability of each prisoner as well as efface the fact that the United States targets black people *as such* rather than for what they do or believe.

In their use of the phrase "Claimin I'm a Criminal," rappers also draw attention to how the term informs the white perception of black men, who are always already *seen* as a threat and as people who cannot be trusted. In this way they contribute to the phenomenology of the white gaze provided by black philosophers, writers, and artists in the field of black existentialism, and further the studies initiated by Fanon in his seminal text *Black Skin, White Masks*. As previously mentioned, Fanon makes use of the term "overdetermined" to illustrate how the discursive category of "black" informs white perception of black skin on the level of sensibility: "But in my case everything takes on a new guise. I am given no chance. I am overdetermined from without. I am the slave not of the "idea" that others have of me but of my own appearance."[3] Fanon draws attention to how the white sensibility of black men as "black" is also, at the same time, to regard them at a distance, through a veil that also produces suspicion and so inhibits epistemic respect. Recently the work of the social psychologist Jennifer L. Eberhardt has revealed that there are empirical grounds for understanding the interdependence of discourse, perception, and oppressive relations of power. Eberhardt conducted a series of experiments to show how "mostly unconscious racial stereotypes can criminalize African-Americans," and has proved that police officers are more likely to judge as criminals those whose faces are the most stereotypically "black." As she explains, "It's almost as if people are thinking of blackness as a crime."[4] Her conclusions support the idea behind the phrase "Claimin I'm a Criminal," namely, that in the United States the criminalization of black men in white sensibility obfuscates the infliction of genocidal anti-black violence that has always been essential to sustaining the foundation of a white supremacist state.

Although African American hip-hop artists have been making use of the term "genocide" for over thirty years to describe the system of anti-black racism in the United States, they cannot "get a witness" who hears the vital importance of their testimony *as a source of knowledge* about the nature and distinct harms inflicted by anti-black racism in the United States, due to the fact that they are *also criminalized* from birth, subject to the "school to prison pipeline." As succinctly expressed in a bar rapped by Flava Flav on the iconic track "Caught, Can We Get A Witness?" on the equally iconic album *It Takes a Nation of Millions to Hold Us Back* released by the group Public Enemy in 1988:

> They claim that I'm violent/Now I choose to be silent
> Can I get a witness?[5]

Although the overdetermination of black rappers as "violent criminals" have prevented scholars from taking their testimony seriously as a source of authority about the nature and effects of anti-black racism in the United States, they have not hesitated to use the term genocide to describe the nature of both American slavery and the criminal punishment system. For example, in 1991 the Lifers Group released a rap album (*Lifers Group*), and at the time of its release all of the members were incarcerated at the Rahway State Prison in New Jersey. In one song titled "The Real Deal," Maxwell Melvins (aka 66064) raps:

> So now I'm in prison and yo, it's like apartheid
> Modernized slavery, straight to the genocide[6]

Melvins refers to the nature of prison life in terms of "modernized slavery" that produces a racial caste system "like apartheid" that advances "straight to the genocide"; in this way he deftly illustrates the continuity and transmutation of genocidal practices over time. In my experience working in the field of Holocaust and genocide studies for twenty years, genocide scholars do not regard the use of the term "genocide" by underground rappers to be a legitimate use of the term (if hip-hop is regarded at all!), nor do they regard the testimony of African Americans about suffering from patterns of state violence to be a significant source of evidence or even relevant to the field of genocide studies (again, if African American history is regarded at all!).

Their refusal to take seriously black testimony about American genocide reflects the larger sensibility of genocide that is operative in the field and *assumes the distinction* between anti-black forms of discrimination and genocidal violence as a matter of fact, as a matter ostensibly too obvious to be considered critically. In our published work together, my co-author Alfred Frankowski and I have illustrated that in the field of Holocaust and genocide studies, this distinction is never challenged or questioned as to what service it provides or what sensibility it means and what it produces. In fact, this lack of interrogation is canonized in the critical philosophical and literary studies that have shaped current scholarship in genocide studies and its discourse.

For example, in Berel Lang's recent book *Genocide: The Act as Idea*, he offers a defense of the importance of the term genocide against its contemporary detractors.[7] He is most careful to defend this category from being applied to anti-black forms of violence: namely, slavery, Jim Crow, and by extension, the political violence of mass incarceration. However, like most other genocide scholars, in his book Lang does not defend his exclusion of anti-black violence in the United States from his historiography of genocide, but instead merely affirms that while American slavery was morally bad, it was not a system of genocide *per se*. It is this *judgement from nowhere* and *based on nothing* that does the critical work of clarifying the term genocide. Lang merely takes this as an assessment that seems true, yet he bases his critical distinction on a type of critical sensibility that is only possible because it produces a failure to be critical about its own aesthetic limits.

The term "genocide" was coined by the Polish-Jewish legal scholar and refugee Raphael Lemkin in the immediate aftermath of the Nazi regime, after he had emigrated to the United States. He coined the term in order to name a new crime in international law that would place new limits on sovereign power by prohibiting the effort to destroy entire groups marked by race, ethnicity, nationality, and religion. With great endurance, patience, and passion, Lemkin successfully lobbied the newly formed United Nations to formalize his concept and adopt the Convention on the Prevention and Punishment of the Crime of Genocide in 1948 in order to establish legal and moral limits on the types of violence that a nation can inflict on its own people, and empower the world community to intervene in the sovereign affairs of a nation when they threaten the survival of a group "as such."

Specifically, the U.N. Convention criminalizes the sovereign intent to destroy racial, ethnic, religious or national communities, "in whole or in part," through a variety of policies that all aim to weaken the cultural and intergenerational bonds between members of these communities. The Convention lists five specific types of genocidal violence that aim to destroy the foundations of a group:

1. Killing members of the group
2. Causing serious bodily or mental harm to members of the group

3. Deliberately inflicting on the group conditions of life calculated to bring about its physical destruction in whole or in part
4. Imposing measures intended to prevent births within the group
5. Forcibly transferring children of the group to another group

Despite the legal recognition of a variety of ways that nations can *over time* undermine the social and intergenerational vitality of a group "as such," genocide scholars have always based their sensibility of genocide on a narrow definition that focuses on the means of killing a large number of the targeted group. This has led to a sensibility of genocide as the "act" or an "event" of mass murder rather than a process that—like every historical genocide— is realized thorough a legal system of exclusion and subordination and violent practices that attack and tear apart the family unit. For this reason, genocide scholars have always based their studies on a specific ontology of genocide as a singular "Event" that always already excludes the *systemic* infliction of anti-black violence in the United States, and this ontology also informs the sensibility of genocide in the political imaginary.

The historical refusal of scholars in the field of Holocaust and genocide studies to question or defend the default, irrational distinction between anti-black violence as a form of systemic *discrimination* and the systemic infliction of violence against racialized communities as *genocide* must be understood in relation to Lemkin's historical refusal to support the effort of the Civil Rights Congress to become the first group in history to make use of the U.N. Convention Against Genocide in order to file a petition in 1951—*We Charge Genocide: The Crime of Government against the Negro People*—to U.N. offices in New York and Paris. The aim of this petition was to formally charge the United States of the (new) crime of genocide for their institutional and systematic destruction and economic exploitation of black communities. At the time it was presented, the United Nations refused to take up the petition or consider the analysis and evidence provided by black scholars, activists, politicians, lawyers, and artists about the genocidal character of anti-black racism in the United States. Their refusal to hear the petition was followed by Lemkin's indignant refusal to take it seriously, and these two refusals informed the sensibility of genocide in academic and popular culture that is marked by limits that prevent us from thinking, imagining, or perceiving the possibility of American genocide. These limits prevent us from thinking about the systemic anti-black violence inflicted through the historical systems of slavery, Jim Crow, and incarceration (consistently inflicted by the police force and the administration of the criminal justice system), as *genocidal* violence that aims to destroy black communities "as such." Despite its historical importance, the *We Charge Genocide* petition remains a largely unexamined founding text for genocide scholarship.

Although the petition references the continuity of genocidal violence against black Americans from slavery through 1951, it focuses its analyses on the persistence of political and legal discrimination *and* violence perpetrated through the (then operative) Jim Crow laws. The most exemplary of these forms of violence is spectacle terror lynching, and the petition includes poignant and graphic accounts of specific lynchings and the terror they inflict on entire black communities. The petition also offers an account of systematic state violence perpetrated through legal segregation that contextualizes black suffering, and it stands out as a methodological document analyzing forms of social death produced by American laws and extra-juridical practices as forms of genocidal violence. The following passages from *We Charge Genocide* could just as easily describe the anti-black logic of our criminal justice system as it does the logic of Jim Crow laws and lynching:

> Mass murder on the basis of race is a powerful source of constant terror, as it is intended to be, to the whole Negro people. As a result of the pattern of extra-legal violence in which they live out their lives, if they do live, the entire Negro people exists in a constant fear that cannot fail to cause serious bodily and mental harm.
>
> Another source of serious bodily and mental harm is the segregation which imprisons United States Negroes from birth to death, marking their status as inferior as a matter of law on the basis of race, cutting them off from adequate education, hospital facilities, medical treatment, and housing, forcing them to live in ghettos and depriving them of rights and privileges that other Americans are accorded of course. This imprisonment which cuts off United States Negroes from the services and privileges of their fellow citizens, which makes them pariahs in their own country, results in a condition which is temperately described by the words "serious bodily and mental harm."[8]

The CRC's demand for international recognition of the distinctly *genocidal* violence perpetrated by Jim Crow laws in the United States between 1890 and 1965 was a direct political critique of its institutions. This critique was more than political since it demanded that the American destruction of black communities be seen as an event and as a pattern within history that marks the severity and structure of the anti-black violence that has been embedded in U.S. law and society in the past and present. The conveners of the petition intentionally used the term "genocide" because they explained that it is necessary to oppose the "pious phrases" and "deadly legal euphemisms" that mask the regularity and brutality of state-sanctioned violence against black Americans. They argue that without this term to describe the system of anti-black violence in the United States, we are not able to actually confront the crime and the violence itself as it is experienced. For this same reason, Claudia Card appealed to the notion of genocide in order to explain and condemn the harm of *social death*—a term originally coined by Orlando Patterson to explain the logic of American slavery—that emerged from the structural discrimination against entire populations in war and in peace, in the legal and medical and academic and domestic areas of human life.[9] When underground rappers insist on using the terms "genocide" and "holocaust" to describe the nature and effects of American anti-black racism, they take up the mission of the now defunct Civil Rights Congress insofar as they similarly believe in the political importance of the term "genocide" to contest the dis-articulation of systemic violence against black communities in American discourse and white sensibility.

At the time of its presentation, the CRC petition was ignored by the world community and it has been largely ignored by scholars who work in the field of Holocaust and genocide studies, following Lemkin's scathing rejection of the CRC's effort. Two years after the *We Charge Genocide* petition had been largely swept into the dustbin of history, Lemkin felt compelled to write an op-ed for *The New York Times* titled "Nature of Genocide: Confusion with Discrimination Against Individuals Seen,"[10] that reiterated his objection to the petition. His editorial is peculiar because despite his heroic and noble efforts to force the world community to regard genocide as an international crime against humanity, Lemkin exhibits callous indifference about the atrocities and effects of American slavery and lynching, as well as denigrates the black activists, artists, politicians, and lawyers who work for the Civil Rights Congress—at the time a prominent civil rights organization—as "the opponents of the Genocide Convention":

> The opponents of the Genocide Convention have been asking, literally, can one be guilty of genocide when one frightens a Negro? Obviously not, because fear alone cannot be considered as serious mental harm as meant by the authors of the convention; the act is not directed against the Negro population of the country and by no stretch of imagination can one discover in the United States an intent or plan to exterminate the Negro population, which is increasing in conditions of evident prosperity and progress.

Lemkin's response is significant because he does not simply dismiss the argument of the petition, but rather he dismisses the legitimacy of comparing instances of racial discrimination with the political violence of genocide (even though clearly inseparable in the logic of Nazism), and dismisses the mental anguish suffered from segregation, lynchings, and police brutality as nothing more than being "frightened." Lemkin insists that "by no stretch of imagination" could one possibly discover any intent to commit genocide in the regular, state-sanctioned murder, torture, and exploitation of black

Americans, or within the legal system of discrimination that serves to preserve the status quo of white economic and political supremacy. And yet, the CRC presented nearly 200 pages of documented evidence that makes just this case; pointing out, that it would take quite a bit of one's imagination to deny the impact of this violence.[11]

As an op-ed, one could argue that Lemkin may simply be conceding that *to him* these charges make no sense. In this sense, his objections are reduced merely to a matter of personal opinion or to a misguided case of him protecting the definition of genocide for European forms of genocide. Neither rationale make sense. Both positions are problematic, the former more so because Lemkin was distinctly concerned with colonialism and its violence globally in many forms.[12] So his rejection is troubling because it seems inconsistent with his larger understanding of global political violence and his sensibility toward it, and he appears to harbor an unusual resentment against African Americans *in particular* for their efforts to draw attention to the genocidal forms of violence that terrorize entire black communities. The fact that the CRC charges *made no sense* to Lemkin who insisted that their petition threatened to reduce the term genocide to *nonsense* is critical to how genocide discourse engages or disengages anti-black violence at the level of the sensible. Not only in Lemkin, but across the discipline, the frequency of such dismissals and the role it plays in the shaping of genocide discourse, is cause for questioning of what it takes to *make sense*, to not be *nonsense,* which is a question of the sensibility that is being deployed and developed as a hallmark of genocide discourse.

In our work, Frankowski and I argue that Lemkin's reaction and the historical refusal to consider the petition or Lemkin's op-ed indicates the moral and political power of the term "genocide" as well as the anti-black *sensibility of genocide* that informs both academic and popular discussions about the history of genocide in western politics. In this context, the use of the term "genocide" in underground hip-hop both co-opts and re-signifies the term outside of the limits of white sensibility. In this chapter I explain how the consistent use of the term "genocide" in underground hip-hop lyrics to describe the system of anti-black violence in the United States can be understood as an effort to take up the mission of the Civil Rights Congress, who first intimated the political importance of the term "genocide" for naming the system of anti-black violence that founded and still informs the structure and procedures of American democracy as a racial caste system that sustains the economic and political supremacy of white men.

As illustrated in chapter 2, underground hip-hop has always contested the narrative of the American Dream through attesting to the traumatic nature of structural racist oppression and its transfiguration from slavery to mass incarceration. The persistent use of the term "genocide" to describe the American penal system and the importance of the phrase "Claimin I'm a Criminal" in hip-hop culture, indicate that hip-hop artists further the mission of the CRC to draw attention to the distinctly *genocidal* system of anti-black violence in the United States. Roughly 70 percent of the prisoners now incarcerated in the United States belong to ethnic or racial minorities, and nearly two-thirds of the women in prison are women of color (African Americans constitute roughly 13 percent of the population). Underground rappers illustrate that the racial disproportion of U.S. prisoners belies the fact that the over-representation of racialized minorities is not a real political problem "to be solved" because the prison system has always functioned as an essential means with which the state prevents the social, economic, and political mobility of black citizens and—like most genocidal regimes—continues to find new ways for white businessmen to profit from the systemic violence against black communities (prison labor, private prisons, private half-way houses, bail bondsmen, phone calls to/from the prison, etc.).

In order to counter the dis-articulation and dis-appearance of American anti-black genocide from our sensibility of genocide in academic discourse, Frankowski and I have recently illustrated how the specific commitments and lines of inquiry in the field of Holocaust and genocide studies are also informed by an anti-black bias—a refusal to think black bodies as vulnerable to genocide—that is produced by the structure of recollection or historical inquiry. This structure ensures that every scholarly effort to remember and record a specific genocide is, at the same time, an act of forgetting that rests on the perpetual displacement of anti-black genocide in the present. Lastly, we have also criticized the ontology of genocide as an "Event" with a discrete beginning, middle and end, and instead have suggested the model of a "social pathology": as a social pathology, we can understand genocide in terms of a pattern of social, political, economic, aesthetic, and legal practices that produce and sustain lethal dysfunctions in human behavior such that entire populations are targeted for state-sanctioned violence on the basis of race, religion, ethnicity, ability, gender, sex, and/or nationality. As rappers illustrate again and again, anti-black genocidal violence is a pathological pattern of socio-political practices that have always informed the racist distribution of power and capital in the United States.

However, the use of scholarship is limited in its ability to contest and interrupt our conditioned sensibility of genocide that re-produces those entrenched discursive practices that reinforce patterns of moral blindness to the extremity of anti-black genocidal violence in the American present. Frankowski and I have referred to the modern sensibility of genocide as a "morbid sensibility" due, in part, to its role in the dis-articulation and repetition of black suffering and un-natural death in the aftermath of the Nazi regime. For as Shakur clearly understood, our failure to reckon with our genocidal past informs our present indifference to the genocidal wounds suffered by African Americans from their mass incarceration. That is, although there has always been a disproportionate number of black men and women in the prison system, we cannot see the criminal justice system as structurally genocidal because we refuse to recognize the founding genocide that established the racial democracy in which we still live. For we continue to interpret the excessive violence in our prisons as the tragic but inevitable consequence of any system of criminal punishment, rather than as the sense-less, brutal infliction of torture against populations already marginalized by the racist and classist distribution of capital in order to sustain our racial democracy.

In this way the cognitive erasure of American slavery as a system of genocide allows for its historical repetition through the state-sanctioned infliction of traumatic violence in our penal system that is also rendered invisible as a "necessary evil' rather than as the contemporary form of American genocide. The ubiquity of the term "genocide" in underground hip-hop indicates that American rappers—like the members of the CRC—believe that the definition of genocide is not merely an academic matter, but pertains to our ability to recognize and thus arrest the genocidal bio-politics that now informs the structure and conditions of incarceration. And their devotion to the term indicates their faith in the ability of hip-hop music to arrest or dis-rupt the conditioned sensibility of genocide and the default criminalization of black men that serve as aesthetic conditions for the repetition of anti-black genocidal violence in the American present. As poignantly expressed by Shakur in his track "They Don't Give a Fuck about Us":

> I'm watchin' my nation die, genocide the cause
> Expect a blood bath, the aftermath is y'alls[13]

As the CRC and underground rappers understand, genocide—the attempt to destroy a population as such—cannot be reduced to a single act of intentional mass murder. If we remain faithful to the U.N. definition and assume Card's notion of genocide as the infliction of social death upon a particular population, then we are in a position to better understand the testimony and text of rap songs about the nature and effects of prison upon African American families. For they testify to the loss of identity and dignity in the penal system, and the separation and destruction of their families who must continually grieve the loss of a father or mother or brother or sister or son who is still alive, but subsisting in the midst of violence and degradation.

In my view underground hip-hop provides an essential aesthetic intervention on our sensibility that is a powerful political weapon to be forged in order to escape the cycle of prison reform that only perpetuates the genocidal wounds inflicted upon black communities through deferring the question of the *everyday* conditions of confinement through the focus on the most apparently extra-legal and indefensible practices (solitary confinement and the death penalty). The traumatic form of hip-hop (illustrated in chapter 2) is distinctly capable of bearing witness to the transfiguration of genocidal policies in the United States from slavery to Jim Crow to mass incarceration, as well as illustrating the structural importance of anti-black genocide to our racial democracy that serves as the originary trauma that returns to the extent that we refuse to see, remember, or acknowledge its presence in the past and in the crisis of the American present.

HIP-HOP AND THE SENSIBILITY OF GENOCIDE

Hip-hop songs testify to the conditions that make life unbearable in U.S. prisons: the physical and sexual abuse from guards and inmates, the inedible food, the slave labor, the isolation, the degradation, the alienation from one's family and the powerlessness to help them, the arbitrary, autonomous system of excessive punishments for disobedience or "disrespect," the inability to mourn or attend the funerals of loved ones who pass away, the substandard medical care, the filthy and toxic conditions in the prison (black mold, contaminated water, etc.). As Brand Nubian raps in "Claimin' I'm a Criminal": "The beast is a bitch and I see it/I do the knowledge to em, so next time I can do em . . . / You can never know the penal til you been locked the fuck up in it." The verse reminds us that the excessive and extra-legal conditions of prison life—like the conditions in a concentration camp—are out-of-sight and thus out-of-mind in the popular sensibility about the "justice" of the criminal justice system.[14]

Hip-hop is a vehicle for the testimony of the oppressed, and in the case of American hip-hop, for those incarcerated and those more vulnerable to incarceration due to their race and class. Underground rap songs about prison life testify to the *pain* of incarceration that is hidden from view, in isolated prisons inaccessible to public scrutiny and free from federal oversight. And the aesthetic expression of this pain—in the traumatic form and content of the music—serves to jolt us out of our indifference to the real, vulnerable human beings who suffer from state-sanctioned torture in the name of "justice" and "public safety."

The public and political debate about prison focuses on the excessive *number* of black men in prison and the more overt forms of carceral torture such as solitary confinement and the death penalty; this discourse presupposes that the prison system would be a just institution if we (1) reduced the number of black men in prison and (2) eradicated specific practices that are exceptions to the norm of prison life. In this way the discourse reinforces the neoliberal sensibility that promotes piecemeal legal reforms as the solution to systemic racism and the post-racial sensibility that views systemic, state-sanctioned anti-black racism as a problem that was overcome with the end of slavery, Jim Crow laws, and segregation. For this reason the public debate about prison reform is dictated by the limits of white sensibility that cannot see, think, or imagine the prison system as an institution that perpetuates anti-black genocide through the everyday conditions of confinement and the administration of penal policies for the sake of sustaining our racial caste system that supports white supremacy.

Underground rappers testify to the pain and effects of confinement in order to resist the *episteme* that both obfuscates and rationalizes the carceral violence from which they suffer. As Brand Nubian raps: "But still I won't bite my tongue/I just write tight shit to incite the young, to fight the one," and contextualizes the moral and political need for hip-hop to oppose the system "Who keeps them on a level that's minimum/That's the number one reason." The conditions of incarceration keep African Americans living "at a minimum" through traumatizing those confined and their families left behind, and rappers hone their craft as a form of resistance against the debilitating effects of these traumas ("I just write tight shit to incite the young"). However, underground rappers are remarkable in their consistent association of the routine carceral traumas inflicted on black communities with the logic and nature of genocide, especially when the term is rarely used by critical race theorists, genocide scholars, prisoner advocates, or scholars who work in critical prison studies to describe the logic, problem, and criminality of the penal system.

The routine association between slavery, prison, and genocide in underground hip-hop is exemplified in a track titled "Modern Day Slavery" by Joell Ortiz from his album *The Brick: Bodega Chronicles* released in 2007. In the first verse he raps "Ain't nothin' changed 'cept the chains/They're restrainin' our physical frame," and deftly connects the legacy of American slavery with the mass incarceration of black men in the present.[15] He continues, "Mentally we're still livin' the same/It's lockdown," attesting to the continuity of the traumatic conditions suffered by African Americans that undermine the well-being of entire communities rather than simply harm those individuals killed or incarcerated by the state. In the second verse Immortal Technique is even more direct about the function of the prison system as a form of genocide that perpetuates the violence of American slavery that first established our racial democracy:

Our people are the product of genocide and slavery
Everything in the ghetto was how it was made to be

And then emphasizes that the exploitation of African Americans is neither accidental nor incidental nor historical:

Designed in a process, Prison Industrial Complex
Niggas transformed into numbers and objects

Immortal Technique refers to American slavery and genocide as part of a single process to transform black people into "numbers and objects," now accomplished by design through the prison-industrial complex that *produces* the black ghetto as the means and effect of its genocidal economy. In the song, the association of the prison system with genocide is not stated but alluded to through the art of rapping in poetic verse that cannot be "understood" the first time it is heard, given the speed of rapping and the grammar and phonology of Hip-Hop Nation Language. For this reason, the verse serve to expose the limits of the sensibility that cannot "make sense" of this association rather than defend this association per se that cannot be "understood" in the academic and popular discourse about genocide.

Rappers' use of "genocide" to categorize the American prison system—with reference to the violent, everyday conditions of confinement—also serves to support the political will to *abolish* the prison system rather than the neoliberal will to *reform* the penal system and sustain the basic structure and conditions of prison life. For the infliction of genocide is a crime organized by the state rather than a legal use of sovereign power, and the public and scholarly debate about prison reform rests on this dis-articulation of the genocidal or traumatic violence inflicted by the prison system as the tragic consequence of an imperfect system. Thus the use of the term "genocide" to describe the prison-industrial complex in the context of American history is both a co-option of the term from its context in white sensibility and a political tactic to disrupt our complacency about the terror inflicted on black communities through our carceral archipelago. Further, the association between slavery, genocide, and the penal system also contests the dominant *sensibility* of genocide that is informed by and reinforces the status quo in order to better expose the historical reality of genocidal violence against its popular and academic distortions.

Rappers are keenly aware that American indifference to the wellbeing of prisoners is reinforced by the vocabulary we use to describe the conditions of incarceration and the categories of prisoners. When we casually use the word "lifers" to refer to those prisoners who have been sentenced to die in prison, or the phrase "solitary confinement" to refer to a form of torture inflicted on prisoners, or the word "cell" to refer to the tiny cage where they suffer from the loss of identity, pride, and health, or the word "criminal" to refer to every single person in prison, we normalize the extraordinary amount of violence and useless suffering in the penal system as the inevitable, legal, rational consequence of breaking the law (or of having been judged guilty of breaking the law). American hip-hop is the only form of popular culture that has consistently testified about the conditions of confinement in order to reveal the perversity of these terms and their centrality in an economy of state violence against African Americans, who are still imagined as "magical" beings able to withstand any pain and survive any brutality.

In fact, the category of the "criminal"—always imagined as a one-dimensional, "evil" individual—has played an essential role in supporting and justifying a large number of genocides in different nations in both the past and the present. In his 2007 book *The Crime of My Very Existence: Nazism and the Myth of Jewish Criminality*, Michael Berkowitz uncovers the important fact that the notion of the Jew as a natural "criminal" was essential to the propaganda that convinced many Germans to support the Nazi state. Berkowitz proves the prominence of the notion of "criminality" in Nazi patter, platitudes, and policy toward the Jews, and explores how Jewish victims experienced the criminalization of their existence.[16] In reality, we have not ceased to assume the category of the one-dimensional "criminal" in order to sanction state-sanctioned violence that has genocidal consequences. Berkowitz's study should lead us to question the larger historical relation between our notion (and the social production) of the "criminal" and genocidal violence, but his study does not consider its larger implications for the current administration of "criminal justice" in democratic nation-states that are organized around a racist distribution of power and capital.

Underground rap songs from the 1970s until today convey the pain perpetuated by the discursive and visual criminalization of black people that both hides and disavows the inexcusable, intolerable suffering inflicted on them by state agencies and institutions. However, popular, radio-worthy hip-hop does not provoke critical thought about racism or carceral violence, and it serves the end of stereotyping *all* rap so as to provide reasons to disregard underground hip-hop as a source of knowledge or authority. As a result of my love of underground hip-hop and my respect for the culture, I started to visit women incarcerated at a medium and maximum security state prison in central Pennsylvania when I attained a faculty position at a university in the area. And in my experience visiting prisoners and teaching philosophy to a group of women sentenced to life imprisonment without the possibility of parole, words always fail to describe the carceral scene in which the infliction of trauma has been so routinized as to make it seem normal and inevitable.

In the United States, the criminal justice system is based on the assumption that punishment must be painful for those incarcerated in jails and prisons; criminals do not only lose their freedom, but must be subject to degradation, mental anguish, humiliation, poor nutrition, substandard medical care, toxic conditions, rape, and torture. In this way, the Justice system is inextricable from a system of vengeance. A society that confuses vengeance and Justice has historically led to an authoritarian regime whose existence depends upon the oppression of certain groups categorized by race, ethnicity, religion, class, or ability. In Nazi Germany the populace came to see and imagine the "Jew" as a criminal, as a threat to social order and moral decency. In the United States, the populace sees and imagines the black man as a "thug," or as a threatening individual ready and willing to break the law. Thus the use of preemptive police force against unarmed young black men is both rationalized and disavowed, even as the police and correctional officers manifest the very irrational violence that they project onto the black men and women they terrorize.

The "criminal" looms so large in our collective unconscious as does our desire for vengeance against those who transgress the law that it is difficult if not impossible for politicians to criticize the conditions of confinement and remain in office. There is no political or social will to fundamentally restructure our Justice system so that the process of punishment no longer rests on the infliction of extreme, gratuitous pain. Underground rappers consistently illustrate that we must understand this indifference in terms of the role the prison system plays in re-producing the genocidal violence against black communities that has always been a condition for the possibility of white supremacy or the racist disparity of opportunity, wealth, legal protection, and power.

Our prison system depends upon the criminalization of racial and ethnic minorities, the poor, and the mentally ill, which rationalizes their civic and social death. And yet it is still impossible to discuss the nature and effects of the American prison system as a form of genocide in the academic and popular discourse about the prison system, genocide, anti-black racism, and American democracy. This indicates that the problem pertains to our sensibility of genocide and the white sensibility of black people rather than a lack of knowledge or reason; it indicates a certain *refusal* to think American genocide that exposes the limits of our conditioned sensibility about how we talk, see, imagine, and interpret our society. These limits to what we can see or think allow us to evade, obfuscate and dis-articulate the carceral traumas inflicted on racialized minorities as the tragic and inevitable consequence of an imperfect but necessary penal system.

In his influential text *The Souls of Black Folk*, Du Bois coined the notion of the "Veil" to refer to the irreducible difference between the sensibilities of those on either side of "the color line." In the field of critical philosophy of race, his notion of the Veil is necessary to expose the limits of white sensibility that is conditioned to *imagine* and thus see black people as criminal, or as deficient in epistemic and moral integrity. As explained in the Introduction, the term "white sensibility" refers to a way of seeing, feeling, and judging experiences in accord with the social, economic, and political privileges of white citizens, or citizens who have been racialized as "white" in contrast to "black." In a society that is structured around the material and ideological needs of white supremacy, it is not the case that every white citizen is consciously "racist," but rather that all white citizens are conditioned to see and think about black people in a way that allows them to defer the reality of systemic state violence against black communities. The consistent refusal to think about or "see" a system of racism allows us to evade the fact that we, too, as white citizens benefit economically, politically, socially, and physically from our racial democracy at the cost of black citizens and their economic, political, social, and physical well-being.

This notion of white sensibility does not preclude the possibility of white citizens from thinking critically about their sensibility and caring about the suffering of black citizens, nor does it preclude the possibility of white citizens protesting their privilege. However, theorists and social scientists have identified patterns of white sensibility marked by (1) moral indifference to the suffering of black citizens and (2) willful ignorance about race and racism in the United States. This notion of white sensibility as structured to both evade and protect its own white privilege was recently explained by George Yancy in his editorial for *The New York Times*, "Dear White America" published on December 25, 2015; as a result of this editorial, he still receives death threats on a regular basis.[17] This indicates the extent to which the *episteme* cannot tolerate the awareness of its own operation on our thought and perception and the lethal means that white people will take to avoid the awareness of their own whiteness (as discussed in chapter 2). In fact, only recently have white scholars started to explore the implications of Du Bois's notion of the Veil and Fanon's phenomenology of the white gaze to grasp that the problem of racism is not a problem of an individual's decision to be racist or due to a lack of knowledge, but rather a problem that pertains to the aesthetic sensibility of experience that belongs to those who "are" white, or who become white and occupy that privileged racial category through perceiving and imagining black people in a certain way despite whatever they consciously decide to believe or affirm.

As previously discussed in chapter 1, Judith Butler writes about the Rodney King trial in order to illustrate that it's not possible to understand the jury's verdict without this focus on the conditioned limits of white sensibility. For in order to make sense of their decision that the police officers who assaulted and tortured Mr. King—caught on video played for the jury—were not-guilty of any wrongdoing, we must consider the *racist saturation of the visual field* and the problems this raises for any appeal to white perception as evidence for our judgments: "If racism pervades white perception, structuring what can and cannot appear within the horizon of white perception, then to what extent does it interpret in advance 'visual evidence?' And how, then, does such 'evidence' have to be read, and read publicly, *against* the racist disposition of the visible, which will prepare and achieve its own inverted perceptions under the rubric of 'what is seen?'"[18] Butler insists that the white perception of black citizens *as* criminal permeates the visual field itself; there is no "seeing" without a simultaneous "reading" in a racially saturated field of vision. When they watched the video, jury members "saw" white police officers using an appropriate amount of force to "defend" themselves against a "dangerous" black man, by repeatedly assaulting him as he lay immobile and defenseless on the pavement.

Butler's view that the evidence read in a court of law occurs within and against "the racist disposition of the visible," which "will prepare and achieve its own inverted perceptions under the rubric of "what is seen," also resonates with the meaning of the phrase "Claimin' I'm a Criminal" which is rapped in order to draw attention to the way in which the collective sensibility of white citizens actually creates the conditions that seemingly "prove" the grounds for their predisposition toward viewing black life *as* criminal. For the phrase draws attention to how the rhetoric of criminality allows white citizens to evade and disavow the racist conditions that force black citizens into compromised, sometimes "criminal" choices in order to blame them for these very conditions that are somehow a product of their collective, "criminal" disposition. In other words, white Americans see and affirm a just Justice system only through criminalizing black Americans for the compromised choices they face as victims of a white supremacist state organized around their subordination and destruction.

As previously cited, when Shakur raps "Crazy, I gotta work with what'chu gave me/You claimin I'm a criminal and you the one that made me," he skillfully illustrates that since black men are *criminalized* from birth, they are in fact *made criminal* as a result of what they are forced to do to stay alive in a system in which they are largely excluded from the labor market and targeted for police brutality, incarceration, and state-sanctioned murder. In the context of underground hip-hop, the phrase also draws attention to the importance of the term "criminal" to the efficient functionality of the anti-black genocide perpetuated through the everyday conditions of confinement and the administration of judicial and penal policies thought to be neutral, inevitable, and reasonable despite the traumatic violence they inflict on African Americans *as such;* of course this violence cannot be seen or imagined as *traumatic* given the limits of the white, neoliberal, and postracial sensibility that is contested by the form and content of underground hip-hop.

As previously mentioned, Card claims that the special evil of genocide lies in the infliction of social death upon a particular population, or an attack upon the rituals and social bonds that unite a group of people together and foster a meaningful life. She adopts the term from the sociologist Orlando Patterson, who coined it to refer to the "natal alienation" suffered by American slaves. As Card explains in her book *Confronting Evils:*

> Genocide not only intentionally strips individuals of the ability to participate in social relationships, activities, and traditions, it aims to destroy the possibility of those particular kinds of relationships, activities, and traditions for others in the future . . . The harm of social death is not necessarily less extreme than that of physical death. In my view, the special evil of genocide lies in its infliction of not just physical death (when it does that) but social death, producing a consequent meaninglessness of one's life and even of its termination.[19]

Card views genocide as an evil; she defines "evils" in relation to intolerable harms inflicted on living things. She explains that intolerable harms are evils when they result foreseeably from culpable wrongdoing, and when the deeds producing them are morally inexcusable. In one application of her definition of evil, Card explains that the death penalty in the United States is an evil policy, because it has been proved that its application has led to many state murders of people wrongfully accused of a crime. Thus despite its ideal aim, we can reasonably expect that the death penalty will continue to inflict intolerable, inexcusable harm on American citizens. Similarly, despite its ideal aim, we can reasonably foresee that the U.S. criminal punishment system will continue to inflict social death on African Americans and undermine the vitality of entire communities.[20]

Nazi Germany targeted Jews for destruction in accord with their "war on crime," and we target African Americans, the poor, and the mentally ill as part of *our* war on crime. Assuming Card's definition of genocide as the infliction of "social death" through a variety of institutional practices that undermine the social vitality of entire communities, we can better understand how the U.S. system of mass incarceration has proved to be genocidal insofar as it has traumatized certain populations already marginalized by the racist, classist, and ableist distribution of power relations, thereby reinforcing and ensuring their powerlessness against violence and discrimination. If we think about Shakur's verse in light of Berkowitz's study and Card's view of genocide, we can see that just as the Nazis created the conditions that necessitated criminal behavior in the Jewish ghettos and the concentration camps, the United States creates and sanctions the socio-economic conditions that necessitate crime in its cities and prisons.

However, the discursive debate about the definition of genocide—while important—cannot affect the general sensibility of genocide that is marked by conditioned limits as to what can be thought as "genocide" and who can suffer from this crime; these limits reinforce the consistent refusal to consider the systemic anti-black violence in the United States as genocidal or traumatic violence. As a form of art that can affect our emotions and elicit awe and sorrow, underground hip-hop can affect our sensibility of genocide by making us aware of our limits to "know" or "categorize" the brutal and systemic violence inflicted by the prison system. Further, through the use of poetic verse in a subversive grammar delivered through distinct and unpredictable rhyming schemes, underground rappers testify to carceral trauma in a way that disrupts the facile distinction between "slavery" and "genocide" as an obvious or helpful distinction that allows us to make sense of the American past and present. Lastly, hip-hop songs co-opt and re-signify the term "genocide" in a way that can elucidate the historical operation of genocide in the twentieth and twenty-first centuries as a *pathological process* endemic to the birth of the nation-state in western politics that was defined by the cultural homogeneity of its members; the need to *produce* nation-states defined by a single culture required the genocide of minority groups to reinforce the norms of the white colonizers and secure their economic and political supremacy through the exploitation of these groups. For these reasons, underground hip-hop should be regarded as an essential source for the field of Holocaust and genocide studies.

Berkowitz's study on the importance of the criminalization of Jews for the justification and implementation of the Nazis' "final solution " illustrates the power of the category of the "criminal" to normalize state violence against minority populations in a nation-state founded on "law and order." He insists that "it is no coincidence that two of the most notorious, unconcealed killing grounds of the Holocaust, Auschwitz and the Ninth Fort (Kaunas, Lithuania), had been, respectively, a 'prison camp' and a prison—in a more conventional sense—which no doubt eased their transition to installations of 'extermination.'"[21] The Nazi genocide was facilitated by the transformation of prisons into death camps and ordinary human beings into "criminals" or moral monsters. If the populace could "understand" or accept state violence against those labeled as "criminal," perhaps we should ask whether this transformation from prison to camp is better described as a radicalization of certain tendencies already operative in the "more conventional" prison.

Berkowitz explains that: "the Nazis cited the supposed criminality of Jews as a reason for their confinement in ghettos, as well as for harassing them with a barrage of legislation that further circumscribed their ability to move about and to provide basic sustenance." The popular indifference to the wellbeing of criminals is tied to the bad utilitarian reasoning that informs most domestic and foreign policies related to national security. According to this view, it is more important to secure the safety of the populace than to protect the wellbeing of prisoners, which are seen as mutually opposed aims. Here, as Giorgio Agamben explains, "the care of life coincides with the fight against the enemy."[22] This is "bad" reasoning because of course it is not true that the infliction of pain against those judged guilty of breaking the law is necessary for public safety. However our insistence on this non-fact is related to the fact that once the Nazis cast the Jews as "criminals," they were better able to explain to themselves and German citizens the "necessity" of their exclusion and death. That is, the criminalization of populations affects our *sensibility* about the legality and morality of harming them, which indicates that the word "criminal" exercises an especially powerful effect on our general perception of state violence against minority groups.

Berkowitz supports his thesis about the importance of the criminalization of the Jews to their destruction in Nazi Germany with the following anecdote: "As the Criminal Police and the Gestapo competed over who was to get greater control of the Lodz ghetto, Kriminalinspektor Bracken supported the extension of his jurisdiction by saying that 'in the ghetto live, at any rate, about 250,000 Jews, all of whom have more or less criminal tendencies.' This statement was considered convincing, and his 'detachment moved in.'"[23] The Nazi state required the participation of the police force in order to marginalize and destroy entire Jewish communities, and this participation was facilitated by the rhetoric of criminality. As Berkowitz summarizes at the end of his book:

> The Nazis' use of the allegation of criminality, of assigning a collective criminal intent to the Jews, has proven to be one of the more resilient but less obvious aspects of their legacy. In the eyes of Victor Klemperer, it was "one of the many paths along which Hitlerism could march." Like many of the Nazis' horrific and bizarre notions, seeing Jews as criminals was unoriginal, even hackneyed. But it probably helped a huge number of Germans and their fellow perpetrators, as well as bystanders, to accept what the Nazis were doing to the Jews.[24]

Thus the Nazi genocide was facilitated by general, widely held presuppositions about the "criminal" who perpetually threatens the domestic order promised by the nation-state and who, in fact, is incapable of respecting civil and social bonds and so undeserving of the human and legal rights guaranteed by citizenship. These are the same presuppositions that justify our own indifference to every person in jail or prison, even though more than half of our prisoner population was judged guilty of non-violent crimes, and at least half of all prisoners suffer from severe mental illness. In the field of genocide studies, the question of how "ordinary Germans" in the Nazi regime so passively accepted the segregation, arrest, and incarceration of German Jews serves to mask the moral hypocrisy of asking this question in a nation that has passively accepted the mass incarceration of *millions* of black men in prisons that serve as labor camps, who live under conditions *designed* to inflict mental and physical pain and sever family bonds. The extent to which we have ignored and normalized the excessively violent conditions of the penal system as somehow inevitable or natural, indicates the need for a political intervention on the level of our general sensibility of the present rather than on the level of discursive debate about the need for "prison reform."

Only in the last two sentences of his book does Berkowitz suggest the larger implications of his study of the criminalization of Jews in Nazi Germany. He writes: "Certainly minority groups who have struggled to gain a foothold, and those in marginal economic spheres, have been (and continue to be) stigmatized because of their supposed propensity to crime. Although genocidal regimes existed before and after Hitler, the Nazi imagination of the Jews as criminals is one of the grossest perversions of the respect for law ever to be instituted."[25] Though Berkowitz recognizes that the current marginalization of populations marked by race, ethnicity, and class is also facilitated by the criminalization of these populations, he nevertheless reinforces the difference between the genocidal use of the "criminal" that rests on a perversion of the law and a non-genocidal (though still problematic) use of the "criminal" in a just legal system. However, what if the genocidal practices made possible by the category of the criminal have always been present in our prison system to a greater or lesser degree? In this case, we cannot make a facile distinction between an illegitimate "genocidal" use of the category of the criminal and a legitimate, "legal" use of the category of the criminal. Rather, the criminal justice system of the modern nation-state allows for and perpetuates a consistent amount of genocidal violence against ethnic and racial minorities, the poor, and the mentally ill.

When prisoners talk to me about the basic conditions of their confinement, which are governed by rules that serve to generate excessive suffering, I often think of a passage in Foucault's essay on *Nietzsche, Genealogy, and History*:

> Humanity does not gradually progress from combat to combat until it arrives at universal reciprocity, where the rule of law finally replaces warfare; humanity installs each of its violences in a system of rules and thus proceeds from domination to domination.[26]

One of the rules of prison life in the United States is that the state does not provide prisoners with products for basic hygiene such as a toothbrush, toothpaste, shampoo, a brush, etc. Many prisoners complain that the only free soap is harsh and causes their skin to break out in pimples. Prisoners must buy hygienic products through the commissary, and corporations make an enormous amount of money by selling their products in the prison at grossly inflated prices. At the state prison for women in Muncy, Pennsylvania, each prisoner is given two pairs of underwear for an entire year (though they can purchase additional pairs at the commissary). Prisoners who do not have family members or friends contributing to their commissary accounts must rely on the salary they make in prison to buy hygienic products. The highest paid position receives twenty cents an hour. Further, most prisoners complain about the quality of the food and many prefer to skip meals altogether and eat the processed food they can buy from commissary. This leads to poor nutrition and poor health, and a disproportionate rate of cancer in the prisoner population. Prisoners can call their friends and family, but only at grossly inflated prices and, of course, under surveillance. Any infraction of prison rules may lead to cell restriction or solitary confinement; if the anguish caused by this isolation further prevents the prisoner from following the rules then she is put back into isolation.

Prisoners cannot go to the funerals of their family and friends, and they are denied the right to vote. Upon release, they are disqualified from most student loans and forbidden from living in section 8 housing (federally subsidized low-income housing). They are also often disqualified from other government assistance programs such as welfare and food stamps. The only logic operating in these rules is the economy of social death, for they reinforce the powerlessness of marginalized populations. Of course, in the prison the law coincides with the suspension of the law, as correctional officers harm prisoners with impunity and prisoners are not arrested for harming each other but rather, in extraordinary cases, "sent to the hole." However in this space of exception the laws governing the carceral space work in tandem with the suspension of the law to inflict social death upon the prisoner population.

Berkowitz's failure to draw implications from his study of the role that the term "criminal" played in the economy of Nazi Germany and the role that it now plays in the genocidal economy of the United States is a reflection of the sensibility of genocide operative in the field of genocide studies and the political imaginary that rests on a sharp distinction between slavery and genocide; this distinction serves to rationalize the exclusion of systemic anti-black racism from its purview. If scholars do consider slavery in relation to genocide, they often claim that slavery is a form of "cultural genocide" as opposed to a "real," or physical genocide. This distinction is defended on the basis of the intent specific to genocide, or the aim to destroy a specific ethnic, religious, racial, or national group, *as such*. Most of the white, male scholars in the field have interpreted this to mean that only if the intent of the perpetrators is to destroy the enemy as a desired end in-itself, does the attack constitute genocide. On the other hand, if perpetrators hope to profit from the destruction of the targeted population through the accumulation of wealth or land or the acquisition of power, then their intent is not for the destruction of this population as such, and in this case their attack does not constitute genocide.

As explained by Yehuda Bauer, the Holocaust was unprecedented because "it was totally non-pragmatic,"[27] and Nazi anti-Semitic ideology was forged and followed in isolation of any practical concerns or economic, social, or political objectives. Similarly, in the midst of defending a more expansive understanding of genocide, David Moshman takes it as self-evident that American slavery should be excluded from a study of comparative genocides because "killing and cultural extermination were not the primary intent."[28] Their remarks illustrate the role that the Holocaust plays in our political imaginary as an "Event" that was *worse-than-slavery*. However the facile distinction between slavery and the Nazi genocide or between "pragmatic" versus "non-pragmatic" state violence requires that we selectively *read-out* important facts about the Nazi genocide such as the importance of slave labor in the ghettos and the camps, as well as the economic utility of the genocide for German corporations who made use of this slave labor, as well as for German citizens who seized Jewish homes, goods, and businesses.

In defending his view that the Holocaust was "unprecedented" because of the non-pragmatic intent of its perpetrators to destroy the Jewish people as a goal in-itself, Bauer claims that the Nazis "did not kill the Jews in order to get their property. They took their property because they wanted, at first, to get rid of them, and then they robbed them on the way to killing them." However, how can Bauer make a gross generalization about the order of every perpetrator's priorities as being to first, kill Jews, and then second, to loot their possessions and property? There is no evidence to support this sweeping claim, which rests on proving that the *overriding* psychological motive for every German who participated in or profited from the Jewish genocide was hatred for the Jews. This view does not take into account the role that our sensibility plays in shaping our motivations or providing us with norms as to what "makes sense" as a citizen, and seems to presuppose the myth of the "criminal" disposition capable of harming people in order to satisfy the desire to harm people (Indeed, Arendt's brilliant critique of this image of the ideologically-motivated Nazi in her text *Eichmann in Jerusalem* was the cause for its notoriety). However, the historical inaccuracy of this view about the "non-pragmatic" nature of the Nazi genocide as opposed to the "pragmatic" nature of American slavery has not prevented esteemed historians from reinforcing it in their accounts of the Nazi genocide, in the process reinforcing our inability to see the repetition of our genocidal past in the atrocities produced by our penal system in the American present.

The rationale behind the traditional view in genocide studies that American slavery was "pragmatic" while the Holocaust was "non-pragmatic" is based on the false assumption that since slaves were valued as property, they were "taken care of" to an extent that the Jewish slaves of Auschwitz were not. This view is expressed by Arendt in her work on *The Origins Of Totalitarianism* when she writes, "Throughout history slavery has been an institution within a social order; slaves were not, like concentration-camp inmates, withdrawn from the sight and hence the protection of their fellow-men; as instruments of labor they had a definite price and as property a definite value."[29] Historians portray the labor in the Nazi camp as a prelude to physical death by exhaustion or disease, whereas they portray the lives of American slaves as possessing a modicum of security and health that was utterly lacking in the Nazi camps. In reality, the lives of the American slaves were no more secure than the lives of Jews in Nazi Germany, and their value as commodities did not serve to guarantee a modicum of safety or dignity or health. This is made clear in the following testimony by Silas Jackson, published in the collection of testimonies of former African American slaves titled *When I Was A Slave:*

> I have heard it said that Tom Ashbie's father went to one of the cabins late at night. The slaves was having a secret prayer meeting. He heard one slave ask God to change the heart of his master and deliver him from slavery so that he may enjoy freedom. Before the next day the man disappeared, no one ever seeing him again . . . When old man Ashbie died, just before he died, he told the white Baptist minister that he had killed Zeke for praying.[30]

As this testimony makes clear, the lives of American slaves were no more "valued" than the lives of Jews in Nazi camps, even though they held commercial value. The view that American plantation owners "took care of" their slaves follows from the popular romanticization of American slavery and the Southern plantation.

In reality, American slavery was enforced through a gratuitous amount of brutal violence whose sadism far outstripped its utilitarian value. Of course, the reality is hard to square with the image of the well-meaning Christian plantation owner, and it threatens to disrupt the patriotic nostalgia for the wisdom of our founding fathers. So the denial of the real conditions of American slavery (reinforced by the traditional distinction between "slavery" and "genocide") also keeps us blind to the centrality of genocidal violence to the founding and structure of the United States. This prevents us from inquiring into the historical transmutation of genocidal violence against racialized populations in the American past and present.

The importance of the distinction between American slavery and genocide for our nationalist narratives makes it clear why we cannot understand the different roles they play in our political imaginary with reference to a general deficit of knowledge about the real conditions of slavery, for this distinction *works to whitewash* the excessive cruelty and useless violence that characterized the American slave trade and still characterizes our penal system. That is, the distinction between slavery and genocide marks a limit of white sensibility that cannot think one in terms of the other without somehow shattering the entire frame of reference for the present. This limit helps us understand the political importance of the association between slavery, genocide, and prison in the lyrics of underground rap songs as an aesthetic intervention and tactic that interrupts our popular sensibility of genocide that is complicit with our moral and political blindness to the genocidal violence now inflicted through the criminal justice system. Like the members of the Civil Rights Congress who wrote the petition *We Charge Genocide*, underground rappers are keenly aware that our refusal to recognize the distinctly genocidal structure of racial discrimination in the United States has played an essential role in the economy and repetition of genocidal practices over time.

In my previous work on Holocaust victim testimonies, I introduced the term "unlivable life" to designate the state-of-being suffered by social death, and I found three conceptual markers of unlivable life expressed in these testimonies: (1) some notion that the suffering endured is "worse than death" (2) the use of the notion of "Hell" to designate one's space of suffering, and (3) psychic pain over the loss of familial and fraternal bonds. All three of these markers are also present in hip-hop songs about prison life, and they convey the traumas of incarceration that can never be healed or forgotten. Underground MCs aim to convey the pain and social harms of incarceration—rather than simply the logic of genocide—through testimony and beats that arrest the senses and our ability to make sense of our prison system. Their effort to provide an emotional register of this experience is also an effort to provoke empathy for black men tortured in the prison system.

Further, these songs testify to the carceral traumas that are dis-articulated and so absent from the popular sensibility of the criminal justice system. For example, in his song "16 on Death Row," Shakur draws attention to the plight of juvenile offenders who are sentenced as adults to life in prison or the death penalty. In 2012, the United States Supreme Court deemed it unconstitutional to sentence a juvenile offender to life without the possibility of parole, but it gave the states the power to decide if this new law had to be applied retroactively to those prisoners who had already been sentenced as juveniles to life in prison and already incarcerated for 20, 30, or 40 years. The State Supreme court in Pennsylvania, where I live, decided that the law would not apply retroactively to those prisoners already sentenced as juveniles to life without parole. In Pennsylvania alone there are 500 "juvenile offenders," and it is hard—if not impossible—to explain what it is like to grow up in prison knowing that you will die in prison, given the terms of the dominant discourse. Shakur's song is achingly aware of this discursive impossibility, and draws attention to it even as he aims to convey something of the pain that can help us feel—if not explain—how the common practice of sentencing black teenagers to die in prison is an *atrocity* rather than a sensible public policy. In his song he raps:

> The brother in my cell, is 16 as well/ It's hard to adapt when you're Black and you're trapped in a living Hell/

Shakur follows the reference to "a living Hell" with the verse:

> I shouldn't have let him catch me/Instead of livin sad in jail I coulda died free and happy.[31]

Later in the song the lyrics reinforce this view that death would have been preferable to suffering from penal violence:

> They got you trapped, you're better off getting shot up
> I'm convinced self-defense is the way/Please, stay strapped, pack a gat every day

These lyrics convey the idea that the conditions under which juvenile offenders suffer in prison are worse than death; that, indeed, they would do better to go down in a blaze of gunfire than to be arrested and subjected to prison life. And the subject-position assumed in the song—the teenager locked up in an adult prison—forces the listener to consider the plight of one of the most vulnerable populations in the United States that belies any neoliberal or post-racial account about the "progress" of the prison system.

Run-DMC released a track about prison titled "Back from Hell," and the rap begins with the lines: "On the lower level where the devils dwell/ Comin from the one, comin back from hell." The first verse is rapped by Run:

> So you do your time and never let the time do ya/He lost his mind that's what the time'll do to ya

And then alludes again to Hell:

> Four years done, another one in a cell/Don't need nobody to come, cause I'll be back from hell[32]

The song provokes us to question whether prisoners can ever leave the Hell of prison even when released, or whether—for many prisoners—their time in an earthly hell so compromises the quality of their lives that, in the words of the artist Antonin Artaud, they are doomed to eternally reenact the traumas of their confinement, thus foreclosing the opportunities offered by their escape. The analogy of Hell to describe prison life was also poignantly used by the group 5th Ward Boys in their rap song titled "Concrete Hell," in order to convey the mental anguish suffered in prison, from the position of an inmate: "342036 is ma id number/My head is fucked up coz the prison took me under." The lyrics include these bars:

And now am living life in a cell/
Trying not to lose ma mind, in this Concrete Hell.[33]

Rappers do not use the metaphor of Hell lightly, but instead require this imagery to convey that the U.S. penal colony serves to ruin lives and transform earthly existence into a nightmare from which one cannot fully wake up. Indeed, the metaphor serves to remind us that despite the provision in the Eighth Amendment of the U.S. Bill of Rights against cruel and unusual punishment, we cannot grasp the nature of prison life as anything other than a diabolical organization of torments that the Devil himself could scarcely surpass and from which one can never fully escape.

The Christian notion of Hell serves to distract us from the man-made sites of "hell" at the margins of society, such as the prison and the camp. This image can be distorted to justify the creation of earthly sites of hell for those who are judged guilty of sin, for it is reasoned that anything they may suffer as punishment for crimes on earth surely pales in comparison with what they will suffer in (the real) Hell. Indeed, casual statements such as "I want them to lock 'em up and throw away the key," indicate the extent to which prisoners are thoroughly excluded from our moral consideration. Even the Christian conception of Hell does not sanction the creation of earthly hells where man acts as God, with the power of life and death over those subject to that hell. And yet that is precisely the nature of prison life, which exists as a surreal counter-image of a free, democratic society that respects the rule of law and human rights. It is this surreal inversion of moral agency present in prison life—where victims "deserve" violence because they "are" violent— that rappers convey with the analogy to Hell. In the past 30 years hip-hop has served to testify for those who have been silenced and excluded and condemned to useless suffering in the name of "Justice," and many of these testimonies have required the analogy of "Hell" in order to convey the extreme, intolerable, and perverse nature of prison life.

Rappers also consistently illustrate that the prison-industrial complex keeps African Americans "at a minimum" through the disintegration of the family caused by mass incarceration and the conditions of confinement. Multiple rap songs testify to the pain caused by the penal attack on the family itself. For example, Sadat X raps alongside a female voice during the following verse from "Claimin I'm a Criminal" that depicts a phone call between a prisoner and his wife:

I love the kids and I teach em to love their father/I'll get you some kicks and try to send some flicks/But it's over, baby, yes it's over

And the next verse is rapped from the prisoner's perspective:

Ain't much you can do when you're holdin a phone/A million inmates but ya still alone/You're not cryin but inside ya dyin.

This verse conveys the visceral pain of incarceration on families who are torn apart and *targeted* for destruction by the hyper-surveillance of black communities and the criminalization of black men and boys. We can better understand how the penal system targets specific kinds of families to break up when we consider certain statistics: One in 9 African American children (11.4 percent), 1 in 28 Hispanic children (3.5 percent), and 1 in 57 white children (1.8 percent) in the United States have an incarcerated parent.[34] Parental incarceration is now recognized as an "adverse childhood experience" (ACE); it is distinguished from other ACEs by the unique combination of trauma, shame, and stigma. 62 percent of parents in state prisons and 84 percent of parents in federal prisons are held over 100 miles away from their residence. About 43 percent of parents in federal prisons are held over 500 miles away from their last residence. Thus many families cannot visit their loved ones who are in prison, and so suffer from the loss of social bonds with their fathers, mothers, sons, and daughters.

Further, according to The National Resource Center on Children and Families of the Incarcerated, "The uneven geographic distribution of incarceration in poor communities and communities of color means that the effects radiate beyond the individual to the broader community, presenting profound long-term consequences for family integrity, public health and general quality of life."[35] Rap songs about prison life often refer to the unique pain produced by the loss of family ties from which multiple generations suffer, and so convey the *genocidal* harm of penal policies that serve to disrupt and prevent familial and fraternal bonds.

Two examples of rap songs that testify to the pain of family disintegration caused by mass incarceration and the conditions of confinement include "Concrete Hell" by 5th Ward Boys and "Family Business" by Kanye West.[36] In "Concrete Hell" the lyrics are rapped from the subject-position of a young black man recently sentenced and doing time for someone else:

And I can still hear the judge when he said 25
See ma mamma cry now am fucked up inside

The verse reminds us that prisoners do not only have to reckon with the pains endemic to prison life but to the pain caused to one's family, and one's inability to restore ties that previously gave one's life meaning. As indicated by the U.N. Convention Against Genocide, the sovereign separation of families targeted on the basis of race is a form of genocidal violence that aims to destroy the targeted group "as such," and underground rappers have always sought to illustrate this genocidal aspect of the prison system that has always targeted black men in order to target the vitality and generational bonds of black families and black communities *as such*, as black men are criminalized from birth, tortured in prison, and removed from their families who suffer from their absence.

There is a common phrase among inmates that is also part of the lyrics of multiple rap songs written to give a "shout-out" to black men in prison and provide support: "Do Your Time, Don't Let Your Time Do You." In his song "Do Your Time," Ludacris repeats this phrase throughout the chorus, and other rappers also spit bars that mention specific friends or family members still incarcerated, who they counsel with the same phrase. In the first verse Ludacris raps:

Born in this way of livin and our youth was stuck
To be safe, it's safe to say the justice system's fucked up[37]

Here Ludacris refers to the carceral space as the space into which black men are *born* in the United States, since they are *criminalized* from birth and forced to navigate lethal threats to their wellbeing so that "our youth was stuck," or prevented and warped by the compromised choices and un-natural though entirely rational fears faced by those targeted by a genocidal regime. Thus "it's safe to say" that a Justice system that is organized around the mass arrest, incarceration and murder of black people is "fucked up" or a moral atrocity.

The counsel that prisoners should "Do Your Time, Don't Let Your Time Do You," reinforces an insight that Primo Levi had while imprisoned at Auschwitz, about the great danger presented by the fact that "the personality is fragile," and subject to disintegrate under traumatic suffering.[38] Many prisoners who regularly suffer from solitary confinement, sexual abuse, and/or hard restraints may never emotionally or physically recover from their suffering. And like many camp inmates, many prisoners in U.S state and federal prisons often lose the social instinct altogether and find themselves unable to form healthy relations with others either during or after release. Our high recidivism rate is related to the mental anguish suffered in prison, as ex-offenders have an extremely difficult time adapting to the conditions of "normal" life. A 2006 Justice Department study found that 75 percent of female prisoners and 60 percent of male prisoners suffer from severe mental illness; what is unclear is how many prisoners developed psychiatric disorders as a result of the conditions of confinement themselves.

As previously mentioned, the public critique of the prisons as presented in the popular media focuses on the vast *number* of young black men in prison, rather than on the conditions of confinement themselves. The public decries the trend of *mass* incarceration instead of the racist system of incarceration that ruins the health and integrity of individuals and entire communities. If all Americans were equally vulnerable to arrest and incarceration as a result of breaking the law, then the system would not inflict distinctly *genocidal* wounds from the regular torture of the prisoner population. The potency of the term genocide as a moral and legal crime against humanity indicates why it does not "make sense" in the dominant discourse and white sensibility to apply this term to the function of the penal system that still serves an essential role in the legal subordination of black citizens and the protection of white supremacy.

The refusal to think about the prison as a site of genocide persists despite the fact that there are visible traces of the Nazi past in the carceral present, beyond the ubiquitous presence of swastikas and the "Aryan Brotherhood"—the most murderous of all of the gangs in U.S. prisons. Like the camp, the judicial system inside the prison is secret and autonomous; there is no government oversight of the punitive decisions made by Department of Corrections (DOC) staff in local jails, state, and federal prisons. This includes decisions to send prisoners into solitary confinement or deny them parole. For this reason, the DOC staff has absolute power over the prisoners.

Finally, prisoners are subject to an infinite number of mental and physical tortures that slowly erode their ability to resist their degradation. Underground rappers draw on the term and history of genocide in order to convey the illegal, inhuman, and irrational infliction of carceral violence against black men. In the fourth verse of "Do Your Time," C-murder raps a bar that evokes the "Camp" as an image of the prison yard that is disproportionately composed of black men: "One fight, dude got stabbed, he lost an eye (uh-huh)/Almost died, in Camp Jay nigga, ride or cry (cry)." Given the radical vulnerability of prisoners in the carceral environment where "anything can happen" because they are *seen* as criminals who are capable of "anything," it is hard to describe this site of "punishment" that is hidden from public awareness and free from federal oversight as anything other than a concentration camp. Underground hip-hop songs about life in prison provide a phenomenology of social death inflicted by the penal system—in poetic verse performed to beats torn from their context and re-signified through their repetition. In this way the form and content of these songs arrest our ability to make sense of the prison system in neoliberal or post-racial terms and disrupt our of "genocide" that serves to exclude carceral violence from relevance.

Some scholars may balk at a comparative analysis between the criminalization of Jewish life in Nazi Germany and the criminalization of black life in the United States, due to the apparent disparity of conditions. However, those who do not think prison life is a scene of gratuitous suffering, violence, and lawlessness have never been to prison or read prisoner testimony or seriously listened to hip-hop. Further, genocide scholars study the conditions that allow for state violence to *become rationalized*, rather than establish a hierarchy of suffering whereby some victims don't "suffer enough" to be proper victims of genocide. Some might object that unlike victims of genocide who are persecuted for who they are, prisoners are punished for what they have done. However, this is not accurate because prisoners are not tortured for the crimes they are accused of committing, but because they are viewed as "criminals" with inherently violent dispositions who are incapable of spiritual renewal. That is, guards do not inflict pain on prisoners because they grew marijuana, or shoplifted, or got a DUI, but instead because these individual transgressions are the sign of a "criminal" disposition or a pathological fixation with harming others.[39]

Though we can intellectually grasp that committing one crime does not make one a "criminal," those who are confined in jails and prisons are *seen and imagined* as inherently threatening, unpredictable, violent individuals who do not respect civil order or social bonds. And prisoners suffer acutely from their misrepresentation as "criminals" and the harsh treatment they receive that is justified by this misrepresentation. Countless women incarcerated in Muncy, PA, have asked me: "Why am I being judged as a "criminal" for the worst decision I ever made?" And of course I do not have an adequate answer.

Though there has been more recent social critique of solitary confinement and the death penalty in the United States, there are few credible, public figures who advocate for the abolition of prisons. In my view, the idea that the prison system is excessive because of the regular use of solitary confinement and the death penalty is akin to saying that the problem with Auschwitz was the existence of the gas chambers. We need to abolish, rather than reform, this network of torture chambers that perpetuates the racist and classist status quo. Insofar as the prison system is autonomous and secret and unaccountable to the government or the public, it represents a "camp" that undermines the ideals of the nation-state. The extent to which the genocidal tendencies of the past still inform the penal system in the present is shocking and morally atrocious. Even more so is its quiet perpetuation. The aesthetic depiction of the American prison system in underground hip-hop as part of the genealogy of genocidal practices that still pervade our political institutions and socioeconomic relations can serve to elicit shock and moral horror at the everyday conditions of confinement; genocide is a term of moral condemnation and action, and it may help to provoke the political will to demand the abolition of modern prisons and the penal culture that informs them.

NOTES

1. 2Pac, "Po' Nigga Blues: Scott Storch Remix," Produced by Scott Storch, Written by 2Pac, Yaki Kadafi, E. D. I. Mean, DJ Daryl, Scott Storch & Ronald Isley, Release Date: December 12, 2004.
2. Nubian, "Claimin I'm a Criminal."
3. Fanon, *Black Skin, White Masks*, 116.
4. Felicia R. Lee, "MacArthur Awards Go to 21 Diverse Fellows," *The New York Times*, September 17, 2014.
5. Public Enemy, "Caught, Can We Get A Witness?"
6. Lifers Group, "The Real Deal," Produced by Doctor Jam & Phaze 5 for Solid Productions, Written by Maxwell Melvins, Release Date: 1991.
7. Berel Lang, *Genocide: The Act as Idea* (Philadelphia: University of Pennsylvania Press, 2017), 1.
8. Civil Rights Congress, *We Charge Genocide: The Crime of the Government Against the Negro People*, ed. William L. Patterson (New York: International Publishers Co. Inc., 2017), 46.
9. Claudia Card, "Social Death is Genocide," in *Confronting Evils: Terrorism, Torture, Genocide* (New York: Cambridge University Press, 2010), 241–266.
10. Raphael Lemkin, "Nature of Genocide," *New York Times*, June 14, 1953, 149.
11. William Patterson, *The Man Who Cried Genocide: An Autobiography* (New York: International Publishers, Co., 1971).
12. Lemkin, *Axis Rule*. In Chapters VII and IX, Lemkin makes particular reference to racial discrimination in labor and feeding as genocidal practices. Furthermore, Ch. II, which concerns policing practices, offer astute analyses of everyday institutions that enable genocidal practices as an extension of political violence. Police are enforcers of colonial rule, and carry out the destruction of nations by other means. The fact that this directly applies to the analysis in *We Charge Genocide* is interesting, but there is a critical difference: Lemkin sees racism and discrimination as part of a larger problem of political violence, but not essential to it. The CRC see state-sanctioned racism as a manifestation of the crime of genocide itself.
13. 2Pac and Outlawz, "They Don't Give a Fuck About Us."
14. Nubian, "Claimin I'm a Criminal."
15. Joell Ortiz, "Modern Day Slavery," Produced by Jonyfraze, Written by Joell Ortiz and Immortal Technique, Release Date: February 27, 2007.
16. Michael Berkowitz, *The Crime of My Very Existence: Nazism and the Myth of Jewish Criminality* (Berkeley: University of California Press, 2007), Xiii.
17. Yancy, "Dear White America." For a description of his experience in the aftermath of this editorial, see his recent book, Yancy, *Backlash*.
18. Butler, "Endangered/Endangering," 16.
19. Claudia Card, *Confronting Evils: Terrorism, Torture, Genocide* (Cambridge: Cambridge University Press, 2010), 265.
20. Card suggested that the U.N. definition should be amended to stipulate that the acts in question are genocidal if committed *either* with the intent to destroy *or* "with the reasonably foreseeable consequence of destroying, in whole or in part" (Card, 2008). This would be an important step in strengthening the power of the document to

110   Chapter 3

force nations to intervene in large-scale atrocities, for then the rationale for intervention would not focus *simply* on the motivations of the perpetrators but instead on the consequences of their actions, on the harms they inflict on others. It would recognize both the intention of the perpetrators and the *system* of violence they help realize as co-determinants of a genocidal process.

21. Berkowitz, *The Crime of My Very Existence*, 53.
22. Agamben, *Homo Sacer*, 85.
23. Berkowitz, *The Crime of My Very Existence*, 54.
24. Ibid., 226.
25. Ibid., 227.
26. Michel Foucault, *Nietzsche, Genealogy, and History*, in *Aesthetics, Method, and Epistemology (Essential Works of Foucault, 1954-1984, Vol. 2)* (New York: The New Press, 1999), 378.
27. Yehuda Bauer, *On the Holocaust and Other Genocides* (Washington, DC: USHMM, 2007), 18.
28. David Moshman, "Conceptual Constraints On Thinking about Genocide," *Journal of Genocide Research* 3, no. 3 (2001): 431–450, 436.
29. Hannah Arendt, *The Origins of Totalitarianism* (New York: Harcourt Brace, 1973), 20.
30. Silas Jackson, *When I Was a Slave: Memoirs from the Slave Narrative Collection*, ed. N. R. Yetman (New York: Dover, 2002), 75.
31. 2Pac, "16 on Death Row," Produced and Written by 2Pac, Release Date: November 25, 1997.
32. Run-DMC. "Back From Hell," Produced and Written by: Jam Master Jay, D.M.C. & Rev Run, Release Date: October 16, 1990.
33. 5th Ward Boyz, "Concrete Hell," Produced by Mike Dean, Release Date: November 28, 1995.
34. Blacks make up 12.3 percent of U.S. population and 43.9 percent of the state and federal prison population. Latinos constitute 12.6 percent of the country's population, but make up 18.3 percent of the prison population. Whites are 69 percent of the general population with only 34.7 percent of those incarcerated.
35. http://nrccfi.camden.rutgers.edu/. In 2010, 93% of Federal Prisoners were convicted of non-violent crimes and 47% of State Prisoners were convicted of non-violent crimes. The vast majority of U.S. prisoners do not represent a threat to the public order and do not need to be removed from their families and subject to mental and physical pain in prison. Instead, they need material assistance, affordable health care, education, and employment.
36. Kanye West, "Family Business," Produced and Written by Kanye West, Release Date: February 10, 2004.
37. Ludacris, "Do Your Time," Produced by Trak Starz, Written by Shamar Daugherty, Alonzo Lee, Pimp C, Beanie Sigel, C-Murder & Ludacris, 2006.
38. Primo Levi, *Survival in Auschwitz*, Translated by Stuart Woolf (New York: Touchstone Books, 1995), 61.
39. Further, the American public rarely considers the vast numbers of prisoners who have been wrongfully accused of crimes. The legal theorist Richard Leo has

shown that the interrogation process itself (in which it is legal for police officers to lie to suspects about what they know or what evidence they already have) creates the conditions for false confessions insofar as suspects become confused, disoriented, and will eventually say anything in order for the interrogation to stop. Although it is impossible to know how many confessions are false, we do know that a vast number of defendants admit to crimes they know they did not commit in order to take a plea deal and avoid the risk of a longer sentence or the death penalty. So given the high number of false confessions and plea deals, and the vast number of prisoners who suffer from severe mental illness, it is not accurate to say that prisoners are harmed for what they have "done."

Chapter 4

But You Don't Hear Me Tho

HIP-HOP AS TRAUMATIC TESTIMONY

In addition to their concern that rappers "keep it real," or respect the values of Hip-Hop Nation rather than produce commercial music that betrays those values, hip-hop artists often express a concern that their fans will not move past their love of hip-hop music to actually being moved-by the music; or motivated to try to dismantle those larger institutions essential to the systemic infliction of anti-black violence in the city and the cell. As explained in the Introduction, with reference to Dead Prez, underground rappers emphasize that "It's Bigger Than Hip-Hop."

In his song "Words I Never Said," Lupe Fiasco articulates this concern in a verse that makes reference to the late Tupac Shakur (Pac): "Just listening to Pac ain't gon' make it stop."[1] Of course he is right to emphasize that listening to music that exposes and critiques our system of anti-black genocide will not, in-itself, create the structural changes necessary to eliminate state-sanctioned practices of anti-black violence. The verse continues: "A rebel in your thoughts ain't gon' make it halt/If you don't become an actor, you'll never be a factor." Here it is less obvious what it means to become an "actor" so that one becomes a "factor" in the collective dismantling of a white supremacist state that is sustained by the military- and prison-industrial complex.

In their hip-hop song about hip-hop, "Sketches of Pain," the group Audible Mainframe expresses a similar concern in the verse "It can weep for you, it can grieve for you/It can open your eyes, but it can't see for you."[2] Here, again, it is unclear how those who listen to hip-hop can better "see" and resist racist oppression, but it is clear that that it is possible to listen to underground hip-hop without hearing it, or to forget that hip-hop is always "bigger than hip-hop"; essentially connected to the struggle for black freedom that provoked the creation of this genre born from the need to Get a Witness to the un-natural forms of traumatic violence that are absent from and obfuscated by the dominant discourse and popular media. In this chapter I will focus on how the role of hip-hop as a form of traumatic testimony—or the aesthetic expression of the pain and collective harms suffered by systemic racism—acts as a form of political resistance against the exclusion of this testimony in popular culture and our nationalist narratives. I will also draw on the lyrics of rappers to illustrate the difference between "hearing" and "consuming" this testimony, a problem that arises from listening to hip-hop as "mere" text or as the testimony of a single individual, unrelated to the larger socio-political condition of black people as a group, who are subject to un-natural and pathological forms of violence internal to our system of governance.

As underground rappers know, most people don't want to hear the testimony of the traumatized, and we come up with all kinds of "reasons" to refuse to listen. In the first part of this text I examined specific discursive practices common to white sensibility called out by rappers that serve to allow white people to perpetually defer awareness of their whiteness, and thus the moral and human cost of their own privileges and opportunities. In this second part, I focus on the power of hip-hop as a form of aesthetic testimony about trauma, as well as the threat this testimony poses to the stability and authority of the dominant discourse that emerges from and sustains white sensibility. In hip-hop songs about hip-hop, rappers often describe the process of producing hip-hop as giving aesthetic expression to emotions—anger and anguish—that need to be expressed, and find expression within the distinct form and language of hip-hop. As expressed by Ludacris in his song "I Do It For Hip Hop": "Now this is what they call poetry in motion/My soul bleeds on the paper, heart screams with emotion."[3]

The discomfort with and exclusion of traumatic testimony from our sensibility is also evident in the fact that those who theorize about trauma often do so in isolation of (1) the contingent social and political conditions that produce and reinforce patterns of violence that provoke the symptoms that characterize the disorder of post-traumatic stress disorder (PTSD); and (2) the concrete experiences and testimony of those who suffer from PTSD. This is reflected in the current trend of scholarship that develops insights about trauma by drawing on observations about how non-human animals are able to process their own near-death experiences through physiological responses like shaking or trembling that prevent them from becoming traumatized, or developing a pathological reaction to these experiences. This line of argument has also informed the development of new practices to help those who suffer from PTSD cope with and process past traumas, such as "Therapeutic Tremoring" in which people are encouraged to "Shake Off Stress and Trauma."[4]

However, we cannot learn about the nature and cause of PTSD from a study of non-human animal life, as the harm of trauma is inextricably linked to the fact that it is violation of our moral and psychic expectations because it need not have occurred and in fact, in the strongest sense, should not have occurred. There is no "Need not have occurred" in the animal kingdom, as non-human animals navigate the world through their instincts rather than through symbolic forms like language and art and number. It's not possible to understand the harm of PTSD if we lose sight of the *un-natural* violation that provokes it; for this reason Freud understands trauma as a "breach" in the psyche that cannot be coped with through the usual mechanisms by which we cope with pain and loss because it violates every rational expectation for what could or should happen. This is why as a pathology, PTSD is so connected with our failure to mediate or "understand" the traumatic violation as it is occurring through linguistic categories. If we did not have rational expectations for what "ought to occur" or if we did not navigate life through "making sense" of it, we would not suffer from PTSD in the way that we do. However, the tendency to regard a distinctly moral violation as a "natural" occurrence reinforces the confusion between traumatic and tragic forms of suffering; as I argued in the first half of this text, the assimilation of traumatic to tragic suffering plays a central role in the white sensibility of anti-black violence as occasional and accidental rather than systemic, institutional and entirely preventable.

PTSD is the only mental disorder that is caused by experience, rather than genetics. This fact—to quote Freud—"astonishes people far too little," for it indicates that the disorder cannot be understood as an evolutionary defect. If we lose sight of this distinctive feature then we run the risk of viewing PTSD as a disorder caused by an individual's weaknesses or genetic flaws rather than by social experiences to which no one should be subject. Humans alone have the evolutionary tool of an advanced form of abstract thought that allows us greater freedom over how and when to satisfy instincts, and so a tool to create a world in which we don't attack each other for food and sex. The severity of the harm that provokes PTSD is related to the fact that we are able to say (unlike animals) that this type of harm should NOT have occurred, given our enhanced ability to control and predict the terms of our existence through its symbolic representation. In this sense the violation suffered by trauma is also a moral violation, and animals don't create a world of moral expectations. So even if non-human animals do suffer from PTSD (and I have no doubt that many do), it does not have the same logic or dynamic of PTSD in human life. Because we are meaning-making creatures, the remedy for PTSD will always require the ability to reinterpret traumatic experiences from the past that invade the present in the form of symptoms like flashbacks and misplaced rage—a deferred response to a traumatic event.

In other words, even if we could tremble in the immediate aftermath of a traumatic violation, we could not heal ourselves without relying on some aspect of human culture to interpret and reinterpret the meaning of that violation; a distinctly human practice that combines sensory with intellectual stimulus to allow us the opportunity to re-experience past traumas in order to re-claim them from the position of having-survived them. In the clinical treatment of PTSD this is done through a psychotherapy treatment called Eye Movement Desensitization and Reprocessing (EMDR), in which the client initiates a process of recollecting emotionally disturbing memories while simultaneously focusing on an external stimulus. The external stimulus can vary and can also incorporate several sensory stimulations that are coordinated with each other, so that a client may be directed to watch a light move from the left to the right side of a standing, horizontal bar to stimulate lateral eye movements, at the same time that the client will feel a vibration in her left hand and a sound in her left ear when her eyes are directed to the left (and a vibration in her right hand and a sound in her right ear when her eyes are directed right). EMDR is marked by two distinct stages: in the first stage, the client bears witness to and reinterprets past traumas from the position of someone who survived them. In the second stage, referred to as the "processing" stage, the client provides testimony about those traumas from a position of authority *as* one who survived them, rather than someone who is somehow responsible for them or feels shame that they occurred.

In this chapter I argue that underground hip-hop has always served the therapeutic role also played by EMDR, insofar as rappers occupy a distinct position of authority from which to testify about suffering from—and surviving the traumatic violence inflicted by—the pathological conditions of our racial democracy. My focus on the parallel between hip-hop and EMDR offers another way to think about the therapeutic value of hip-hop that has already been documented and established in the interdisciplinary volume on the *Therapeutic Uses of Rap and Hip-Hop*, edited by Susan Hadley and George Yancy. However I am also claiming that the therapeutic value of hip-hop as a form of EMDR that helps people cope with, reinterpret, and process traumatic suffering also indicates its political significance as a form of resistance against the discursive violence that excludes and dis-articulates and so exacerbates this suffering. Given the political importance of excluding the testimony of black citizens from the dominant discourse in order to normalize routine patterns of state violence that serve to murder them, attack their social vitality, moral integrity, and psychic wellbeing, it is not surprising that hip-hop artists who do testify to trauma in a form of art inspired by this need also repeatedly insist: "But you don't hear me tho." At the same time, if we take hip-hop seriously as a form of therapy that can help people cope with this violence, then we can understand another sense of the frequent claim "Hip-hop (literally) saved my life." If we do try to hear the traumatic testimony of hip-hop artists and respect the authority of those attacked rather than those protected by the state, then we can discover insights about how the dominant discourse about trauma also serves to dis-articulate the nature and causes of traumatic suffering in the service of white or anti-black sensibility. For example, the discourse that seeks remedies for PTSD through a study of non-human animal behavior is complicit with racist and sexist narratives that blame victims for being victimized, as it suggests that individuals suffer from PTSD due to their failure to adapt to their environment rather than due to socio-political patterns of violence that serve to exclude entire communities from the protection of the law and moral consideration.

In fact, the entire discussion about animals and trauma is based on a false analogy between animal and human life in order to defer critical attention away from the actual source of traumatic violence, or the contingent conditions that sustain a racist, heterosexist, and classist distribution of power and capital. The discussion is informed by the question: "Why don't animals suffer from PTSD?," and so will always lead us away from those questions that need to be asked in order to assess how and in what way the conditions of social and civic life create and in fact require a pathological arrangement of power relations that inflicts patterns of traumatic violence that undermine the social vitality of entire communities—whether or not every person subject to these conditions develops the symptoms of PTSD. In this way the discussion about animal trauma reflects something about "professional" discourse that hip-hop artists and critical race theorists have always sought to convey, or that the way in which we talk about trauma in the terms of the dominant discourse—whether the dominant clinical or academic or popular discourse—only reinforces our moral blindness to and epistemological ignorance about the systemic and lethal harms inflicted on racialized and gendered groups *as such*.

The tendency to ignore, exclude, deny, and distort the testimony of those who have suffered from systemic state or social violence is reinforced by the clinical sensibility of PTSD as an individual pathology that requires therapeutic intervention and clinical expertise to treat and "cure" a client. For this sensibility all too often reinforces the authority of the therapist as the "expert" who diagnoses clients with PTSD rather than someone who serves as a witness to their traumas and listens to the testimony that emerges from their recollection of painful memories. We can better shift our perspective if we listen to the testimonies of trauma that we are so determined to exclude from our sensibility and our academic work. In his reflections on living-through his years in Auschwitz, "At the Mind's Limits," Jean Améry expressed his admiration for those prisoners who could better adapt to and resist the conditions of camp life, though he insisted that he could not and did not want to be like them.⁵ For he suggests that there is something pathological about perfectly adapting to a pathological set of conditions. From this perspective, we can better appreciate the insights offered by those who suffer from PTSD or suffer from the moral horror and shock of specifically traumatic violations that need not and should not occur, for their testimony acts as the emotional register of the social violence that we ignore and obfuscate and exclude in our dominant discourses.

The critical question is not why some people develop the symptoms of PTSD after suffering from un-natural forms of violence and others do not, but rather how the rest of us are able to reconcile ourselves and adapt to the lethal conditions of American society such that we cannot feel or see its horror. This doesn't mean that we can't process or heal from or learn from trauma, but we should not reconcile ourselves to it as an "inevitable" part of human life, akin to tragic suffering, but rather as indicating the moral necessity to radically transform the terms of social and political life that consign racialized and gendered minorities to a position of un-natural vulnerability to PTSD. When we lose sight of the distinct conditions that provoke the symptoms of PTSD, we run the risk of viewing all pain and loss as potentially traumatic and so naturalizing and reconciling ourselves to patterns of social violence.

HIP-HOP AS FORM AND STIMULUS FOR TRAUMATIC RECOLLECTION

After his release from prison in 2018 when he was sentenced to 2–4 years for supposedly violating the terms of his parole, the hip-hop artist Meek Mill dropped a new album—*Championships*—with a track titled "Trauma" that recounted his recent experience in prison in relation to his past and present as a black man in America, targeted from birth for incarceration and exploitation. In the hook of the song he raps:

> When them drugs got a hold of your mama
> And the judge got a hold on your father

Followed by the bar:

> Go to school, bullet holes in the locker[6]

After every verse in which he describes the varieties of institutional violence that he has suffered, Mill returns in the hook to specific adversities or conditions-of-life to which black children are disproportionately subject, to remind us that the source of his trauma cannot be separated from the

American system of anti-black violence that tears apart the family and turns school into a war zone. In one verse he explicitly mentions PTSD:

> Ain't no PTSDs, them drugs keep it at ease
> They shot that boy 20 times when they could've told him just freeze

Here he connects the widespread use of drugs in black communities with the need to medicate the symptoms of PTSD suffered from entirely preventable forms of police brutality and murder that are systematically inflicted on black citizens and normalized as standard operating procedure. The verse also bears witness to the recent police murder of Stephen Clark in downtown Sacramento, who was shot 20 times by police in his grandmother's backyard, to illustrate the un-natural, unnecessary, and entirely preventable nature of traumatic violence inflicted against black communities by police officers trained to treat black life as entirely expendable. The liminal status of black life as always already in a position of un-natural vulnerability to violence and death is traumatic in-itself, as it produces an environment in which anything can happen and anything is possible, and in which to "be black" is to suffer from everyday violations of moral and civic expectations.

In a later verse, Mill reminds us that state violence against black life is neither an accident, an oversight, an aberration, or a tragic state of affairs, but instead the basis of our racial democracy:

> And in the 13th amendment, it don't say that we kings
> They say that we legally slaves if we go to the bing

Here Mill draws attention to the fact that the Thirteenth Amendment in the United States constitution legally sanctions slavery or "involuntary servitude" as a form of punishment, so that the legal subordination and torture of black communities that sustains the white monopoly of power and capital could shift from the plantation to the criminal justice system as a whole. When we lose sight of the difference between tragic forms of pain and loss (or forms of suffering that cannot be prevented, and can be understood/ reconciled with our narratives) and traumatic violations (forms of suffering that can be prevented and cannot be represented by or reconciled with our narratives), then we run the risk of naturalizing a contingent state of human affairs that need not occur and can be prevented. This is why PTSD is not really an individual but instead a social pathology, provoked by the pathological conditions of human culture. It's a mental disorder that reflects the fact that we really can't adapt to these conditions and still "make sense" of human life, which indicates the moral necessity of eradicating them.

Forms of violence that are potentially traumatic are neither natural nor inevitable, but instead inextricably linked to the contingent arrangement of social and political relations. Mill's lyrics suggest that we cannot adopt a "non-political" approach to trauma in the name of scientific objectivity or description without distorting the nature and distinct harm of PTSD. The study of trauma should always lead to an identification of social conditions that are pathological or "bad" precisely because they predictably provoke the disorder. And indeed, this is how hip-hop artists testify to their own traumas, as they consistently trace their symptoms of psychic suffering to the contingent conditions of our racist economy and the forms of violence inflicted to systematically subordinate and exploit entire black communities. The clinical view that does not distinguish between tragic and distinctly traumatic forms of violence and instead views all forms of pain, danger, and loss as potentially traumatic reinforces the ability of white sensibility to (mis) perceive traumatic as tragic violence in order to perpetually defer awareness of the moral and human cost of its whiteness.

In the therapeutic practice of EMDR, the recollection of painful memories is affected by the presence of an external sensory stimulus so that the entire sensibility is stimulated during the imaginative re-creation of past traumas. This corresponds to the form and content of underground hip-hop, where the MC provides a lyrical recollection of past traumas that still haunt the present and threaten the future, in a distinct "flow" that upsets discursive and rhythmic expectations, against a beat that stimulates the senses.

However in the rapper's recollection, the memory of past traumas always leads to reflection about forms of everyday violence that still traumatize black communities in the present, so that the harms suffered by an individual in the past are re-signified as a moral violation against the entire community and as indicating the moral demand in the present to bear witness to and dismantle the system of anti-black violence. In this way the form of testimony in hip-hop reveals those distinct features of traumatic violence that are obfuscated or absent from the clinical sensibility of PTSD as an individual pathology, and so act as a form of "subjugated knowledge" about the nature of traumatic violence and the means to recover in order to navigate a world in the present that is no less lethal. The current clinical focus on observing animal reactions to life-threatening situations in order to find a "cure" for PTSD interprets the (apparent) absence of the disorder in other species as a sign of our natural deficiencies rather than as a sign of the un-natural conditions of human culture that produce forms of violence that we cannot and should not adapt to. This focus also permanently defers the fact that the harm that provokes PTSD is not simply a physical but a moral violation.

It is much easier to believe that traumatic violence is a natural part of our world than to take the time to trace the cultural sources of so many different forms of traumatic suffering, but this is essential for those who suffer from PTSD and it should be essential to the practitioners of EMDR, so that they do not mistake the moral violation at the source of all trauma with the natural vulnerability of human life. Further, this perspective precludes the path to recovery as those who suffer from PTSD also tend to suffer from two feelings that exacerbate the symptoms of the disorder: (1) the feeling that I am somehow to blame for traumas suffered in the past as I am "not good enough" and/or (2) the feeling that I am not safe, because the person or people who violated me in the past are evil, and there are other evil people who want to harm me. These feelings are reinforced by clinical and popular representations of PTSD as a failure to adapt to natural—if violent and overwhelming—conditions and by popular representations of "criminals" who inflict harm for the sake of harm.

As a disorder provoked by the inability to describe or understand how and why one suffered from violence in the past, PTSD and the path to recovery are saturated in language. This is evident in the fact that traumatic flashbacks recur to the extent that an episode of traumatic violence was never integrated into the narrative of the person who suffered from the assault; that is, she never found a way to assign it meaning. In my experience with this symptom, it was not possible to reduce the frequency and intensity of flashbacks until I found the *right words* to describe my past traumas and found some way to assign meaning to having suffered them—or, more accurately, some lesson I could draw from the experience to guide me in the future. And for this reason, my progress was also stunted at various times when my therapist would say the wrong thing at the wrong time, or mis-characterize my pain and my symptoms in language that reinforced the clinical view of PTSD as a pathology caused by an individual's failure to adapt to a near-death experience. A few weeks after I started therapy with the clinician who would also guide me through EMDR, I expressed my concern that previous therapists hadn't been "smart" enough for me to work with, or hadn't caught my various strategies to deflect and avoid their questions. She responded: "Well, I appreciate that you're smarter than me in many ways, but really you're an emotional infant." At that moment I did not have the grace to reflect on what she could have meant, but instead I shut down and could not see her again for several weeks.

The tendency to blame oneself for past traumas can preclude the effort to recollect and re-signify those distressing experiences that I feel guilty for having suffered, and the tendency to demonize one's perpetrator only exacerbates the feelings of rage and hyper-vigilance that are common symptoms of PTSD. In my experience, it is not possible to process past trauma until one can trace the source of past violations to a larger system of violence that also contextualizes the behavior of those who assaulted me as the sign and product of our pathological organization of socio-political and economic conditions. We can only calm down our need to perpetually "complete" our resistance to past traumas in the form of deferred responses to them in the present, by actually honoring those ego states that suffered from the force of their assault. We can only do this by easing our libidinal attachment to blaming them or demonizing those who harmed them. In my view, this process is modeled every time an MC demands a witness to his recollection of the brutal conditions to which he was subject—inseparable from the political subordination of his community—that have compromised his moral agency and undermined the social vitality of his family.

As a disorder, PTSD is characterized by symptoms—like hyper-vigilance and rage—that are triggered by a specific external stimulus and act as types of "deferred response" to past traumas that one did not and could not prevent or emotionally process at the time they were suffered. However there are also symptoms—like flashbacks and depression—that do not require a "trigger" and are not so much deferred responses to traumatic violence as the intrusion of the un-mastered, traumatic past into the sensibility that once suffered from the failure to mediate or process this trauma. That is, these symptoms force us to "see" or "feel" the past that cannot be integrated into the present, indicating that trauma and traumatic history "need a witness" and recur to the extent that they are repressed, denied, and impossible to understand or affirm as part of our past at all. Both types of symptoms indicate that PTSD involves a psychodynamic relationship between past and present ego states in which the failure to fully experience one's past consistently hijacks or over-determines one's sensibility of the present. And they indicate the importance of finding a way to testify about past traumas despite the impossibility of their symbolic representation in the categories and concepts of our dominant discourses.

While the process of EMDR allows us to adjust the psychodynamic relation between the past and the present, it's not the case that someone who suffers from PTSD also suffers from a completely pathological relation to the past or that they have not already developed adaptive skills to cope with and process past traumas. Indeed this is why my therapist's early remark that I was an "emotional infant" was so devastating to me, as my path from being assaulted to surviving in the aftermath could not be reduced to a set of pathological symptoms that had stunted my emotional development.

After my therapist's remark, I listened to the song "Battle Cry" by Angel Haze to affirm what my therapist had been unable to understand, or that victims of trauma *already* have "post-traumatic wisdom" as survivors; the path to recovery allows the adaptive skills we already have to be more effective as we find a way to bear witness to our past traumas without shame or rage, and so to extract the wisdom we already have from the symptoms that make us feel like we are forever "completing" something that we once failed to do. To her credit, my therapist had the humility to own her mistake, and my ability to work-through the impasse (with the help of hip-hop) and return to therapy was essential to my own therapeutic progress.

Haze's "Battle Cry" is an excellent example of how hip-hop can provide a counter-model to the clinical approach toward trauma, as it provides a form of traumatic testimony that facilitates the intellectual and sensory stimulus necessary to affect our sensibility about traumas in the past that recur in the present. In "Battle Cry," Haze spits bars that both recollect her traumatic past of sexual violence and re-enact the different ways in which she re-signified the meaning of this trauma in her effort to live in the present, or reduce her pain and resist the current threats to her wellbeing.

The video for the song features Haze "watching" herself as a little girl who is coerced into a car with an adult man, trapped and helpless as he reaches for her. In multiple interviews, Haze has talked openly about her past growing up in a cult in which she suffered sexual assault as a young child, and has also reported that the cult did not allow its members to listen to music, so that she was only able to first hear and acquire music at the age of 16. Her talent and her exceptional skills as a lyricist and performer are all the more extraordinary given the obstacles she has faced and overcome, but this is precisely why she can assume a position of authority and spit bars with confidence about her path from trauma to recovery. In the therapeutic process of EMDR, the client does not verbally communicate with the therapist while she initiates painful memories about her past, so that it is largely a therapeutic process of self-willed introspection that is guided or affected by an external stimulus; in this way the client always retains the position of authority over the process.

Recall that the therapeutic process of EMDR is marked by two distinct stages, where the first stage corresponds to the need to bear witness to re-signify past traumas and the second stage corresponds to the ability to testify from a position of authority *as* one who survived them, rather than someone who is somehow responsible for them or feels shame that they occurred. In "Battle Cry," Angel Haze offers testimony from inside the experience of PTSD, and her language evokes each stage of her sensibility as she works through and learns to re-signify her past for the sake of carving out a meaningful present. The first bar of the song "It seems like yesterday that I was nothing," bears double significance as an expression of the traumatic past that is not fully past ("It seems like yesterday") and an expression of what it feels like to be traumatized, attacked against one's will and reduced to "nothing" one can affirm or accept. The next few bars describe the feelings of rage and conceit that often accompany the early sensibility of past traumas before one is able to re-signify or testify about them:

Then all of a sudden I'm a volcanic eruption
Then all of a sudden it's like spontaneous combustion

As it becomes impossible to hold back rage, being "all up in your face, yelling":

"Bitch, you can't tell me nothing"
Cos I came from the bottom[7]

This verse doesn't "sound" like a pathological reaction to a past trauma, but instead an emotional disposition that "makes sense" in the aftermath of surviving an attack, when one feels the need to aggressively defend one's right to self-determination and one's authority *as* someone who just "came from the bottom" or survived the loss of agency and authority. In this verse—as in every verse of the song—Haze finds the right language to acknowledge her pain and the real violation she suffered at the same time that they are very words needed *at* each stage of her recovery to progress to a new form of sensibility that allows her to re-signify the meaning of her past trauma for the sake of thriving in the present. For this reason, "Battle Cry" models a path for the recollection and re-signification of past traumas that allows for a psychic re-orientation toward them; one that enhances the ability to cope with pain and find strength in the present. In the course of the song, her past trauma becomes her "battle cry" to discover and assert her own authority and wisdom, as well as devote her life to attending to others who have suffered from violence. This is illustrated in a later verse:

I woke up one Sunday morning, stopped believing in Jesus
Stopped believing in churches, I stopped believing in preachers

Here she illustrates that the process of recovering from trauma requires faith in our own ability to make-sense of our past and organize the present:

I realized I was a teacher, not just one of the heathens
I'm going to destroy the fallacies, start creating believers

Here Haze connects the path of her recovery to her realization that she didn't need "others" to heal or judge or diagnose her but instead as a *survivor* she already had the wisdom attained through her path of recollection to define herself and help others do the same.

Start creating the leaders, tell them who should they follow
Nobody but themselves, especially if they hollow

It's precisely those who are "hollow" or were desolated by the loss of will and agency who can "see" and "feel" a dimension of our social reality that is lost or obfuscated in our narratives about ethics and the human condition.

And in this verse she reclaims her authority to question those narratives and expose the fallacies that mis-represent those who suffer from trauma as "heathens" (or patients or criminals) and preclude their empowerment. Lastly, she draws attention to the importance of language and discursive resistance to our ability to process and heal from trauma.

> So now I spit it for people who say their cords missing
> Inspire life into anybody that's forfeiting

In the last verse, Haze conveys the final way in which she has signified her past in a way to find meaning in the present:

> Cause it's easy to keep pretending that there's nothing wrong
> But it's harder to keep your head up and be fucking strong

Here Haze conveys that her ability to heal from traumas in the past is dependent on her enhanced ability to attend to the suffering of traumatized others in the present—a sentiment expressed by artists in countless hip-hop tracks that recount the traumas of being-black in the United States. Haze understands her role in hip-hop culture to "spit it" for people who are hollow, to inspire them to resume the fight to "keep your head up and be fucking strong" against the social conditions that threaten to overwhelm and destroy us.

Practitioners and trauma theorists should take seriously the testimony from inside PTSD to examine and critique their own discursive patterns of talking about trauma. I can't emphasize enough how much "language matters" to the ability to process and heal from trauma, and hip-hop artists are keenly aware of the importance of discursive resistance for the sake of our psychological wellbeing. Indeed, hip-hop artists had to invent a new genre *and* language to provide a testimony of trauma that is excluded and obfuscated by dominant discursive practices, and yet they are still criminalized just for testifying about the socio-political conditions that provoke their trauma. The criminalization of hip-hop reinforces the white refusal to listen to testimonies of trauma suffered from the systemic infliction of state-sanctioned anti-black violence. As mentioned in the Introduction, the recent refusal of the Supreme Court to review a case in which a rapper was sent to prison for the lyrics in his song "Fuck the Police" indicates just how much is at stake in the continued criminalization of hip-hop and the mis-representation of testimony as a "real threat" to public safety.

The political threat posed by hip-hop is inseparable from its power as a form of counter-testimony to white sensibility that coopts and re-signifies words, melodies, and beats from popular music and discourse in order to expose the *limits* of that sensibility and provide an emotional register of what these limits exclude and perpetuate, namely, the routine and entirely preventable infliction of traumatic violence against black communities, as such, through the practices internal to our social and political and economic institutions. The distinct form of testimony made possible in hip-hop allows rappers to get a witness to their traumas for themselves and their community, despite the white refusal to listen sanctioned by the frequent judicial prosecution of this testimony as a criminal act. This is not a minor accomplishment but instead a major, creative task and underground hip-hop is *still* the only form of popular culture that bears witness to the systemic state violence and traumatic suffering that is obfuscated and distorted by popular media and culture.

As mentioned in the Introduction, there is a common refrain in hip-hop culture that "hip-hop saved my life," and hip-hop heads often add "No, *literally*. Hip-hop literally saved my life." The literalness of this sentence is actually meant in two senses, which are both expressed in the song "Hip-Hop Saved My Life" by Lupe Fiasco. First, hip-hop testifies to the structural conditions that aim to subordinate and destroy black communities and simultaneously illustrates the ability to resist these conditions; this allows for a sense of pride and hope to counter the sense of shame and despair felt in relation to the inevitable and senseless infliction of anti-black violence. Second, hip-hop has always provided material opportunities for black artists otherwise locked out of the labor market, and thus a means of survival in a racist economy. For this reason, hip-hop culture offers an essential "life-force" for black Americans, and underground rappers frequently express their devotion and appreciation for hip-hop culture in songs about hip-hop—as previously mentioned, there are thousands of songs simply titled "Hip-Hop" that express love for the culture and a concern for the future of hip-hop itself. The life-saving qualities of hip-hop also mark its political importance as a form of resistance against the *genocidal* structure of American racism that targets black communities *as such*, for it has enhanced the social and economic vitality of black artists. Further, underground hip-hop is effective as a means to cope-with-trauma precisely because its form and content are based on the distortion and re-signification of the dominant narratives and melodies that exclude and obfuscate systemic traumas as isolated, tragic accidents. Thus the aesthetic testimony of trauma is also a form of political resistance against the ubiquity of the neoliberal and post-racial sensibility that refuses to see or think about the United States as *system* of anti-black violence.

HIP-HOP AS POST-TRAUMATIC WISDOM

While it is obviously not the case that every hip-hop song is about trauma or that every song is informed by a mood of anger or anguish, there is still a sub-text of trauma in so many apparently light-hearted underground rap songs, as the past and present infliction of anti-black violence provides the context for the need or value of the joy and love that is expressed because it is *hard-won* against the daily assaults to life and liberty. For example, an important sub-genre of hip-hop is music about marijuana, or songs that express appreciation for the herb and the euphoria brought by smoking it. Indeed the group Cyprus Hill became known for the variety of their songs that celebrate the culture of smoking weed, most notably "I Wanna Get High" and "Hits From the Bong" from their album *Black Sunday*. In these songs, artists express far more than their love of getting high, insofar as they celebrate their *right* to get high from a natural *herb* in order to cope with the un-natural conditions of violence to which they are subject. Further, they act as protest songs against the criminalization of marijuana that has always served to rationalize and justify the mass incarceration of black men—even now, when white businessmen are profiting from the legalization of marijuana in largely white states.

The paradox of the situation can be grasped in light of the aforementioned verse by Tupac: "You claimin I'm a criminal and you the one that made me." Our nation criminalizes a natural substance in order to criminalize the very means with which so many people cope with the trauma, depression, and rage provoked by our national policies and dysfunctional institutions. Thus our system "produces" criminals by criminalizing the natural herb that helps so many people cope with the criminal conditions of American society or the systemic infliction of violence against black communities.

Though the medical community has now established that marijuana has medicinal value as a substance that can alleviate some of the symptoms of PTSD, it is still regarded by our criminal punishment system as a Category I substance, so that the mere *possession* of marijuana still serves to justify the incarceration of black men who do not live in one of the few states that has legalized it for largely white residents. The criminalization of marijuana has always been essential to the "War on (Black) Drugs" that still serves to criminalize all black men, and so in hip-hop culture the songs that celebrate the herb serve to re-claim its medicinal value at the same time that they (1) serve to protest its criminalization and (2) draw attention to the violent conditions of American life that provoke the need to find a means to get "high" to cope with them rather than lose-oneself in psychic pain and suffering.

These sentiments are all expressed in a new song titled "Four Twenty," produced by Wyclef Jean in his 2019 album *Wyclef Goes Back to School: Volume 1*. The need for these songs in hip-hop culture has never abated, and the chorus to the song reinforces the political importance and perils of smoking weed in a police state that targets black men *and* the herbal means to cope with the condition of being-targeted. The chorus begins "Took a trip to Cali just to smoke some herbs," and continues:

Cause where I'm from, man, this shit ain't legal
But I brought it home anyway[8]

In pot culture, "Four Twenty" is a slang term that refers to something like a universal designated time for smoking weed, or a time reserved in the late afternoon for taking a break and smokin some herb to cope with the day's events and recharge for the next. So the ability to go to a state where one can legally consume the innocuous herb that helps us cope with the traumatic conditions of social life feels like "four-twenty every day," or occupying a social space that affords the opportunity to cope with pain.

In the third verse, Wavie D raps about why "this simple thing" of being *allowed* to smoke weed is so important for his wellbeing:

California, lately I've been having so much on my mind
Thats why I'm smoking everyday

When black rappers write hip-hop songs that celebrate the culture of smoking marijuana, they always trace the love of the herb to its medicinal power to ease the psychic suffering provoked by their un-natural vulnerability to trauma and death *every day*, simply in virtue of being-black in the United States. The verse continues:

My struggles, my troubles, left 'em all behind
Now I'm in a whole new way

The experience of trauma or being traumatized by the genocidal conditions of American life act as sub-text in these otherwise light-hearted and fun songs. It's hard to overstate just how helpful the use of marijuana can be in coping with the symptoms of PTSD for so many people, and so just how perverse it is to criminalize this natural substance in order to criminalize an essential means with which victims of state violence can better cope with and resist this violence. In those states that have legalized the use of THC to treat the condition of PTSD, the process of attaining the necessary license is extremely expensive and it is not always easy to get to a dispensary. So even the way in which select states have sought to legalize the medical use of marijuana already excludes those who do not have the financial means to afford the license or get to a clinic. The criminalization of marijuana is not an arbitrary or accidental fact but instead follows from the genocidal logic of American anti-black racism that aims to destroy the social vitality of black communities *as such,* and so attacks all forms of cultural practices and natural resources that allow black citizens to cope with and resist patterns of traumatic violence.

There is also a sub-genre of hip-hop songs in which rappers express their love and gratitude for their mothers, and a related sub-genre of "woman-centered" rap songs in which rappers come to terms with their own sexism and express empathy for the distinct struggles faced by women. Though these songs are positive and uplifting, they are also informed by a sub-text of trauma or, more accurately, they illustrate the type of "post-traumatic wisdom" that helps those who suffer from PTSD recover from and even gain strength from the recollection of past traumas that still recur in the present. Tupac Shakur's song "Dear Mama" is arguably the most famous hip-hop song written by a rapper to express love and gratitude for his mother, and in my view it is not surprising that he also wrote what is arguably the most famous hip-hop song that honors the struggles and strength of women, "Keep Ya Head Up."

I will focus on this particular sub-genre in hip-hop despite the fact that hip-hop—like every popular genre of music—has also accommodated and sometimes encouraged a masculinist perspective that perpetuates or sanctions heterosexist beliefs and violence against women and the LGBTQ community. I am indebted to the work of Tricia Rose, Imani Perry, and Kathryn Sophia Bell for their foundational and nuanced analyses of hip-hop culture and gender identity, and the varieties of ways in which women have been able to navigate and subvert the limited roles that they were able to occupy in a male-dominated genre in a sexist record industry.[9] Further, I have sought to learn more about the position of black women in the underground scene by talking to women who are talented MCs and in particular, with BL Shirelle and Bates—two members of my crew who frequently perform after I present my work on hip-hop at colleges and universities.[10]

While the feminist critique of certain trends and songs in hip-hop culture as emerging from and reinforcing a culture of violence against women is no doubt essential to Hip-Hop Nation, this analysis is beyond the scope of my argument and beyond my limits as a white woman writing about black musicians. I am not comfortable with nor certain of my ability to criticize black musicians as "sexist" in their lyrics and behavior given the default mis-perception of black men internal to my sensibility or in how I "make sense" of the world *as* a white woman. Lastly, I am always amazed that while hip-hop has been singled out by politicians and cultural critics as somehow "more" sexist than other genres, it is also the only genre in which artists and scholars have devoted concerts, panels, books, and documentaries to exposing and rectifying the problem. In focusing on underground hip-hop that honors women, I do not mean to side-step the problem of sexism in hip-hop culture but rather highlight the types of songs that are often overlooked in this discussion and complicate any sweeping generalizations that someone unfamiliar with the genre may otherwise entertain.

In his song "Dear Mama," before Shakur spits the bars of the song he states: "You are appreciated."[11] And in the course of the song Shakur illustrates the process of *how* he came to better appreciate his mother, as he recollects the pain of his own childhood traumas to identify the source of his misplaced anger toward his mother in his past, and create an empathetic bridge to better feel his mother's own struggles; this allows him to better appreciate the depth of her love, wisdom, and strength *as a mother*—a subject-position that Shakur cannot occupy. This also resonates with the process of EMDR, in which one recollects the traumas of the past in order to better discern how they overdetermined one's feelings and behavior in the present, and re-signifies them in such a way that enhances the ability to empathize with the pain of others.

This dynamic is illustrated in the first verse, in which Shakur's recollection of his childhood traumas "I shed tears with my baby sister, over the years/ We was poorer than the other little kids," leads him to discover why he was unable to appreciate his mother in his youth: "And even though we had different daddies, the same drama/When things went wrong we'd blame Mama." Shakur's effort to understand how his own struggle with trauma in the past compromised his empathy and love for his mother, allows him to re-signify those traumas as a shared experience: "I reminisce on the stress I caused, it was hell/Huggin' on my mama from a jail cell." This allows him to "see" the strength of his mother and "feel" gratitude for her as the woman who suffered-with and sustained him. He writes that he can: "finally understand/For a woman it ain't easy tryin' to raise a man," as he is able—in recollecting his own traumas—to better appreciate the specificity of her position as a woman, as a mother, subject to a different form of systemic discrimination. And his empathy for his mother enhances his awe for her strength and perseverance: "You always was committed/A poor single mother on welfare, tell me how you did it." Shakur's aesthetic recollection of his traumatic past leads to a shift in his sensibility whereby he can better appreciate and honor his mother in the present, such that he has a desire to learn from her.

In the hook of the song Shakur explains "And there's no way I can pay you back/But my plan is to show you that I understand/You are appreciated." Shakur understands the need for women to *feel* appreciated, and the need for men to check their own patterns of mis-recognition and indifference toward the pain of women before they are able to appreciate them. The song also provides a model for how the aesthetic recollection of painful memories can shift our sensibility of both the past and present in order to affect our relations to others and allow us to better navigate the future. Similarly, in his feminist anthem "Keep ya head up," Shakur's lyrics move from describing his own traumatic experiences and moral failings toward women in the past to describing the distinct forms of violence to which women are routinely subject, to describing the shared conditions of their traumatic history which indicate the need to "keep ya head up" not despite but because of how they have survived them together.

J. Cole's song "Crooked Smile" also illustrates the sub-text of traumatic experience that provides the context for his song that honors women, as he recollects his own struggles affirming himself against a classist and racist standard of beauty to better empathize with women and bear witness to the psychic harms inflicted by their objectification. His enhanced empathy allows him to take strength in their shared history of oppression without distorting or minimizing past and present forms of suffering. His emotional bridge from his own concerns about his "crooked smile" to feeling empathy for women who are ruthlessly sexualized then leads back to a description of the shared conditions of American anti-black violence:

Look at the nation
That's a crooked smile braces couldn't even straighten

He follows this with a description of the personal and collective traumas to which his entire community is subject:

Seem like half the race is either on probation or in jail
Wonder why we inhale, "cause we in Hell already"[12]

Though they do not overtly appear to be about trauma or offer a model for the recovery from symptoms of PTSD, hip-hop songs that pay homage to women illustrate the means to process and re-signify past traumas, as they tend to begin from the recollection of emotionally difficult memories and dialectically move through stages of interpreting them, where each stage corresponds with a way of being-in-the-world that lays the ground for the next stage of re-signifying the past until it bears immediate implications for how one can better resist and find meaning in the present.

As a final example of how trauma often serves as the sub-text for underground hip-hop that is not explicitly about trauma, I will claim that the more recent expression of hip-hop that emerged from the younger generation of "SoundCloud rappers"—scorned as "mumble rap" by the older generation of hip-hop heads—can also be heard as an aesthetic response to the continuity of anti-black genocide and the traumas they inherited as the generation born into and already decimated by the War on Drugs. The tension between the more traditional form of hip-hop that privileges lyricism and novel rhyming over the style innovated by the teenaged SoundCloud rappers that privileges a mood of post-apocalyptic nihilism and the rhythm of songs, has now provoked hundreds if not thousands of diss tracks between artists in each camp, calling the other out for failing to keep it real. As explained in the Introduction, these beefs between rappers play an important role in underground hip-hop culture as they sustain on ongoing, collective conversation about the difference between underground and commercial rap, and an ongoing examination of the past, present, and future of hip-hop as political praxis.

Perhaps no other SoundCloud rapper has been the target of as many diss tracks as the young rapper Lil' Pump, who rose to fame at the age of 17 with his song "Gucci Gang" (2017). The song repeats the phrase "Gucci Gang" over and over again in the hook, and includes the bar: "Your momma still live in a tent, yuh/Still slangin' dope in the 'jets, huh? (Yeah)" as well as the memorable verse: "Me and my grandma take meds, ooh (Huh?)."[13] Though dismissed as narcissistic and counter-productive to the struggle, Lil' Pump provides a form of testimony about the collective traumas of his community that departs from the aim of testimony in old-school hip-hop to get a Witness to the history, source, and nature of these traumas. Instead Lil' Pump and many of the other "Lil'" rappers modify the style of rapping to testify to the historical *failure* of hip-hop artists to get a witness through the aesthetic genius of their music, and depict the repetition of psychic and existential harms suffered from their failure to be heard. In this sense they "mumble" through their lyrics to depict the failure of the failure to be heard, and the continued impossibility of being heard against the post-racial and neoliberal sensibility of American society that continues to distort and deny their traumatic experiences of racist violence as so many tragic accidents that could not have been prevented.

In their innovative approach to hip-hop, the "Lils" depict both the failure to bear witness and the cost of this failure which has essentially abandoned their generation to medicating themselves through drinking "lean" (liquid opiates) to anesthetize themselves to the repetition of traumas that have already hijacked their young lives. The controversy between the OGs and the SoundCloud rappers regards two different sensibilities regarding the history and political function of hip-hop that also illustrate the different generational sensibilities of the youngest and the oldest members of hip-hop nation. From my perspective, they both reflect the ethos and subtext of underground hip-hop, as they regard two different sensibilities about traumatic violence inflicted against black communities and two different approaches about how to testify to their suffering that is still disavowed and dis-articulated by the dominant discursive practices.

By their own accounts, this aesthetic effort to reckon-with and re-signify past traumas allows rappers to find resilience in having-survived them, and extend empathy to traumatized others to enhance their collective efforts to better recover from and resist the traumas in the present. The traumatic testimony in underground hip-hop—at once personal and collective—is *political* because the traumas inflicted by our system of anti-black genocide recur to the extent that they are rendered invisible by our narratives about American history and democracy. So the creation of a genre uniquely capable of depicting and evoking and processing how the traumas suffered from state violence in the past survive in the repetition of violence in the present, responded to the *political* need to resist the post-racial and neoliberal sensibility of anti-black violence that regards systemic racism as a problem of the past, overcome in the present organization of American life. Again, the consistent criminalization of hip-hop and persistent judicial practice of sending rappers to prison for the lyrics in their songs indicates just how threatening this testimony is to the racist *episteme* that sustains white ignorance and moral indifference about black suffering.

NOTES

1. Lupe Fiasco, "Words I Never Said," Produced by Alex da Kid, Written by Skylar Grey, Alex da Kid and Lupe Fiasco, Release Date: February 8, 2011.
2. Audible Mainframe, "Sketches of Pain," Release Date: January 1, 2005.
3. Ludacris, "I Do It For Hip Hop," Produced by: Wyldfyer, Written by: Youtha Fowler, Wyldfyer, JAY-Z, Nas and Ludacris, Release Date: November 24, 2008.
4. https://www.acesconnection.com/blog/therapeutic-tremoring-shake-off-stress-and-trauma.
5. Jean Améry, *At The Mind's Limits: Contemplations by a Survivor on Auschwitz and Its Realities*, Translated by Sidney Rosenfeld and Stella P. Rosenfeld (Bloomington: Indiana University Press, 1980), 14.
6. Meek Mill, "Trauma," Produced by: DJ Don Cannon, Written by DJ Don Cannon and Meek Mill, Release Date: October 30, 2018.
7. Angel Haze, "Battle Cry," Produced by: Greg Kurstin, Written by Sia, Greg Kurstin & Angel Haze, Release Date: December 30, 2013.
8. Wyclef Jean, "Four-Twenty," Written by: Wavie D and Wyclef Jean, Release Date: March 8, 2019.
9. See especially: Kathryn Sophia Belle (Published under the name Kathryn T. Gines), "Queen Bees and Big Pimps: Sex and Sexuality in Contemporary Hip-Hop," in *Hip Hop and Philosophy: Rhyme 2 Reason*, edited by Derrick Darby and Tommie Shelby (Chicago: Open Court, 2005). Imani Perry, *Prophets of the Hood: Politics and Poetics in Hip Hop*, "B-Boys, Players, and Preachers: Reading Masculinity" and "The Venus Hip Hop and the Pink Ghetto: Negotiating Spaces For Women" (Durham, NC: Duke University Press, 2004). Tricia Rose, *Black Noise: Rap Music and Black Culture in Contemporary America*, "Bad Sistas: Black Women Rappers and Sexual Politics in Rap Music" (Hanover, NH: University Press of New England, 1994) and *The Hip Hop Wars: What We Talk About When We Talk About Hip Hop–and Why It Matters* (New York: Civitas Books, 2008).

10. I recently interviewed BL Shirelle about her experience as a rapper in the underground scene and her view about sexism and hip-hop for the website Aestheticsforbirds.com, for a special feature on "HIP-HOP, GENDER, AND LANGUAGE WITH UNDERGROUND RAPPERS BL SHIRELLE AND BATES," January 27, 2020 by aestheticsforbirds. https://aestheticsforbirds.com/2020/01/27/hip-hop-gender-and-language-with-underground-rappers-bl-shirelle-and-bates/#more-7963.

11. 2Pac, "Dear Mama," Produced by: Tony Pizarro, Written by: 2Pac, Tony Pizarro, Joe Sample, Terrence Thomas, Charles Simmons and Bruce Hawes, Release Date: February 21, 2015.

12. J. Cole, "Crooked Smile," Produced by: Elite and J. Cole, Written by: Meleni Smith and J. Cole, Release Date: June 4, 2013.

13. Lil' Pump, "Gucci Gang," Produced by: Gnealz and Bighead, Written by: Gnealz, Bighead and Lil Pump, Release Date: August 27, 2017.

Chapter 5

You Feel Me?

In underground hip-hop, the iconic phrase "Can I Get a Witness?" indicates the extent to which rap serves as a plea for others to acknowledge the systemic infliction of anti-black violence that is absent from the media and perpetually deferred by dominant discursive practices. The frequency of the phrase indicates that "trauma needs a witness," as those who suffer from PTSD need to bear witness to their past in order to gain greater control of the future, and our nation must bear witness to the history of traumas inflicted by our system of anti-black genocide in order to arrest their repetition. Further, another iconic phrase in underground hip-hop—"(Do) You Feel Me?"—indicates the extent to which rap music also serves as a plea for others to empathize with black people who suffer from these un-natural and entirely preventable forms of state violence that are rendered invisible by the criminalization of black life in popular culture and discourse.

Rappers turn to the affective power of music to try to induce empathy for their plight—you feel me?—since they cannot hope to be "understood" given the terms of the dominant discourse and the framework of white sensibility. In chapter 1, I drew on hip-hop as a form of counter-text to the post-racial and neoliberal narratives that provide the discursive framework for white sensibility that also inform how white people *read* what they *see*. As a form of counter-text, hip-hop rejects these narratives at the same time that it consistently draws attention to how their outsized influence on thought and sense makes it impossible for rappers to "get a witness" or to be *heard*, evident in other iconic phrases such as "But You Don't Hear Me Tho" and "Know What I'm Sayin?"

However, these phrases indicate more than the inability of rappers to "get a witness" to systemic anti-black violence from those "outside" of the Veil, as they also indicate the need of those racialized as "white" to acknowledge and *reckon with* this inability in order for them to "feel" the music even if they cannot fully understand the lyrics. In other words, these phrases convey the need for white people to bear witness to the *limits* of our ability to bear witness, or the limits of white sensibility to know or understand the experience of being-black in the United States.

In this chapter, I will focus on the power of hip-hop as testimony to disrupt the white sensibility of the present in order to make us aware of our cognitive and perceptual limits *as white people*; this enhanced awareness of our limits allows us to better feel moral anxiety about what these limits exclude, or at least to feel the absence of our moral horror about the system of racism that we cannot describe or understand or imagine or see despite (or because of) the fact that we benefit from this system. Throughout this text I have drawn on hip-hop and critical race theory to argue that it is not possible to question or expose the limits of white sensibility in the terms of the dominant discourse. In this chapter I argue that this requires, instead, an aesthetic stimulus for the interruption of sense-making that momentarily disrupts the totalizing hold of this discourse on sensibility. Specifically, I argue that underground hip-hop can serve as one aesthetic intervention to rectify what Janine Jones describes as "The Impairment of Empathy in Goodwill Whites for African Americans."[1]

As explained in chapter 1, Jones argues that goodwill whites cannot empathize with the suffering of African Americans because they perpetually defer awareness of themselves *as* white, which prevents them from grasping that they are in a fundamentally different and more privileged position, in need of a better understanding about the plight of black people in a white supremacist state from which they themselves benefit. This refusal-of-one's-whiteness is synonymous with the refusal to acknowledge the *limits* of one's perception *as* a white person, and allows white people to regard their sensibility as objective and universal (to quote George Yancy again, "white people assume that they know *everything* about me").[2] This refusal also entails the inability to imagine an actual system of anti-black racism that would otherwise implicate them as white, and this often translates into the judgment that there is no system of anti-black racism (see my analysis of the CNN interview with Meek Mill in chapter 1). For this reason, the effort of goodwill whites to comprehend the experience of black citizens as a group will always lead to a dis-articulation of anti-black violence as tragic, accidental, or deserved.

Goodwill whites refuse to acknowledge their whiteness in order to avoid negative emotions such as shame and guilt, and yet the awareness of what it means to be-white in a society that targets black communities for destruction, as such, is necessary to feel any moral obligation to make a better effort to hear and learn from black people. For this reason Jones concludes that the real problem is not the possibility of white empathy for black suffering, but instead the problem of the goodwill white's motivation to empathize at all, or interrupt the deferral of her whiteness to better comprehend the condition of being-black at the cost of her own moral and epistemic confidence. In other words, goodwill whites can feel empathy for racialized "others" only when they can admit and feel the limits of their own knowledge and perspective about race and society, and yet they lack motivation to do this, for it leads them to suffer from the loss of certainty and moral complacency. As Yancy explains, the white refusal to admit the limits of white sensibility is connected to the refusal to feel vulnerable, or accept the vulnerable position of one's fallibility and epistemic vulnerability to untruths ("fake news" in the parlance of the day).

Though I cannot definitely "prove" the power of hip-hop to expose the limits of white sensibility and create a space in which to *feel* the moral horror of anti-black racism in the present, I will draw on evidence from clinical psychology, hip-hop culture, and personal experience to argue that as a genre of music, hip-hop can disrupt our sense of what "makes sense" as a form of "common sense" to better grasp the limits of being-white in knowing, representing, or imagining the experience of being-black. The form of hip-hop—based on sampling and distortion—exposes the traumatic cracks in our tragic narratives about the United States that present anti-black violence as both a problem of the *past* and as an *exception* in American history, through the auditory interruption and co-option of those narratives to disrupt our sense-making so that we can *hear* the indecipherability or the *senselessness* of the American present. Further, underground rap music cannot be "listened to" in the same way as a song where it is easy to hear every word and understand the lyrics; instead in order to "hear" rap music it is necessary to let go of the need to understand every word or the ability to predict what words will follow from others. The novelty of the rhyming schemes and the spontaneity of freestyle rap preclude the ability for anyone to "master" the flow of a talented MC, and the novel combinations of discursive terms yield an infinite variety of interpretations.

This is not to claim that it is possible to "lift" the Veil that separates the sensibilities of those on either side of the color line, but it is possible for hip-hop—as a form of poetic testimony—to expose its existence, or to affect our sensibility of our sensibility such that we become aware of our limits as white people to understand, define, or judge the nature, cause, and effects of anti-black racism. This enhanced awareness of our distinctly white sensibility places goodwill whites in a better position to empathize with the plight of black Americans, or feel some of the discomfort and moral horror of *being-white* that is perpetually deferred by the sense-making of our discursive practices. Aesthetic works affect the emotions rather than simply the intellect, and temper the discomfort that attends our cognitive dis-orientation with awe at the beauty and poetic excellence of the work itself.

Scholars who write about the relation between music and empathy have suggested that since music can provoke a type of unconscious "emotional contagion" in which a person feels the emotion that is evoked by a song, it can play an important role in developing our conscious capacity for empathy. Drawing on their insights, we can better understand how hip-hop can address the problem raised by Jones about the lack of motivation among "goodwill whites" to empathize with black people, for the aesthetic enjoyment of rap music induces those emotions that normally escape the limits of white sensibility; these emotions do not "make sense" in the post-racial or neoliberal interpretations of American society that provide the framework for white sensibility. When white people are open to hearing hip-hop as a form of testimony, then they can experience the disruption of their moral and epistemic certainty in the process of aesthetic appreciation which is neither defensive nor reactive. And this can allow white people to feel empathy or to want to empathize with black people not despite but rather because they are white, and grasp the limits of what they can understand about the un-natural vulnerability of black citizens to state violence.

HIP-HOP AND EMOTIONAL CONTAGION

Despite the popular view that greater empathy requires greater knowledge of "others" who we often exclude from our moral concerns, rappers illustrate that the ability to *feel* something in relation to another's pain is enhanced when we are no longer able to make sense of it. Tupac Shakur illustrates this dynamic in the following bars in his song "Starin Through my Rearview": "In the cell, countin' days in this livin' black hell/Do you feel me?"[3] Here the ability to feel concern about the details of Shakur's testimony arises from the failure to "understand" what it's like to be locked in a cell, "countin- days in this livin' black hell," which provokes the moral anxiety required to "feel" a sense of horror at the un-told and un-known horrors that—for a white person—are out of sight and out of mind. Shakur's song can provoke a form of moral anxiety about racism that is not comparable to the anxiety and pain felt by Shakur, but which nevertheless can be felt as a response to his experience as a way to "bear witness" to the importance and authority of his testimony.

Clinical psychologists have referred to this tendency to feel emotions that are similar to and influenced by the emotions of others as the largely unconscious process of "emotional contagion," and have also identified music as a particularly powerful means with which to induce certain emotional states and behavioral attitudes that resonate with the mood of the artist and the emotional tenor of the song. As explained by Jacques Launay, Roger T. Dean, and Freya Bailes in their article "Intentional Sounds Induce Motor Empathy": "This evidence suggests that believing that human agents intentionally create sounds leads to them being empathically acted out in motor regions of the brain."[4] Additionally, in his article "Is it Empathy? Contagion, Perspective-Taking, and the Listener's Shoes," Deniz Peters argues for a distinct form of "musical empathy" characterized "as a mode of emotionally engaged, as opposed to distanced, listening" that—under the right conditions—can enhance the musical experience itself, such that "genuine musical empathy may occur, leading us first into, and then perhaps beyond, ourselves."[5] The term "emotional contagion" is used to describe this phenomenon whereby I feel or "catch" the emotion expressed by an artist in a song as an unconscious process of being affected-by the music, and our penchant for emotional contagion is related to our aesthetic enjoyment of music as that which "moves us" beyond ourselves and our immediate concerns. Thus part of the aesthetic enjoyment of hip-hop is the ability to feel emotions provoked by the anguish, anxiety and despair evoked by rappers that takes us "outside of ourselves" so that we are affected-by the pain and experience of others—this aesthetic appreciation of emotions evoked by music also tempers the pain of cognitive dis-orientation felt by the inability to immediately understand or master the lyrics and meaning of the song.

While there is a general consensus among clinical psychologists that the unconscious process of emotional contagion allows for and/or enhances the capacity for empathy, there is less consensus on how to define empathy itself, which is often explained as the capability "to share and understand another's emotion and feelings" or to "in some way experience what the other person is feeling." Departing from this conception of empathy, I will again follow the definition of empathy developed by Paul Thagard and Allison Barnes as "the attempt to comprehend either positive or negative [mental] states of another," as this conception identifies empathy as the *effort to* better comprehend the mental state of another rather than the ability to actually "understand" or "experience" the feelings of another who is subject to conditions that are altogether other than what I have experienced. For I am not convinced that it is possible to "understand" or "experience" the feelings of someone who I identify as radically "other" to myself, but I am convinced that the white *presumption* to be able to understand the nature of anti-black racism and the experience of black people plays an essential role in sustaining the willful ignorance about and moral indifference to black suffering that are defining characteristics of white sensibility.

Further, the more popular conception of empathy is not able to recognize the moral and epistemic value of making a better effort, in itself, to understand the position and pain of someone else. For the attempt to better understand someone else's position is made possible by the ability to grasp the limits of one's own sensibility to immediately "know" or accurately judge someone else's pain, and so requires some additional effort to learn more about the conditions this person faces; this effort is made possible, then, by the ability to recognize the authority of different perspectives and testimonies that I do not share and with which I cannot identify. Thus it is the effort to empathize across the color line rather than the actual ability to "feel" what others are feeling that allows white people to hear and respect the authority and epistemic value of black testimonies and texts.

When rappers ask "You feel me?," they are also making an appeal to those who listen to momentarily suspend their need to understand or judge them in order to feel something in relation to their pain and the suffering of their community. Thus it is not surprising that the phrase appears in a large number of Shakur's songs, given his insight (discussed in the Introduction) that the problem of anti-black racism is not essentially a problem of ignorance but rather a problem of sensibility such that white people "don't give a fuck about us," or appear radically in-sensitive to the atrocities inflicted on black communities and the entirely preventable traumas from which they suffer.

Shakur includes one last appeal to the empathy of those who listen to his testimony in the first verse of his last recorded single, "Made Niggaz": "My life in exchange for yours, born hated as a thug . . . Do you feel me? World, do you hear me?"[6] Here Shakur dis-arms the ability of a white person to "understand" the experience of being "born hated" before he asks "do you feel me?" And even more "World, do you hear me?," which conveys the feeling of being abandoned by a world in which you are consigned to suffer in virtue of having been born. Shakur's appeal is powerful precisely because it is delivered in a novel rhythm, so that we can *hear it* in a distinct register, with which we are unfamiliar, even (and especially) because we cannot immediately comprehend it in the post-racial or neoliberal register of meaning about American history and democracy.

Cognitive scientists have also identified six emotional and cognitive abilities that are necessary to develop the ability to empathize with the suffering of strangers, and the emotional traits—identification, emotional contagion, and true empathy—are viewed as preconditions for the cognitive traits—theory of the mind, perspective taking, and cognitive empathy. Further, they view the emotional traits as a sequence of developmental stages such that it is not possible to attain "true empathy" without first having experienced "identification" with others and then emotional contagion. Misuchi Sakurai describes the first stage of identification as an unconscious process "through which a person absorbs and incorporates facets of others, assimilating this information to produce their own identity."[7] This stage is essential to the formation of one's personality and influences our interactions with others "in subtle and powerful ways that lie beyond our conscious awareness." He describes the second stage of emotional contagion in which "another person's emotions are taken as one's own," as the ability to emotionally identify with the emotions expressed by someone else.

However, in accord with the analysis of white sensibility offered throughout this text, it is clear that these stages occur within the context of one's racialization. Clearly, our identification is formed in relation to and shaped-by our identity as "white" or "black" which plays an essential role in how we learn to interact with others and, indeed, with whom we can interact. From this perspective, we can better understand why the phrase "Fuck Tha Police" serves as an important warning to black people who learn to fear the police as a threat to their safety, dignity and survival at the same time that the phrase is heard as a threat by white people who learn to trust and depend on the police force for their safety. Indeed, in its decision to decline to review the recent judicial decision to send Jamal Knox to prison for writing a new version of the N.W.A song "Fuck Tha Police," the Supreme Court reinforced the white sensibility of the police force and their own *refusal* to consider why rappers coined that phrase and the role that it plays in black sensibility and culture.

In relation to moral psychology and our capacity for empathy, the refusal of the Supreme Court Justices to review the case also indicates that our racialization and identification as white people can actually preclude our ability to experience emotional contagion in relation to the feelings of people who are not-white. For those white judges who sentence black men to prison in order to criminalize the aesthetic expression of their fear and rage at their un-natural vulnerability to police brutality, arrest and murder ("Fuck Tha Police"), have never been affected-by or felt the anguish of black citizens who are "born hated as a thug," or routinely harassed, humiliated, arrested, and killed by police officers who criminalize the fact of being-black. If they had, they could grasp the lethal threat that the police force poses to black citizens rather than hear the pain of being-threatened as some sort of "threat" to individual police officers. This is not an accidental mis-perception but essential to the veneer of American democracy as a "post-racial" society where all citizens are protected under the laws.

This white sensibility of American society produces the moral blindness to routine patterns of anti-black violence also essential to white ignorance about our system of racism. The court's refusal reinforces the white *right* to this moral blindness that produces the dis-articulation of anti-black violence inflicted by the police force as occasional, tragic, and accidental rather than systemic and genocidal. And in this way the court's decision also reinforces one of the central lessons of hip-hop discussed in this text: the socio-political repetition of traumas inflicted on black communities is connected to our collective disavowal of their existence through clinging to the very narratives that are made possible by a revisionist history in which they never occurred.

The post-racial contours of white sensibility helps explain the context for the moral perversity of perceiving black rappers—the victims of police violence—as criminals who plot to harm the police—the perpetrators of routine violence against their communities. And of course the criminalization of hip-hop is not new, but has always indicated the political power of this genre and the threat it poses to the white establishment and the systemic infliction of anti-black genocide. This is succinctly expressed by the group Brand Nubian in their song "Claimin I'm a Criminal": "They want to send us to war and they want to ban rap/What they really want to do is get rid of blacks."[8]

The famous MCs who went to the Supreme Court on behalf of Knox were well aware of the fact that the Justices had not heard or been affected by underground hip-hop, which is why they had to insist in their legal brief to the court that hip-hop is "a work of poetry," "not intended to be taken literally, something that a reasonable listener with even a casual knowledge of rap would understand." Their defense of hip-hop as an important form of art also served to chastise the ignorance of the Justices whose refusal to listen to hip-hop allowed them to criminalize black artists. However, this statement also illustrates their faith that had the judges who sentenced Knox to prison actually listened to hip-hop and sought to learn from the poetic testimony of young black men, they could better see the injustice and moral perversity of sending men to prison for producing art. Their faith is grounded on their skills as DJs and MCs to produce music from the interruption, distortion, and co-option of beats and words that can disrupt the sense-making of white sensibility so that we can better feel the emotional tenor of the music and the horror of the traumas that provoke the need to testify.

HIP-HOP AND THE AESTHETIC DISRUPTION OF SENSE

As illustrated in chapter 1, the form of rap music (based on interruption, co-option, and distortion) and the subject of underground hip-hop culture (everyday forms of anti-black violence rendered invisible by the media and the dominant discourse) aim to disrupt our complacency and our comfort as citizens in a racial democracy that depends on the systemic, useless, gratuitous suffering of black citizens that our politicians would rather not confront or address. In the culture of underground hip-hop, the ethical injunction to "keep it real" serves to provide a standard by which artists and fans are judged as either "true" hip-hop or merely posing as hip-hop for the sake of material success in ways that are decidedly anti-hip-hop. The effort to keep it real regards the sensibility with which one listens to and orients oneself toward the music, for those who listen to hip-hop and actually *hear it* or allow themselves to be affected-by it, are able to adopt a critical stance toward discursive practices and perceptions that serve to evade, defer, or dis-articulate the extremity and regularity of state-sanctioned, anti-black violence in the United States. This explains why hip-hop has been essential to the Black Lives Matter movement, as well as to independent films and documentaries that aim to counter post-racial narratives about the American past and future.

As explained in chapter 1, the lyrics of underground rap songs are formed from a variant of Black American Speech referred to as Hip-Hop Nation Language that serves to oppose the discursive practices of the reigning *episteme*, and so cannot be immediately "understood" or mediated within the terms of the dominant discourse. Further, rappers produce novel rhyming schemes that defy our sonic expectations and deliver their lyrics in a distinct flow that bewilders the senses. In this way, the aesthetic enjoyment of hip-hop is inseparable from the dis-orientation of sensibility produced by the effort to hear a form of music that cannot be immediately understood or judged or anticipated. For this reason, hip-hop can disrupt the totalizing hold of white sensibility such that it can be *grasped* as a limited form of sensibility, and we can better detect its limits. In the space opened up between understanding and hearing hip-hop music, there is room to feel something that one could not anticipate or predict, a form of emotional contagion internal to the experience of musical empathy. And the emotions one feels when affected-by hip-hop will correspond to the rage and anguish expressed in the testimonies of black rappers that serve as an emotional register of the moral horror one ought to feel in relation to the genocidal violence inflicted on black communities.

The two predominant moods of underground hip-hop—righteous indignation and mourning—also represent aesthetic expressions of the two psychic responses or existential orientations to the routine traumas to which rappers are subject. The emotional contagion by these moods made possible through hearing hip-hop as a form of testimony can serve to pierce the moral insensitivity to black suffering that is reinforced by white sensibility, so that we can learn to adopt a more critical stance toward the limits of what we can know and understand as white people.

Throughout this text I have drawn on hip-hop as text and testimony to illustrate that white sensibility is largely characterized by patterns of discourse that serve to reinforce its limits and render them invisible. For this reason *aesthetic interventions* are necessary to disrupt our "sense" of reality and oppose the discursive frame of white sensibility with images and narratives that it cannot understand; the aesthetic dis-orientation of white sensibility can expose its limits in making-sense of being-black and provoke discomfort and concern about those limits. In chapter 1, I illustrated this point by referring to the white rapper Eminem and citing his testimony about his discomfort using the N-word in his lyrics, *as a hip-hop artist.* The form of hip-hop disrupts our sensibility through 1. the interruptive force of sampling and the scratch that create a form of music dependent on the interruption of linear, coherent, predictable melodies and 2. The rapping of words over novel rhyming schemes that distort, co-opt, reconfigure, and reinterpret discursive terms central to the *episteme.*

Those who identify with the political mission of hip-hop culture (also referred to as Hip-Hop Nation) often proudly declare "I am hip-hop," to signify its importance for how one feels, sees, and acts in the world. After taking my course on philosophy and hip-hop, so many of my white students who had not previously listened to underground hip-hop declare themselves "hip-hop heads" to indicate a shift in their sensibility and sense of responsibility. Hip-hop nation acts as a nation within our nation, as its members form a community with a distinct set of values reinforced by the music that produce specific commitments in thought and action opposed to the moral blindness and willful ignorance to black suffering perpetuated by white sensibility.

One of these commitments include prisoner advocacy, and my own journey as a hip-hop head led me to pursue opportunities to visit prisoners in state prisons throughout Pennsylvania, as well as volunteer to teach courses in philosophy at a women's state prison. On one occasion when I was waiting on line at a men's prison to go through the metal detector and into the visiting room, I started talking to two black men with dreadlocks who had complimented me on my own long dreadlocks. When they asked if I was visiting a friend, I told them no, and then they asked why I was there. So I explained that as an "official visitor" with the Pennsylvania Prison Society, I was able to visit any prisoner in a state prison who requested a visit, and I did not need to get prior approval. They looked at me in surprise and said: "Why would you do that?" I responded "hip-hop nation," and they immediately understood. We exchanged information and later that day shared some of our favorite new tracks over social media. I am not recalling this anecdote in order to boast about how "woke" I am or insist that white people need to visit prisoners, but instead to illustrate the shared sensibility of hip-hop heads that informs underground culture and builds our nation within and against the nation of Amerikkka sustained by post-racial sensibility and the refusal to feel or care about the traumatic suffering of black communities.

NOTES

1. Jones, "The Impairment of Empathy in Goodwill Whites for African-Americans."
2. Yancy, *Backlash*, 11.

3. 2Pac, "Starin Through my Rearview," Produced by: 2Pac and Johnny J, Written by: E. D. I. Mean, Yaki Kadafi and 2Pac, Release Date: October 7, 1997.

4. Jacques Launay, Roger T. Dean, and Freya Bailes, "Intentional Sounds Induce Motor Empathy." *Music and Empathy: Sempre Conference Proceeding*, November 2, 2013, edited by Caroline E. Waddington, Evangelos Himonides. London: International Music Education Research Centre (iMerc) Press (2013), 27.

5. Deniz Peters, "Is it Empathy? Contagion, Perspective-Taking, and the Listener's Shoes." *Music and Empathy: Sempre Conference Proceedings*, November 2, 2013, edited by Caroline E. Waddington, Evangelos Himonides. London: International Music Education Research Centre (iMerc) Press (2013), 34.

6. 2Pac, "Made Niggaz," Produced by: Johnny J and 2Pac, Written by: Yaki Kadafi, Kastro, Napoleon (Outlawz), E. D. I. Mean, Hussein Fatal and 2Pac, Release Date: October 7, 1997.

7. Misuchi Sakurai, "Emotional Contagion vs. Empathy" (April 16, 2009) accessed at: https://empathicperspectives.wordpress.com/2009/04/16/emotional-contagion-vs-empathy/.

8. Nubian, "Claimin I'm a Criminal."

Chapter 6
Fuck Tha Police

Since the completion of this text, the phrase Fuck Tha Police has gained more currency in popular discourse in the aftermath of George Floyd's murder on May 25, 2020, by a Minneapolis police officer who—in the course of arresting him—knelt on Floyd's neck to strangle him for 8 minutes while his colleagues helped restrain him and prevent bystanders from intervening. Floyd's murder became the impetus for the largest civil rights movement in American history because it occurred during a global pandemic that exposed the genocidal economy of our racial caste system in the stark and clear terms of *who* was dying from the lack of essential medical care. The ongoing nationwide protests have popularized the hip-hop call to defund and abolish the police force that has always functioned as a state agency to terrorize and kill black people for the sake of our American white supremacy. However, while it appears that more white Americans now understand the political sense of Fuck Tha Police, and thousands are even willing to risk being assaulted by police with tear gas and rubber bullets to protest their right to say it, Jamal Knox remains in prison serving time for producing a song titled Fuck The Police as MC Mayhem Mal.

The history and criminalization of the phrase "Fuck Tha Police" indicate that it hits a particularly sensitive nerve in the psyche of white sensibility and poses a distinct kind of threat to the *episteme* and the white establishment. This is reinforced by the juridical judgment of this phrase as a "a true threat" that must be silenced rather than protected as free speech; the phrase clearly provokes a crisis for white sensibility that must banish it from sight, sound, and thought. In this sense the phrase acts as a form of discursive resistance or critical theory—a field in the Western philosophical tradition initiated by the Frankfurt school that rose to prominence in the aftermath of the Nazi Genocide. The Frankfurt school sought to correct for the historical failure of the Western tradition to respond to and oppose the present by adapting different tools of analysis for critical reflection on our contingent *system* of political oppression for the sake of emancipation from useless suffering.

The creation and focus on critical theory shifted the moral burden in philosophy from theory to political praxis; no longer could philosophers ignore social violence and declare—with Hegel—that the owl of Minerva spread her wings only at dusk, always already too late to critique or change the shape of human affairs. The legendary rapper Chuck D, a member of the seminal underground hip-hop group Public Enemy, famously said that "rap is black America's CNN." For the form and content of underground hip-hop were provoked by the need to bear witness to and describe the varieties of harms suffered in virtue of being-black in America that are absent from our nationalist narratives, popular discourse, and media. It is therefore surprising that it is still rare for philosophers who work in the field of critical theory to draw on hip-hop as a source of insight and evidence about the economy of racist oppression and strategies of resistance against new tactics and forms of genocidal violence.

Given the limits of white sensibility and the dominant discourse, the pursuit of critical theory in the academy cannot seal itself off from aesthetic interventions and aesthetic productions in black culture that act as counter-narratives and affect the sensibility rather than simply appeal to the intellect. In their counter-narratives, rappers present a different sensibility of the present from the perspective of black citizens who suffer and die from the everyday conditions of being-black in America; a sensibility that contests and contradicts the post-racial sensibility that cannot "see" or "admit" the existence of systemic, institutional racism. For this reason, the language that emerges from hip-hop sensibility can feel threatening to someone who is invested in a post-racial reading of the American present even and especially when it evokes or depicts something that this person must continually defer, deny, and dis-articulate in order to sustain the post-racial interpretation of American society. This interpretation, in turn, allows someone who is white to defer the need to think about being-white, as she reasons that we "no longer" live in a society where slavery is legal and black citizens are excluded from the protection of the law. "Therefore," the reasoning goes, to be white is not to be in an essentially different position than someone who is black, and every occurrence of police brutality against black citizens is an accidental, occasional exception to the norm of a Just Justice system.

As Jamal Knox's case and its dis-appearance in the crisis of the present indicates, the phrase "Fuck Tha Police" provokes a crisis of a different order, one that appears to threaten the very terms in which white Americans can make-sense of their own experience. For central to the myth of a post-racial society is the claim that since all citizens are now protected by and enjoy equal rights under the law, we have "overcome" the racist enforcement of the law that once sustained the historical institution of slavery, the policy of segregation and the practice of lynching. However this view presupposes two beliefs that only make-sense to a white sensibility of American society: 1. White citizens no longer enjoy economic and socio-political privileges through the exploitation and subordination of black citizens and 2. The police protect black citizens. The emotional tenor of the phrase Fuck Tha Police that evokes both anguish and righteous indignation serves to oppose these lies central to what Charles Mills refers to as the "epistemology of ignorance" (discussed in the Introduction) that provides the framework for white sensibility and is enacted as a shared practice of dialogue and deferral among white citizens. The collective anguish evoked by the phrase Fuck Tha Police testifies to the continuity of systemic state violence against black communities, and the sense of righteous indignation evoked by the repetition of the phrase in hip-hop music and culture testifies to the genocidal role of the police force that enforces white supremacy and safeguards white privilege. We can gauge the power of the term by the fact that white people feel so threatened by it that the state has criminalized it *as a form of poetic testimony*. The threat emerges from the fact that the phrase "Fuck Tha Police" belies the two beliefs so central to white ignorance and moral indifference about anti-black violence that it threatens to pierce the veneer of American democracy that justifies our apathy about traumatic and entirely preventable harms inflicted on black communities as such.

Originally coined by Ice Cube in his song "Fuck Tha Police" for his group N.W.A, the phrase inspired an entire genre of hip-hop songs about specific occasions of police brutality and murder covered in the national media. These songs provide counter-testimony about their significance from an aesthetic sensibility that runs counter to the media's post-racial and neoliberal lens through which this violence is seen and understood as a series of accidental, tragic accidents. They serve to memorialize the victims of police violence who are so often mis-represented by the media, courts, and public opinion as criminals who somehow "deserved to die" and need not be mourned. And these songs often combine a mood of mourning for the victim with a renewed call-to-arms to fight the power that kills black people with impunity.

The first song of this kind that deeply affected me and arrested my sensibility of the American present was "A Tree Never Grown," which appeared on the EP *Hip Hop for Respect* released by Rawkus records in 2000 as a collaborative project organized by Mos Def and Talib Kweli. The aim of the four-track EP was to speak out against police brutality in general, and the case of Amadou Diallo in particular—a 23-year-old immigrant from Guinea—who was shot at 41 times and killed while he stood in the vestibule of his own apartment building by four New York City police officers on February 4,

1999. The officers claimed to have mistaken him for a rape suspect from one year earlier, and all four officers were acquitted of second-degree murder at their trial in Albany, New York. In the first verse Fre raps the bars: "Thinkin about brother Diallo/I find it hard to swallow/Cause 41 is a hard act to follow/ Who is it, it can happen tomorrow/Goes down all the time in some African community."[1] As traumatic testimony, the song memorializes the individual fate of Diallo by tracing it to the unnatural and oppressive conditions to which black citizens are collectively subject.

In hip-hop culture there is a long tradition of mourning for the loss of black lives to racist oppression in the United States, through the use of graffiti and rap music informed by a mood of resigned weariness rather than anger about racist oppression. Tupac Shakur's classic song "How Long Will They Mourn Me?" voices both the inevitability of his senseless death in a system designed to destroy him, as well as his need to be mourned and thus remembered after his death: "Damn! They should've shot me when I was born/now I'm trapped in the motherfucking storm. How long will they mourn me?"[2] Other, more recent rap songs such as "Just a Moment" by Nas and "Soundtrack 2 My Life" by Kid Cudi also aim to enact an elegiac practice on behalf of African Americans murdered in the past and for those vulnerable to an unnatural and premature death to police brutality in the present.

This tradition of mourning acts as a form of political resistance against the failure of our society to mourn the loss of black lives to state violence *as a loss* to our community or to register the loss of black lives subject to routine carceral tortures in our jails and prisons that for many white Americans are out-of-sight and out-of-mind. All of these songs indicate the need to perpetually acknowledge and mourn for our prisoners who are overdetermined as "criminals" and subject to unnatural forms of violence made possible by their institutional exclusion from the protection of the law and moral concern. Rappers mourn for their brothers in prison who are regarded as unworthy of being-mourned, and it reflects the fact that there has always been a social and aesthetic interrelation between hip-hop culture and penal culture that informs the moral and political commitments of Hip-Hop Nation.

For example, the two moods of anguish and righteous indignation that characterize the emotional tenor of the phrase Fuck Tha Police correspond to two general orientations toward carceral violence that prisoners refer to with the slang terms of the "inmate" and the "criminal" (prevalent in prisons throughout the United States). As prison slang, these terms refer to two psychic responses or existential orientations to prison life, The "convict" is characterized by his anger toward the prison system and opposes it through breaking the rules designed to break him. The "inmate" is characterized by his mood of weary resignation toward the system and tends to follow the rules to avoid the possibility of other harms such as hard restraints or solitary confinement to better cope-with the conditions of confinement. These subject-positions are neither entirely separable nor enduring, but instead characterize the shifting moods of prisoners over the course of days, weeks, and years as they navigate the traumatic conditions of confinement. We can also recognize these existential orientations in rap music about prison and prison life (Compare *Claimin I'm a Criminal* by Brand Nubian to *Family Business* by Kanye West), as well as in the dominant moods of righteous indignation and anguish that inform the emotional tenor of underground hip-hop music.

This indicates the distinctly *philosophical* value of underground hip-hop as critical theory and anti-racist practice, as it based on the subversive production of "subjugated knowledges" that contest the *episteme* with the testimony of the marginalized—those abandoned to routine carceral violence—in order to expose the contingent, *genocidal state of affairs* masked by our discourse and media. In other words, the interrelationship between underground hip-hop and penal culture illustrates that hip-hop is an effective form of subjugated knowledge precisely because it provides a voice to the voiceless, or testifies to the testimony of black citizens subjugated and silenced by genocidal violence inflicted by the officials and authorities charged with their protection. As a potent form of subjugated knowledge that contests the racist organization of the *episteme* with the testimony of the oppressed, hip-hop can incite local ruptures in the organization of power relations that sustains the systemic infliction of anti-black violence. Indeed, the commitment to the aesthetic practice of mourning in underground hip-hop songs has influenced the tactics of new civil rights groups such as the Black Lives Matter movement as well as new directions of inquiry in critical race theory and aesthetics.

In her essay "The Condition of Black Life Is One of Mourning," Claudia Rankine connects a sense of mourning to the politics of anti-racism: "The Black Lives Matter movement can be read as an attempt to keep mourning an open dynamic in our culture because black lives exist in a state of precariousness. Mourning then bears both the vulnerability inherent in black lives and the instability regarding a future for those lives."[3] Rankine describes mourning both as the expression of an unnatural vulnerability to state sanctioned violence and as an "open dynamic" able to bear witness to the loss that is suffered and the wounds that can never be healed. It acts as the emotional register of that fact that "something is wrong everywhere and all the time, even if locally things appear normal." The politics of mourning becomes acute when entire communities must *pre-emptively mourn* for the inevitable loss of more family and friends to violence, targeted on the basis of their association with communities marked by race, gender, ethnicity, class, ability, and sex. Here *a sense of* mourning is necessary to register and recognize the fact of social death and the severity of its harm, a sense of mourning that cannot be overcome by mourning the loss of individuals subject to state violence and social death.

In his book, *The Post-Racial Limits of Memorialization: Toward a Political Sense of Mourning*, Alfred Frankowski claims that a sense of mourning can exert political resistance against post-racial representations of violence that treat racial oppression as a problem of the past. As he explains:

> The violence of *post-racial discourse* and *post-racial memory* employs memory and representation to such a great extent that our responses lose all meaning—and yet this makes a political sense of mourning all the more important and dangerous because it is that ability to reconnect with our living experience of a past and of deaths that I have become aware of at a distance . . . When we *mourn* a friend's death, that death lives on with us and it is our task to keep the sense of that life alive. The task of mourning is the process of *living with* the death within our context . . . mourning requires a recasting of what it means to respond to violence now, but also a shattering of both this question and our answers. To *respond to* is first and foremost to be a *taking in*. Taking, in a particular sense, allows for that which is shattered to be navigated-through as opposed to being settled, reconciled, or simply represented.[4]

Post-racial discourse reinforces a liberatory narrative of the civil rights struggle in the United States that allows us to represent every police murder of an unarmed black man or woman as an "exception" to the norm of a legal system that is *no longer* informed by the racist distribution of power and capital. In this way, as Frankowski explains, post-racial discourse transforms acts of remembrance into acts of forgetting at the same time. We saw this dynamic during the vice presidential debate in 2016, when Mike Pence chided Tim Kaine for Hilary Clinton's use of the terms "implicit bias" and "institutional racism" that—he asserted—distort and politicize a "tragedy," as well as demean our police officers. The frequency with which white people defer any criticism of the police force that terrorizes black communities through the defensive need to "protect the honour of our police officers" indicates the sort of cognitive pattern that sustains post-racial sensibility and the myth of American equality. Against the refusal of our politicians to recognize the predictable and systematic state violence inflicted on African Americans as a matter of policy and judicial procedure, the collective act of mourning for black lives registers the traumatic violation of useless violence and our unreconciled relation to the past and present.

In Frankowski's words, this mourning forces "a recasting of what it means to respond to violence now" (viz. it was just an isolated "tragedy"), but also "a shattering of both this question and our answers" (viz. Q: "Why do police continue to shoot unarmed black citizens?" A: "We need new legal reforms."). In this way, the political sense of mourning interrupts the neoliberal and post-racial narratives that normalize state violence and exposes the failure of discursive practices to represent or arrest the systemic state violence against black communities. The political sense of mourning interrupts our tragic narratives about the "exceptional" and "accidental" nature of police brutality, in order to expose that which cannot be represented in our post-racial discourse, or the state's systematic destruction of black lives for the sake of white supremacy. Tragic narratives represent difficult truths about the human condition, whereas trauma violates every expectation we have and can represent about what should or could happen to human beings. In this sense victims of trauma suffer from "useless" violence insofar as it is entirely preventable and the product of one or more systems of domination that empower certain individuals to inflict violence on others with impunity.

Frankowski explains that "Like the Sublime, mourning makes the context in which we live appear now as a problem."[5] When we cultivate a political sense of preemptive mourning, we aim to carve out meaning for a life that has already been denied meaning, and to expose this as a *problem* that is disavowed in our narratives about the moral and legal progress of our nation. Because of its disruptive or interruptive potential, preemptive mourning can be read as a powerful way to unhinge the time of the present and to resist or interrupt the relentless forward movement of everyday life in which the past is a present that is no longer and the future is a present that is not yet. By testifying to the past lives of those lost to anti-black state violence, this mourning is a mode of being temporal that opens up the future that approaches as a time of inevitable loss—and both of these aspects reveal the true present state of vulnerability and instability in which those who mourn find themselves.

The distinct temporality of the political (preemptive) sense of mourning in which the unmastered past invades and overdetermines both the present and the future, illustrates what Frankowski refers to as the "generational trauma" inflicted by social death that provokes the need for and the sense of mourning. As he explains: "this question [of preemptive mourning] speaks to the generational trauma that not only exceeds the acts of violence performed by police, but also the way that the present is saturated in the historical. Each police shooting, whether or not it happens in your neck of the woods is the anti-black violence that contextualizes you, your kids, and your future relatives. The violence that contextualizes us also binds us—and in this way, anti-black violence is also the possibility of violence against transgendered people—it is not their violence but the possibility of this violence that frames their existence as precarious, as being already structured by vulnerability and violation."[6] Frankowski's comments echo the meaning of the phrase "Fuck Tha Police" in underground hip-hop that draws attention to the unrelenting violence inflicted by this state institution that is always felt and always already structures the unnatural perils of being-black that compromise the terms of agency and the social vitality of one's community.

The political sense of mourning cannot overcome loss to restore hope in the future, but rather serves to problematize the present and so expose the complicity of all efforts to "overcome" the past *in the very perpetuation* of the present iterations and modalities of state violence against racialized groups. Thus the political sense of mourning disrupts any form of hope based on post-racial representations of state violence. At the same time, the political, public sense of mourning resists nihilistic resignation about the perpetual amount of state violence that produces endless amounts of useless suffering. As Frankowski explains: "A political sense of mourning does more than make room for a reflective stance in which we rethink our lives. It requires that our passivity be turned into an activity, and our philosophical questioning leads to a reformulation of our political agency."[7] In the transition from private grief to a communal sense of mourning, sorrow becomes the mode for the political rejection of narratives that continue to obfuscate and disavow the violence produced by our structurally racist and heterosexist distribution of power relations.

The rap songs cited above are part of a tradition in underground rap music that also performs the *preemptive mourning* that exposes the moral horror of a structurally racist society where senseless state violence is disavowed as a natural and inevitable part of "national security." In a more general way, hip-hop culture has always served to provide counter-narratives to the post-racial discourse that serves to minimize the extremity of racist oppression in the neoliberal nation-state. The entrenched nature of post-racial discourse that obfuscates the continuity of systemic racist and heterosexist violence indicates the need for a political shift incited by aesthetic means. As Frankowski explains in a recent response to a review of his book, "aesthetics gives us a different sense of the violence of the political because its focus is on the way the sensible becomes strange in reference to the political . . . memorializations are politically powerful to the extent that they make the present strange."[8] Under the current American regime where the hate speech of anti-black racism, heterosexism and Islamophobia is the now the norm of political discourse and presidential tweets, and in a milieu in which we have already normalized the creation of detention camps for children who were violently separated from their parents at the border, cultural expressions of mourning that serve to disrupt white indifference to structural oppression will become all the more important. A sense of mourning-without-end is political for any marginalized population that suffers from social death and from the disavowal of their suffering through the dis-articulation and normalization of violence against them.

Throughout this text I have drawn from underground hip-hop as text and testimony to illustrate how it acts to counter the framework of white sensibility through the cooption and re-signification of words, beats, melodies, and phrases from popular music and the dominant discourse to expose their limits and—as testimony—provide an emotional register of what these limits exclude and perpetuate, namely, the routine and entirely preventable infliction of traumatic violence against black communities, as such, through the practices internal to our social and political and economic institutions. The distinct form of testimony made possible in hip-hop allows rappers to get a witness to their traumas for themselves and their community, despite the white refusal to listen or make an effort to hear them, a refusal now sanctified by the judicial prosecution of this testimony as a criminal act. That is, our Supreme Court Justices are so unwilling to listen to hip-hop in order to *hear* the phrase "Fuck Tha Police" that they are willing, instead, to affirm the right of the courts to send hip-hop artists to prison for rapping the phrase in a song. Their moral callousness also betrays the threat that Hip-Hop Nation Language poses to the stability and force of the *episteme* on the American psyche and white sensibility.

I wrote this book as a preliminary study to provoke renewed academic and popular interest in underground hip-hop as text and testimony about race, anti-black racism, trauma, genocide, white sensibility, musical empathy, and American society. After the 2016 presidential election, I felt compelled to write this book as a response to the crisis of the present; one in which the criminalization of hip-hop has taken on a greater urgency in political, social, and educational institutions that now serve to legitimate and enforce the racist phantasies of a narcissistic and sociopathic rich white man who is above the law and beyond accountability. At the university where I attained tenure, roughly 70 percent of our students voted for the man who won, the first presidential candidate to ever receive an endorsement from the Klu Klux Klan. In the immediate aftermath of the election, there were so many swastikas painted on walls and carved into bathroom stalls that the university president announced that he would no longer announce the presence of swastikas around campus in order to avoid bad publicity. A few weeks later, as I was working on the proposal for this book, the administration sent out another notice to students and faculty that condemned a recent poster created and distributed by a student, that pictured a group of Disney princesses saying "Fuck Tha Police" in unison. The notice stated that the school would not tolerate this hate speech that denigrated our police officers, and demanded that the students responsible for these posters come forward so that they could be escorted off campus (the notice added that the administration would happily refund their tuition costs from the current semester), for, as the notice explained, someone who would create such a poster does not deserve to graduate with a college degree from our university.

At this largely white, liberal arts college with a Christian affiliation where the majority of the student body supported our white supremacist, misogynist president, the message of the two notices sent so soon after the election was clear: swastikas were to be tolerated but disavowed, and the phrase "Fuck the Police" was to be condemned as a criminal offence that warrants the maximum penalty of immediate expulsion from the university. My response to this notice that effectively criminalized the phrase "Fuck Tha Police" on campus was neither professional nor prudent. I did not schedule a series of meetings with members of the administration to express my objection to the notice, nor did I attempt to file a complaint about the new policy through the bureaucratic process for doing so. Instead, for the remainder of the semester, I frequently initiated a conversation about the new policy with my students in all of my classes so that we could pursue and develop the critical examination of its intent, logic, and socio-political and psychological significance.

I can't defend my actions that exasperated tensions that already existed at the school and imperilled my career. However, I understand why I felt compelled to oppose the new policy by bypassing the purely perfunctory action of expressing my objection to the criminalization of hip-hop to administrators who serve the neoliberal interests of a private university. For it was more important to me to create a space for my students to question the moral and epistemic value of the new policy without fear of recrimination or censorship. I don't know if my actions helped the situation, but I felt compelled by my love of hip-hop and my commitment to Hip-Hop Nation to privilege the need to say "Fuck Tha Police" over the need to act in a "professional" or prudent manner. However this decision placed me in a vulnerable position, at odds with the administration, under constant suspicion of insubordination. Eventually I found that the criminalization of hip-hop on campus created a hostile environment that undermined academic freedom, so I left.

My guiding model for the need to take such risks to keep it real—even at the cost of one's career—is the example set by the iconic group Wu-Tang Clan, during their infamous 1997 performance at Hot 97's Summer Jam at the Meadowlands Arena in New Jersey. At the time they were invited to perform they were on a national tour with Rage against the Machine, and they were told that if they refused to leave their tour to perform for the Hot 97 concert *without compensation*, the station—at the time the dominant source of hip-hop on the airwaves—would no longer play their music. Not only did they have to pay for their own airfare to New Jersey, but when they arrived they were shocked to find huge crowds; once the extent of their exploitation became apparent, they could no longer sanction it. During their set, Ghostface Killah led the crowd in chanting "Fuck Hot 97!" over and over again. As a result, they were blacklisted from Hot 97 and all the other major radio stations for the next 10 years. Although this prevented them from attaining commercial success at the height of their career, it also solidified their status as underground MCs who privilege principles over profit. And when we strive to do this in institutional settings, we will eventually be pushed past our limit—at which point I have to say "Fuck Hot 97" rather than sanction whatever form of exploitation I've been asked to ignore.

I hope this book has conveyed even a little bit of the wisdom and values that I have received from Hip-Hop Nation, which allow me to understand the political importance of saying Fuck Tha Police and the moral importance of defending our right to say it or rap it as a form of poetic testimony and political praxis.

NOTES

1. Hip-Hop for Respect, "Tree Never Grown," Produced by: 88-Keys, Written by: Wordsworth, Tame One, Rubix, Yasiin Bey, Jane Doe, Kofi Taha, J-Live, Invincible, Grafh, Fre and A. L. Release Date: January 1, 2000.
2. Thug Life, "How Long Will They Mourn Me?"
3. Rankine, "The Condition of Black Life Is One of Mourning."
4. Frankowski, *The Post-Racial Limits of Memorialization*, 96.
5. Ibid., 98.
6. Private email correspondence on May 15, 2017.
7. Frankowski, *The Post-Racial Limits of Memorialization*, 98.
8. Alfred Frankowski, "Beyond the Dissensus Schema," reply to the review essay "Resistance and the Reconfiguration of the Sensible," by Adam Burgos. In *Syndicate Philosophy*, symposium on *The Post-Racial Limits of Memorialization: Toward a Political Sense of Mourning* by Alfred Frankowski. First published in the online symposium https://syndicate.network/philosophy/, May 15, 2017.

Conclusion
The Aesthetic Politics of Underground Hip-Hop

I have often wondered how anyone understands anything about America without hip-hop. When I was a teenager in the 1980s in DC, confused about the physical proximity of the Congress and crack houses, and how our politicians could ignore the suffering just a few blocks away from where they governed "for the people," my (white) parents and teachers and rabbis did not provide answers but instead just agreed that it was terrible. However, underground MCs "broke it down" in a way that I could grasp the disparity between the appearance and the reality of America and the disparity between my world and the precarious world to which these black artists were subject. I still think there's a huge difference in sensibility between white people who have sought out, enjoyed, and heard underground hip-hop and those white people who have refused to listen.

Part of the difference is that white people who love and hear hip-hop can better grasp that they are white, understand that they see and feel the world in a distinctly "white" way that allows them to be relatively unaffected by and unaware of the system of anti-black genocide that supports their own social and economic privilege. However their awareness of their limits is also part of their love of hip-hop, for they appreciate the aesthetic experience of being-affected by testimony and music that emerges from a different sensibility—here the experience of difference and the dis-orientation of sense is experienced through awe. On the other hand, when I talk about race and anti-black racism with white people who do not listen to hip-hop, they tend to be easily offended by the very term "white person," and my use of this term often leads them to defensively insist: "I'm not racist!" These conversations are rarely helpful, and the refusal of white people to talk about being-white supports their refusal to talk about or acknowledge the system of anti-black violence that allows us to be and benefit from being-white.

As I have illustrated throughout this book, their refusal to acknowledge this system is also essential to reinforce the post-racial and neoliberal sensibility of the American present.

While I am devoted to scholarship and dialogue, these conversations always leave me feeling like discourse can just make shit worse or reinforce white complacency and denial about being white. As I illustrated in chapter 1, this problem can be explained with reference to how the terms of the dominant discourse reinforce the status quo, and both emerge from and reinforce the neoliberal and post-racial sensibility of the United States; this perspective regards racism as a problem of the past, overcome in the present, and regards every instance of state-sanctioned, anti-black violence as an exception to the norm that indicates the need for specific legal reforms to our criminal justice system. As features of our sensibility, the "post-racial" and "neoliberal" stances inform patterns of how we interpret the facts of American life and how we "read" what we "see"; thus it is hard—if not impossible—to present facts that can challenge or disrupt the certainty of this framework for "making sense" of senseless violence. And the neoliberal and post-racial interpretations of American life preclude the ability to feel sorrow or anger at the continuity of this violence, and—for so many white citizens—preclude the ability to empathize with black victims of state terror or take their persecution seriously as genocidal violence inflicted against black communities *as such*.

My concern that dialogue is not effective for helping white people acknowledge their whiteness *and* a system of anti-black racism has only deepened in the current political climate, in which hate speech is now *spoken as political discourse* and spewed in presidential tweets in order to sanctify misogyny and white supremacy as the priorities of our highest authority.

We can no longer accuse our politicians of hypocrisy when they no longer feel the need to justify their policies with reference to facts or American ideals. And this has promoted a model of discourse that has made the animosity and division between Americans so much worse, as the refusal to limit one's claims about our society with reference to facts or moral ideals is also a refusal to engage in a real dialogue with a standard of truth, where one accepts the possibility of learning something from the person one speaks with.

In this climate, people are so preoccupied with repeating certain discursive practices that drown out all opposition that discourse only reinforces the invisibility of our *sensibility* that is invested in and reinforced by these practices. For this reason we require an *aesthetic* stimulus for the interruption of sense-making that momentarily disrupts the totalizing hold of this discourse on sensibility so that we can *feel* something about the present precisely because we can't "make sense" of it. The ability for white people to acknowledge they are white or acknowledge that they see and feel the world in the way they do only because they are not-black, is not simply a matter of learning more about the history of race and racism but a matter of *feeling* the limits of one's sensibility to "understand" the experience of being-black. For this reason, the question of how our sensibility is affected is not simply a question of aesthetics but a critically important question of politics key to the possibility of resisting the current regime and the forty million Americans who support the sociopath in office. Obviously, white people cannot be allies in the effort to dismantle the racist structures and institutions that support our racial caste system until they acknowledge or feel the moral horror of its existence. Part of the aesthetic brilliance and political power of underground hip-hop is that it is able to expose specific discursive practices that continue to dis-articulate the harms of anti-black racism and the genocidal conditions of American society that are minimized and obfuscated by this discourse.

My personal and professional experiences with underground hip-hop have led me to make certain connections between white sensibility, empathy, and hip-hop as a source of philosophical wisdom that I have detailed in this text. When I refer to hip-hop as a source of wisdom, I mean to refer to the dual role that it plays as a source of ideas that can be read as counter-text to dominant views about race, anti-black racism, trauma and American politics, and a form of music and poetic testimony that is a source of aesthetic experience that can affect our sensibility in distinct ways.

HIP-HOP AS TEXT

In chapters 1 and 2, I illustrated that underground hip-hop exposes the dis-articulation of systemic anti-black violence as occasional, individual, and accidental through the sonic and lyrical depiction of the traumatic cracks in our tragic narratives about beingvablack in the United States. I also illustrated that underground hip-hop provides counter-text to the view that the problem with racism or racist bias is a problem of ignorance that can be "overcome" with greater knowledge and more finely tuned perceptual awareness in our encounters with black people. Instead, hip-hop testifies that racism is a problem of moral and emotional indifference to the freedom and wellbeing of black people, and it is a problem connected with the refusal of white people to acknowledge the limits of their knowledge and understanding.

In chapter 3, I illustrated that in their poetic testimony about carceral violence, underground rappers illustrate at least five specific reasons why the term "genocide" is the only way to make sense of the American past and present, as (1) black men are targeted for arrest and incarceration *as such*; (2) they are subject to gratuitous violence through the *everyday* conditions of confinement that erode their mental and physical health; (3) the mass incarceration of black men attacks entire black communities or undermines their social vitality and the strength of the familial and fraternal bonds between its members; (4) the penal system is essential to the *systemic* persecution of black citizens, who live in a state of un-natural vulnerability to state violence; and (5) the United States criminal justice system is organized around the same genocidal logic that informed the legal institution of slavery that first established our white supremacist state; our racial caste system sustains itself through the transmutation of its institutions that serve to target and inflict routine violence on black people *as such* to prevent their economic, social, and political mobility.

I also drew attention to the fact that when underground rappers co-opt the terms "genocide" and "holocaust" in their lyrics in order to re-signify them as terms that *explain* the system of anti-black racism in the American past and present, they also expose the gap between our *sensibility* of genocide and the historical reality of genocidal violence. This is especially evident when they co-opt the term "holocaust" and re-signify it beyond its dominant designation for the Nazi destruction of European Jewry, in order to expose (at least) four historical features of western genocides that are ignored or neglected in the field of Holocaust and genocide studies: (1) the larger structure of racist discrimination in western politics that rationalized both the destruction of African slaves and European Jews; (2) the continuation of genocidal logics from the past in the system of anti-black violence in the American present; (3) the *system* of genocidal violence as a process of degradation, torture, and exclusion (from the protection of the law and moral consideration) that precludes a decent life and death; (4) the role of our discursive practices about the Holocaust in the obfuscation and repetition of genocidal forms of anti-black violence in the American city and the cell. These insights are especially evident in the song "Never Again," written and performed by Remedy, the only Jewish member of the iconic group Wu-Tang Clan for their 1998 album *Killer Beez*, as well as throughout the entire album titled *Da Holocaust*, also released in 1998 by the group Concentration Camp.

From my perspective as a genocide scholar, it is striking that underground rappers have used the term "genocide" so consistently over the past thirty years in their poetic verse to indicate the foundational importance of anti-black violence to our racial democracy *at the same time* that white genocide scholars have just as consistently refused to consider anti-black violence in the United States as a system of genocide. Indeed, their refusal to think or imagine American anti-black genocide has informed entire lines of inquiry that are based on the taken-for-granted distinction between systemic anti-black violence and genocidal violence. I do not believe that white genocide scholars have consciously excluded consideration of American anti-black violence from their domain of concern and scholarly interest, but rather that their refusal is produced by the default distinction between "slavery" and "genocide" essential to the academic and popular *sensibility* of genocide that serves to preclude thinking one in terms of the other. This distinction perpetually defers any thought or awareness of the distinctly genocidal violence inflicted through slave labor on the plantation and in the American penal system. The academic and popular sensibility of genocide is shaped by its limits or its impossible application to historical systems of anti-black violence in the United States and in this way supports the neoliberal and post-racial sensibility about the American present.

HIP-HOP AS TESTIMONY

The disparity between the sensibility of Hip-Hop Nation and the sensibility of academic culture was also made clear to me when I discussed this project with various hip-hop artists who all expressed confusion that I had to defend certain views—such as the idea that the prison system inflicts genocide—that they viewed as so obvious as to not need to be defended at all. Of course, this is obvious to them because their sensibility is shaped by hip-hop culture that in all of its forms—graffiti, breakdancing, scratching, sampling, and rapping—contests the post-racial and neoliberal sensibility that are framed by limits that prevent the ability to see, hear, imagine, or think about the systemic and routine infliction of violence against black people *as such* in the United States. In the second part of this text, I tried to account for this disparity with an analysis of how underground hip-hop can affect the sensibility in a way that disrupts or problematizes the neoliberal and post-racial interpretations of American society that perpetually defer the moral horror of the present and preclude the possibility for empathy for black citizens who are not "seen" as victims but instead as a "criminal" threat to the social order. I argued that as an aesthetic intervention based on the interruption of linear melodies to create a cyclic loop that arrests our senses, the form of hip-hop evokes the structure of post-traumatic stress disorder as a psycho-social and historical pathology, and this correlation helps explains the existential impact of hip-hop on our sensibility of the present.

In chapter 4, I argued that the therapeutic value of underground hip-hop as a form of EMDR that can help people to reinterpret and process traumatic suffering also helps explains its political value as a form of resistance against the exclusion and obfuscation of this suffering in the dominant discourse. Further, I illustrated how the depiction of traumatic violence in underground hip-hop departs from and contests the depiction of trauma in professional academic and clinical discourse. Specifically, I illustrated that: (1) departing from the professional discourse about PTSD that views it as an *individual* pathology, underground hip-hop depicts trauma as a social pathology and depicts PTSD as the symptoms of a pathological arrangement of sociopolitical conditions that negatively affect entire communities—whether or not every person subject to them suffers from this disorder; (2) departing from the current trend in trauma theory to naturalize PTSD by looking for a cure in animal behavior, underground hip-hop illustrates that we suffer from PTSD due to un-natural, contingent conditions to which no one should be subject; (3) thus we should not reconcile ourselves to PTSD as an "inevitable" part of human life, akin to tragic suffering, but rather as indicating the moral necessity to radically transform the terms of social and political life that consign racialized and gendered minorities to a position of un-natural vulnerability to PTSD; and (4) hip-hop artists illustrate that the way in which we talk about trauma only reinforces our moral indifference to and epistemological ignorance about the systemic and lethal harms inflicted on racialized and gendered groups *as such*. Hip-hop can act as a sonic expression of trauma, as an emotional register of the social violence that we ignore and obfuscate and exclude in our dominant discourses.

In chapter 5, I defended the view that hip-hop can act as a sonic register of the traumas that violate and exceed the discursive terms with which we could re-present them. For this reason it can affect the sensibility of goodwill whites who cannot "see" a system of racism so that we might better *feel* the moral horror of a system we cannot understand. In this way, hip-hop can act as an aesthetic stimulus to enhance the ability of goodwill whites to feel empathy for black citizens as victims of the racial caste system from which they themselves benefit. Specifically, I argued that (1) the aesthetic enjoyment of rap music induces those emotions that normally escape the limits of white sensibility as they do not "make sense" in the post-racial or neoliberal interpretations of American society; (2) when white people are open to hearing hip-hop as a form of testimony, then they can experience the disruption of their moral and epistemic certainty in the process of aesthetic appreciation which is neither defensive nor reactive; and (3) this can allow white people to feel empathy or to want to empathize with black people not despite but rather because they are white, made possible by their ability to grasp—through aesthetic awe—the existence of limits to what they can understand about the un-natural vulnerability of black citizens to state violence.

In chapter 6, I argued for the philosophical value of the traumatic testimony in underground hip-hop as a form of "subjugated knowledge" essential to our critical analysis of race and anti-black racism in the United States. As a form of testimony that evokes the moods of righteous indignation and a sense of mourning, hip-hop can affect and disrupt our sensibility of the present so that we can grasp how our discourse does not reveal but instead conceals the nature of our social reality in order to sanction and re-produce the status quo of our racial democracy. Specifically, hip-hop is a form of subjugated knowledge that contests the *episteme* with the testimony of the marginalized—those abandoned to routine carceral violence—in order to expose the contingent, *genocidal state of affairs* masked by our discourse and media. I defended this view through illustrating three points: (1) the interrelationship between hip-hop and penal culture shows that hip-hop is an effective form of subjugated knowledge that can oppose the stability and force of the *episteme* on the American psyche and white sensibility; (2) The two predominant moods of hip-hop—righteous indignation and a sense of mourning-without-end—represent two existential responses to systemic trauma and aim to disrupt the white complacency toward the present supported by neoliberal and post-racial sensibility; (3) The criminalization of the phrase "Fuck Tha Police" and the recent prosecution of Jamal Knox ("Mayhem Mal"), indicate the threat that hip-hop poses to white sensibility and the white establishment.

HIP-HOP AS POLITICS

Some scholars in the field of hip-hop studies have raised concerns that the political significance of hip-hop is misconstrued as *politics itself*, or as an action that disrupts the systemic infliction of anti-black violence or serves to dismantle the racist distribution of capital and power that requires this violence to sustain itself. This concern has been raised most prominently by Lester K. Spence in his book *Stare in the Darkness: The Limits of Hip-Hop and Black Politics* (2011), and more recently by P. Khalil Saucier and Tryon P. Woods in their article "Hip Hop Studies in Black" (2014) in the *Journal of Popular Music Studies* (26:2). They both argue against the common view in underground hip-hop (and a presupposition of this book) that hip-hop culture represents a form of political activism, a view aptly summarized by Spence in the Introduction to his book:

> MCs, activists, pundits, and citizens alike believe that rap lyrics communicate politics; they believe that hip-hop can be used to circulate and generate a new form of political activism, and they believe that rap consumption shifts political attitudes. Rap and hip-hop are not only "Black America's CNN" (Chuck D 1997); they are also the key to generating a new black political movement. They are spaces in which blacks create new meanings of "blackness" and develop critiques that offer alternatives to the status quo.[1]

In contrast to this view about the subversive power of hip-hop, Spence argues that "hip-hop's productive, circulative, and consumptive politics both mirror and reproduce" the neoliberal narrative that individual freedom and liberty are best attained by reducing the role of government in the alleviation of social suffering and relying instead on the market.[2] He defends this claim with reference to how the commercial distribution and popular consumption of hip-hop undermines the subversive aim of the culture and instead circulates and re-produces the discursive practices that allow us to evade the structural oppression of black people in the United States. Further, he argues that hip-hop culture is not a real form of politics or political resistance since it has not significantly affected the distribution of resources in the United States in order to dismantle the structure of white supremacy.[3] Spence's argument is supported by his focus on the effects of a specific form of commercial rap on the status quo of anti-black oppression, as opposed to the space of the underground and its effects on individuals and groups who suffer from anti-black violence. In other words, Spence does not consider the *aesthetic affect* of underground hip-hop on our sensibility of the American past and present as politically significant.

Drawing on Spence's work, Saucier and Woods claim that "Hip hop does not have a politics; it cannot be read as progressive or retrograde by simply analyzing its expressive content." They continue:

> In fact, racism is a structure—historical, epistemological, ontological, axiological, social—in which our preconscious interests, unconscious desires, and conscious identifications are constituted in racial violence. Hip hop studies implicitly desires a causal link between performance (by the MC, the dancer, the student learning how to read/write/think through rap, etc.) and emancipation—or, in its liberal universalist variant, a nebulous (from the vantage point of blackness) "social justice."[4]

Even though Saucier and Woods explain that racial violence is sustained by "our preconscious interests, unconscious desires, and conscious identifications," they do not regard the aesthetic effort to expose and dis-rupt our unconscious affiliations and desires as a politically significant form of opposition to this violence. For their view—like Spence's view—rests on a specific conception of politics as emancipation from a system of domination through the destruction of its institutions and the redistribution of power and capital.

Since the publication of Derrick Bell's book *Faces at the Bottom of the Well: The Permanence of Racism* (1992), critical race theorists have explored how the expectation that we can somehow "end" the system of anti-black racism has precluded our ability to theorize new possibilities of resistance in the present against the degenerating effects of this system. As Bell explains: "Freed of the stifling rigidity of relying unthinkingly on the slogan 'we shall overcome,'" "we are impelled both to live each day more fully and to examine critically the actual effectiveness of traditional civil rights remedies."[5] In his alternative conception of the civil rights movement beyond the opposition between the neoliberal call for piecemeal legal reforms versus the call for revolution, the aim is to "fashion a philosophy that both matches the unique dangers we face, and enables us to recognize in those dangers opportunities for committed living and humane service."

Bell's book provides the theoretical foundation to better understand the relation between black aesthetics and black politics that Taylor also illustrates in his previously cited book *Black is Beautiful*. Bell initiates a reorientation away from the "end" of racism and toward the present organization of power relations and the forms of violence they predictably inflict on black communities. This reorientation also helps us to better understand *how* the aesthetic effort to affect our sensibility and cope with the harms of collective suffering are forms of *political resistance* against our white supremacist state. Further, Bell's view of political action presents a model that takes into account the distinct existential position faced by victims *who are born into* a genocidal regime in which the system of oppression from which they suffer is entrenched in historical, social, and political institutions, perpetuated and enforced by the modern military-industrial complex. In such a milieu—contrary to the Socratic view that actions taken on behalf of one's "life" preclude actions taken on behalf of the "good life"—the effort to stay alive in a nation organized around one's destruction contains political and moral value in-itself. Hip-hop culture provides a space for those targeted by our state to find some respite and so better cope with and resist the harms inflicted by a system that they cannot escape or destroy. In a genocidal state, this is a profound form of resistance against the logic of group destruction.

For Socrates, we should protect the moral integrity of our souls, rather than the safety of our bodies, "at all costs." His worldview is compelling and poignant, given that he chose to die rather than to commit the unjust act of breaking the law or breaking out of prison to escape an unjust sentence of death. However, there are no resources from within Socratic theory to affirm the right of victims of state violence to prioritize their self-preservation over their fidelity to the laws or traditional values. In an environment of distinctly *genocidal* suffering where the state targets an entire group for destruction, the value of an individual person as a member of this group also represents the value of the group that is under attack. In other words, when a group is threatened with destruction through systemic state violence against its members, then when one member fights for her life, she is simultaneously fighting for the survival of the group under attack. Her desire to stay alive is necessary in order to preserve the existence of the group, as such, and her effort to stay alive represents a moral protest to the logic of genocide and an affirmation of an individual's right to exist as well as the value of the group to which one belongs (*Black Lives Matter*). In this sense when rappers claim that "hip-hop (literally) saved my life," they are also giving voice to the political power of hip-hop to help victims of racist violence to "Keep Ya Head Up" and resist the degenerating, genocidal effects of social and institutional violence.

In his own time, Socrates did not appear to protest the exclusion of select communities from the rights of citizenship (women, slaves, and foreigners).[6] His life and moral theory are inadequate to reflect upon the plight of marginalized populations who are excluded from the protection of the law, and they cannot help us to evaluate the political and moral value of decisions made by victims of state violence whose very "lives" have been criminalized and judged superfluous to the human community. Instead, we must set aside his sharp dichotomy between acting on behalf of the "good life" vs. "life itself" in order to better appreciate the political relevance of aesthetic works created by victims of anti-black genocide to contest, defy, and better cope with the existential vulnerability to state violence and the communal harms inflicted by state institutions.

For these reasons, I disagree with the critique set forward by Spence, Saucier, and Woods that evaluates the political in-significance of hip-hop in terms of its complicity with the neoliberal economy of our anti-black genocidal regime that promotes the individual accumulation of wealth as the solution to historical and systemic systems of oppression. Their view neglects the political value of hip-hop culture as a means of resistance in the city and the cell, and as a form of aesthetic intervention against neoliberal and post-racial sensibility—despite the fact that commercial rap is consumed and distributed in such a way as to reinforce neoliberal norms and values. However, given their view of politics as the *destruction* of the racial caste system that has always informed western politics, it is not possible for them to understand the political significance of the aesthetics of hip-hop and underground hip-hop culture that allow communities to contest and better cope with the conditions of anti-black racism. Instead, their view of properly political action regards the aim to destroy a system that appears entrenched in political institutions and our sensibility as a way of knowing, sensing, and understanding the world (in Butler's terms, given the *racist saturation of the visible*). For this reason, I argued that the aesthetic effort to arrest, interrupt, and dismantle the sensibility that criminalizes black men is no less significant as a form of political resistance against our entrenched system of anti-black violence than the effort to overthrow an oppressive institution through the forced appropriation of power and capital—an effort that appears futile against the modern power of the military-industry complex.

NOTES ON HIP-HOP PEDAGOGY AND PRACTICE

However, the concern raised by Saucier and Woods about the failure to move past the enjoyment of hip-hop to opposing racist structures in everyday practices is a real problem, similar to the problem of moving past one's love of Jesus Christ to acting on his principles of love and moral concern for the poor, the sick, and the oppressed. I don't have a solution, but taking this problem seriously has helped me better understand my own complicity working as a white professor in private colleges that are not in-tension with but rather essential to and dependent on, the neoliberal project to advocate piecemeal legal and economic reforms that serve to sustain the structure of anti-black racism. For example, given the exorbitant costs of a college education, the system of higher education still serves to privilege wealthy—largely white—students who can afford tuition or who stand a good chance of getting a job after college that will allow them to pay off school loans.

The social and economic difficulties faced by students of color in private colleges with a largely white student body are masked by the neoliberal narrative—central to all college brochures—that a college education expands all minds and guarantees greater job opportunities for those who graduate. Amid institutional initiatives to enhance diversity in the student body, our colleges still largely serve to perpetuate and exacerbate the racist distribution of wealth and power. Taking seriously the problem of my complicity in this system, and my view that hip-hop is essential to political resistance and personal commitments, I have initiated certain programs, created new courses, and defied specific administrative policies at the small, private liberal arts colleges where I have worked as an assistant and associate professor of philosophy. I do not think these actions have been adequate to the task of opposing the systemic racism and classism of academia, nor have they soothed my concerns about the value or efficacy of my work. However, I will detail some of the projects that I have initiated in my efforts to keep it real, in order to share how my love of hip-hop has influenced my everyday practices as a professor and employee of a neoliberal institution.

Although I went to college in upstate New York and graduate school in Atlanta, Georgia, my career led to tenure track positions at liberal arts colleges in Iowa and then central Pennsylvania, in small, largely white and Christian communities. I had never before been in communities where so few people listened to hip-hop or so few people had any real interest in African American culture. I introduced certain programs that—at other universities—would not have been as controversial or unusual for the student body. However at these small schools, these programs did alter the social and political climate and—at the university where I received tenure—created a controversy that placed my career at risk (as detailed in chapter 6). This was not that surprising, given that hip-hop is controversial precisely because it contests those post-racial and neoliberal narratives essential to the economic success of private colleges. Hip-hop culture has also taught me that in order for white people to better strive to keep it real and oppose those policies that protect them at the expense of black people, we need to be willing to take risks and make real sacrifices. I don't think I do it enough, but I am striving to do it better.

My own hip-hop interventions include the introduction of a course on "Philosophy and Hip-Hop" that serves as an introduction to the genre and the philosophy of race. My overwhelmingly positive experiences teaching this course to largely white, middle-class students convinced me of the pedagogical and existential value of underground hip-hop in the college classroom. In designing this course, I departed from traditional pedagogical requirements in order to add a performance component that represented 20 percent of the final grade. This changed the dynamic of a philosophy course in such startling and productive ways that it led me to re-think our notion of "diversity" in the academy, as well as the problems with the traditional standards and categories of excellence in Anglo-American Universities. These insights led to an article that I co-authored with Sheila Lintott titled "Inclusive Pedagogy: Beyond Simply Content" (2016) for the journal *Hypatia: A Journal of Feminist Philosophy*. I am grateful for having had the opportunity to teach this course for several years, which provided me with insights about how to be a better teacher for all of my students.

Following the introduction of a course on hip-hop, I facilitated an arrangement between our university and the Pennsylvania Prison Society to train and empower our students to become "official visitors" to women incarcerated in a nearby medium and maximum security state prison. In my view, this is essential to honor the mission of hip-hop to care about and attend to those oppressed communities who are all too often "out of sight" and "out of mind" to academics—even as they affirm the need for more "diversity" on campus and support the abstract goal of "social justice." In order to encourage our students to sign up for this program, I started a lecture series that invited women who were formerly incarcerated at this state prison to speak to our students, faculty, and staff about their experiences. Not only did these speakers have a profound effect on our students, but I was able to compensate them with honoraria at a time when they needed material support and encouragement. And again, all of these efforts—never adequate, never perfect—were inspired by my effort to keep it real in the academy.

Lastly, I organized a series of "hip-hop happenings" at our university that brought together underground rappers, b-boys, and b-girls, DJs and graffiti artists from Philadelphia, New York, and New Jersey for a collective celebration and performance of hip-hop culture in our concert venue. This became a regular occurrence after some of my students organized to create a hip-hop society on campus, able to receive funds from the student government to support their mission of enhancing the visibility of hip-hop culture in the community. It is hard to explain how much these events meant to those of us who felt marginalized on campus or how our collective aesthetic awe also enhanced our pride and our sense of community. I'm hoping that the ideas I presented in this book can help compensate for the failure of words to describe the beauty and impact of these hip-hop happenings. And I hope this book inspires more academics to consider integrating hip-hop into pedagogy and research, as a vital source of knowledge and aesthetic experience that can enhance our ability to examine ourselves.

I Do It for Hip-Hop, and Hip-Hop Saved My Life. One Love.

NOTES

1. Lester K. Spence, *Stare in the Darkness: The Limits of Hip-Hop and Black Politics* (Minneapolis: University of Minnesota Press, 2011), 3.
2. Ibid., 11.
3. Ibid., 2.
4. P. Khalil Saucier and Tryon P. Woods, "Hip Hop Studies in Black," *Journal of Popular Music Studies* 26, no. 2 (2014): 275.
5. Derrick Bell, *Faces at the Bottom of the Well: The Permanence of Racism* (New York: HarperCollins, 1992), 199.
6. It is clear in Plato's *Euthyphro* that the historical Socrates was not morally shocked by slavery, as he questions Euthyphro's effort to prosecute his own father for killing a slave. Since a slave does not have the same legal rights as a citizen, Euthyphro is going out of his way to prosecute his own father and it is this insistence on bringing his father to court *on behalf of a slave* that Socrates questions as impious.

Playlists by Chapter

INTRODUCTION: IT'S BIGGER THAN HIP-HOP

1. "Hip-Hop," Dead Prez
2. "Hip-Hop," Pace Won and Mr. Green
3. "Hip-Hop," Yasiin Bey (as Mos Def)
4. "Hip-Hop," DJ Jazzy Jeff feat. Twone Gabz
5. "Hip-Hop," DJ Khaled feat. Scarface and Nas
6. "I Do It for Hip-Hop," Ludacris feat. Nas and Jay-Z
7. "Love of My Life (An Ode to Hip-Hop)," Erykah Badu feat. Common
8. "Hip-Hop Is Dead," Nas feat. Will.i.am
9. "Hip-Hop Saved My Life," Lupe Fiasco
10. "Say," Method Man feat. Lauryn Hill

CHAPTER 1: KNOW WHAT I'M SAYIN?

1. "Know What I'm Sayin'," Mike Jones feat. Lil Keke & Bun B
2. "Do You Know What I'm Sayin'," Ugly Duckling
3. "Know What I'm Saying," Plies
4. "Words I Never Said," Lupe Fiasco feat. Skylar Grey
5. "C.R.E.A.M," Wu-Tang Clan
6. "Nowhere2Go," Earl Sweatshirt
7. "Mr. Nigga," Mos Def
8. "Pimps (Free Stylin at the Fortune 500 Club)," The Coup
9. "Homeland and Hip Hop," Immortal Technique feat. Mumia Abu Jama
10. "Sound of Tha Police," KRS-ONE

CHAPTER 2: CAN I GET A WITNESS?

1. "Caught, Can We Get a Witness?," Public Enemy
2. "Can I Get a Witness?," Run-D.M.C.
3. "Fear Not of Man," Yasiin Bey (as Mos Def)
4. "Changes," 2Pac
5. "How Long Will They Mourn Me?," Thug Life, feat. 2Pac, Macadoshis, Rated R, Big Syke & Nate Dogg
6. "Hard Knock Life (Ghetto Anthem)," JAY-Z
7. "Trauma," Meek Mill
8. "Traumatized," Meek Mill
9. "Traumatized," Dave East
10. "Traumatized," YoungBoy Never Broke Again

CHAPTER 3: CLAIMIN' I'M A CRIMINAL

1. "Claimin I'm a Criminal," Brand Nubian
2. "The Tower," Ice Cube
3. "16 on Death Row," 2Pac
4. "One Love," Nas
5. "Do Your Time," Ludacris feat. Pimp C, C-Murder & Beanie Sigel
6. "Pick a Side," BL Shirelle
7. "Family Business," Kanye West
8. "Concrete Hell," 5th Ward Boyz
9. "The Real Deal," Lifers Group
10. "Prisoner 1 & 2," Lupe Fiasco feat. Ayesha Jaco

CHAPTER 4: BUT YOU DON'T HEAR ME THO

1. "But You Don't Hear Me Tho," Statik Selektah feat. The LOX & Mtume
2. "Battle Cry," Angel Haze feat. Sia
3. "Dear Mama," 2Pac
4. "Hey Mama," Kanye West
5. "Conspiracy," Gang Starr
6. "Four Twenty," Wyclef Jean feat. Wavie D
7. "Crooked Smile," J. Cole feat. TLC
8. "I Get Out," Lauryn Hill
9. "Soundtrack 2 My Life," Kid Cudi
10. "Sunday Morning," Noname feat. K.O.

CHAPTER 5: YOU FEEL ME?

1. "Sketches of Pain," Audible Mainframe
2. "The Mystery of Iniquity," Lauryn Hill
3. "The Writing on the Wall," V.I.T.A.L. Emcee
4. "Tearz," Wu-Tang Clan
5. "Holy Are You," Rakim
6. "This Is America," Childish Gambino
7. "Alright," Kendrick Lamar
8. "My Life," Foxy Brown
9. "Starin' Through My Rear View," 2Pac
10. "Casket Pretty," Noname

CHAPTER 6: FUCK THA POLICE

1. "Fuck Tha Police," N.W.A.
2. "Fuck Tha Police," Bone Thugs-N-Harmony
3. "Fuck Tha Police," The Black Squad
4. "Fuck Tha Police 2005," Daz Dillinger
5. "Police State," Dead Prez
6. "They School," Dead Prez
7. "Still Alive," BL Shirelle
8. "Amerikkka's Most Wanted," Ice Cube
9. "Tree Never Grown," Hip-Hop for Respect
10. "Modern Day Slavery," Joell Ortiz

CONCLUSION: THE AESTHETIC POLITICS OF UNDERGROUND HIP-HOP

1. "Strange Woman," Bates
2. "Crash," DonChristian feat. bbymutha
3. "Shiny Suit Theory," Jay Electronica feat. The-Dream
4. "Strap on My Lap," Globalthugz feat. Ty-Stick
5. "God Bless," BL Shirelle
6. "Stay Shinin'," Dynasty feat. Talib Kweli
7. "I'm in a Mood," Mykki Blanco
8. "Campfire," Amine
9. "I'm the Best," Nikki Minaj
10. "The Glorious Five," Logic

Discography

2Pac. 1995. "Dear Mama." Track 9 on Me Against The World. Interscope Records.
———. 1997. "16 on Death Row." Track 9 on Disc 2 R U Still Down? (Remember Me). Interscope Records.
———. 1998. "Changes." Track 1 on 2 Pac Greatest Hits. Interscope Records.
———. 2004. "Po' Nigga Blues: Scott Storch Remix." Track 14 on Loyal to the Game. Interscope Records.
2Pac and Outlawz. 1997. "Starin' Through my Rearview." Track 8 on Gang Related: The Soundtrack. Death Row Records and Priority Records.
———. 1997. "Made Niggaz." Track 1 on Disc 2 Gang Related: The Soundtrack. Death Row Records and Priority Records.
———. 2002. "They Don't Give a Fuck About Us." Track 13 on Disc 2 Better Dayz. Interscope Records.
5th Ward Boyz. 1995. "Concrete Hell." Track 2 on Rated G. Rap-a-Lot Records.
A Tribe Called Quest. 2016. "Solid Wall of Sound." Track 4 on We got it from Here . . . Thank You 4 Your service. Epic Records.
Aminé feat. Injury Reserve. 2018. "Campfire." Track 1 on Campfire. Universal Records.
Angel Haze. 2013. "Battle Cry." Track 9 on Dirty Gold. Island Records and Republic Records.
Audible Mainframe. 2005. "Sketches of Pain." Track 7 on War to be One. Self-Release.
Bates feat. Mz Tigga, Cedes Cedes, Phenom Ionos, Chill and G.A. Barz. 2017. "Strange Woman." Track 1 on Strange Woman. Bates/She Dope Publishing Company.
BL Shirelle. 2019. "Pick a Side." Track 11 on Restricted Movement 2. BL Shirelle.
———. 2019. "God Bless." Track 3 on Restricted Movement 2. BL Shirelle.
Bone Thugs-N-Harmony. 2017. "Fuck The Police (Remix)." Track 5 on Living Legends. Mo Thugs Records.

Brand Nubian. 1994. "Claimin I'm a Criminal." Track 11 on Everything is Everything. Elektra Records.
Childish Gambino. 2018. "This Is America." Track 1 on This is America. Wolf + Rothstein/RCA Records.
Dave East feat. Kiing Shooter. 2018. "Traumatized." Track 4 on Karma 2. The DisPensary.
Daz Dillinger. 2005. "Fuck Tha Police." Track 19 on Tha Dogg Pound Gangsta LP. Dogg Pound Online.
Dead Prez. 2000. "Hip-Hop." Track 4 on Let's Get Free. Loud Records.
———. 2000. "It's Bigger Than Hip-Hop." Track 16 on Let's Get Free. Loud Records.
———. 2000. "Police State." Track 5 on Let's Get Free. Loud Records.
———. 2000. "They School." Track 3 on Let's Get Free. Loud Records.
DJ Jazzy Jeff feat. Twone Gabz. 2007. "Hip-Hop." Track 2 on The Return of the Magnificent (Explicit). Rapster Records.
DJ Khaled. 2012. "Hip Hop." Track 7 on Kiss the Ring. Cash Money Records and Republic Records.
DonChristian feat. Bbymutha. 2018. "Crash." Track 4 on Where There's Smoke. Palm Out Sounds.
Dynasty feat. Talib Kweli. 2013. "Stay Shinin'." Track 1 on A Star in Life's Clothing. Dynasty/ D. Maria E Music.
Earl Sweatshirt. 2018. "Nowhere2Go." Track 1 on Nowhere2go. Tan Cressida/ Columbia
Records.
Erykah Badu feat. Common. 2002. "Love of my Life (An Ode to Hip Hop)." Track 2 on Brown Sugar. Brown Sugar/MCA Records.
Foxy Brown. 1999. "My Life." Track 3 on Chyna Doll. Def Jam Records/RAL.
Gang Starr. 1992. "Conspiracy." Track 12 on Daily Operation. Chrysalis Records.
Globalthugz feat. Ty-Stick. 2018. "Strap on my Lap." Track 1 on Strap on My Lap. Tz EnterPriZe.
Hip Hop for Respect. 2000. "Tree Never Grown." Track 4 on Hip-Hop for Respect. Rawkus Records.
Ice Cube. 1990. "Amerikkka's Most Wanted." Track 3 on Amerikkka's Most Wanted. Priority Records.
———. 1991. "The Tower." Track 23 on O. G. Original Gangster. Sire/Warner Bros.
Immortal Technique feat. Mumia Abu Jama. 2004. "Homeland and Hip Hop." Track 12 on Revolutionary Vol. 2. Viper Records.
Jay Electronica. 2020. "Shiny Suit Theory." Track 5 on A Written Testimony. Roc Nation.
Jay-Z. 1998. "Hard Knock Life (Ghetto Anthem)." Track 2 on Vol. 2. Hard Knock Life. Roc-A-Fella Records.
J. Cole. 2013. "Crooked Smile." Track 14 on Born Sinner. Roc Nation and Columbia Records.
Joell Ortiz. 2007. "Modern Day Slavery." Track 7 on The Brick: Bodega Chronicles. Koch Records.

Kanye West. 2004. "Family Business." Track 20 on The College Dropout. Def Jam and Roc-A-Fella Records.

———. 2005. "Hey Mama." Track 16 on Late Registration. Roc-A-Fella Records.

Kendrick Lamar. 2015. "Alright." Track 7 on To Pimp a Butterfly. Top Dawg Entertainment / Aftermath Records.

Kid Cudi. 2009. "Soundtrack 2 My Life." Track 2 on Man On The Moon: The End Of Day. G.O.O.D./Dream On/Universal Records.

KRS-One. 1993. "Sound of da Police." Track 7 on Return of the Boom Bap. Jive Records.

Lauryn Hill. 2002. "I Get Out." Track 4, Disc 2 on MTV Unplugged No. 2.0. Columbia Records.

———. 2002. "Mystery of Iniquity." Track 2, Disc 2 on MTV Unplugged No. 2.0. Columbia Records.

Lifers Group. 1991. "The Real Deal." Hollywood Records.

Lil Pump. 2017. "Gucci Gang." Track 2 on Lil Pump. Warner Records.

Logic. 2018. "The Glorious Five." Track 4 on YSIV. Def Jam Recordings.

Ludacris. 2006. "Do Your Time." Track 11 on Release Therapy. Def Jam Records.

———. 2008. "I Do It For Hip Hop." Track 13 on Theatre of the Mind. Def Jam Records.

Lupe Fiasco. 2011. "Words I Never Said." Track 2 on Lasers. Atlantic Records.

Lupe Fiasco feat. Nikki Jean. 2007. "Hip-Hop Saved My Life." Track 9 on Lupe Fiasco's the Cool. 1st & 15th/Atlantic Records.

Lupe Fiasco feat. Ayesha Jaco. 2015. "Prisoner 1 & 2." Track 6 on Tetsuo & Youth. 1st & 15th/Atlantic Records.

Meek Mill. 2018. "Trauma." Track 2 on Championships. Atlantic Records.

Method Man feat. Lauryn Hill. 2006. "Say." Track 13 on 4:21… The Day After. Def Jam Records.

Mike Jones feat. Lil Keke & Bun B. 2005."Know What I'm Sayin'." Track 13 on Who is Mike Jones? Warner Records.

Mos Def feat. Q-Tip. 1999. "Mr. Nigga." Track 15 on Black on Both Sides. Rawkus Entertainment.

Mos Def. 1999. "Fear Not of Man." Track 1 on Black on Both Sides. Rawkus Entertainment.

———. 1999. "Hip Hop." Track 2 on Black on Both Sides. Rawkus Entertainment.

Mykki Blanco. 2016. "I'm in a Mood." Track 1 on Mykki. Dogfood Music Group.

Nas feat. Q-Tip. 1994. "One Love." Track 7 on Illmatic. Columbia Records.

Nas feat. Will.i.am. 2007. "Hip Hop is Dead." Track 5 on Hip Hop is Dead (Bonus Tracks). Columbia Records/Def Jam Records.

Nicki Minaj. 2010. "I'm the Best." Track 1 on Pink Friday. Nicki Minaj/Cash Money Records Inc.

Noname. 2016. "Casket Pretty." Track 7 on Telefone. Noname.

N.W.A. 1988. "Fuck Tha Police." Track 2 of Straight Outta Compton. Ruthless and Priority Records.

Pace Won and Mr. Green. 2008. "Hip-Hop." Track 7 on The Only Color That Matters is Green. CD Baby.

Plies. 2014. "Know What I'm Saying." Track 2 on Da Realest Nigga Left 2. Plies Music.know

Public Enemy. 1988. "Caught, Can We Get A Witness?" Track 8 on It Takes a Nation of Millions to Hold Us Back. Columbia Records.

Rakim. 2009. "Holy Are You." Track 7 on The Seventh Seal. SMC Recordings.

Run-D.M.C. 1990. "Back From Hell." Track 9 on Back From Hell. Profile Records.

———. 1993. "Can I Get a Witness." Track 11 on Down With the King. Profile Records.

Run the Jewels. 2016. "Talk to Me." Track 2 on Run the Jewels 3. Run the Jewels Inc.

Statik Selektah feat. The Lox, Mtume. 2017. "But You Don't Hear Me Tho." Track 7 on 8. Showoff Records/Duck Down Music Inc.

The Black Squad. 2018. "Fuck Tha Police." Track 9 on The Classic Tape. Street Cred Music Group.

The Coup. 2008. "Pimps (Free Stylin At the Fortune 500 Club)." Track 3 on Genocide & Juice. Melee / Wild Pitch Records.

Thug Life. 1994. "How Long Will They Mourn Me?" Track 6 on Thug Life Vol. 1. Interscope Records.

Ugly Duckling. 1999. "Do You Know What I'm Sayin'." Track 6 on Fresh Mode. 1500 Records.

V.I.T.A.L. Emcee feat. Maylay and Matt Embree. 2006. "The Writing On the Wall." Track 3 on The Secret of the Invisible Man. Mdb Records.

Wu-Tang Clan. 2004. "C.R.E.A.M." Track 1 on Legend Of The Wu-Tang: Wu-Tang Clan's Greatest Hits. SBME Strategic Marketing Group.

———. 2007. "Tearz." Track 11 on Enter The Wu-Tang (36 Chambers). RCA Records Label.

Wyclef Jean. 2019. "Four-Twenty." Track 7 on Wyclef Goes Back to School Volume 1. Head's Music.

YoungBoy Never Broke Again. 2018. "Traumatized." Track 9 on Until Death Call My Name. Never Broke Again, LLC.

Bibliography

Agamben, Giorgio. *Homo Sacer: Sovereign Power and Bare Life*. Translated by Daniel Heller-Roazen. Palo Alto, CA: Stanford University Press, 1998.

Alcoff, Linda Martín. "Epistemologies of Ignorance: Three Types." In *Race and Epistemologies of Ignorance*, edited by Shannon Sullivan and Nancy Tuana. New York: SUNY Press, 2006.

Alim, H. Samy. "'Bring It to the Cypher': Hip Hop Nation Language." In *That's the Joint!: The Hip-Hop Studies Reader*, edited by Murray Forman and Mark Anthony Neal. New York: Routledge, 2011.

———. *Roc the Mic Right: The Language of Hip Hop Culture*. New York: Routledge, 2006.

Améry, Jean. *At The Mind's Limits: Contemplations by a Survivor on Auschwitz and Its Realities*. Translated by Sidney Rosenfeld and Stella P. Rosenfeld. Bloomington: Indiana University Press, 1980.

Arendt, Hannah. *The Origins of Totalitarianism*. New York: Harcourt Brace, 1973.

Baldwin, James. "Going to Meet the Man." In *Going to Meet the Man: Stories*. New York: Vintage, 1995.

Bauer, Yehuda. *On the Holocaust and Other Genocides*. Washington, DC: USHMM, 2007.

Bell, Derrick. *Faces at the Bottom of the Well: The Permanence of Racism*. New York: HarperCollins, 1992.

Belle, Kathryn Sophia. "Queen Bees and Big Pimps: Sex and Sexuality in Contemporary Hip-Hop." In *Hip Hop and Philosophy: Rhyme 2 Reason*, edited by Derrick Darby and Tommie Shelby. Chicago: Open Court, 2005.

Berkowitz, Michael. *The Crime of My Very Existence: Nazism and the Myth of Jewish Criminality*. Berkeley: University of California Press, 2007.

Burgos, Adam. *Political Philosophy and Political Action: Imperatives of Resistance*. Lanham, MD: Rowman & Littlefield Publishers, 2016.

Butler, Judith. "Endangered/Endangering: Schematic Racism and White Paranoia." In *Reading Rodney King, Reading Urban Uprising*, edited by Robert Goodings Williams. New York: Routledge, 1993.

Butler, Paul. *Let's Get Free: A Hip-Hop Theory of Justice*. New York: The New Press, 2009.

Card, Claudia. *The Atrocity Paradigm: A Theory of Evil*. New York: Oxford University Press, 2005.

———. *Confronting Evils: Terrorism, Torture, Genocide*. Cambridge: Cambridge University Press, 2010.

———. "Genocide and Social Death." *Hypatia: A Journal of Feminist Philosophy* 18, no. 1 (2003): 63–79. https://doi.org/10.1111/j.1527-2001.2003.tb00779.x.

———. "The Paradox of Genocidal Rape Aimed at Enforced Pregnancy." *The Southern Journal of Philosophy* 46, no. S1 (2008): 176–190. https://doi.org/10.1111/j.2041-6962.2008.tb00162.x

Caruth, Cathy, editor. *Trauma: Explorations in Memory*. Baltimore: Johns Hopkins University Press, 1995.

———. *Unclaimed Experience: Trauma, Narrative, and History*. Baltimore: Johns Hopkins University Press, 1996.

Civil Rights Congress. *We Charge Genocide: The Crime of the Government Against the Negro People*. Edited by William L. Patterson. New York: International Publishers Co, 2017.

Crenshaw, Kimberle. "Mapping the Margins: Intersectionality, Identity Politics, and Violence against Women of Color." *Stanford Law Review* 43, no. 6 (1991): 1241–1299. DOI: 10.2307/1229039.

Dotson, Kristie. "Tracking Epistemic Violence, Tracking Practices of Silencing." *Hypatia: A Journal of Feminist Philosophy* 26, no. 2 (Spring 2011): 233–251. https://doi.org/10.1111/j.1527-2001.2011.01177.x.

Du Bois, W. E. B. *The Souls of Black Folk* (1903). New York: Dover Books, 1994.

Fanon, Franz. *Black Skin, White Masks* (1952). New York: Grove Books, 2008.

Forman, Murray and Mark Anthony Neal, editors. *That's The Joint!: The Hip-Hop Studies Reader*. New York: Routledge, 2012.

Foucault, Michel. "The Confession of the Flesh." In *Power/Knowledge: Selected Interviews and Other Writings, 1972–1977*, edited by Colin Gordon. New York: Pantheon Books, 1980 (194–228).

———. "Nietzsche, Genealogy, and History." In *Aesthetics, Method, and Epistemology Essential Works of Foucault, 1954–1984, Vol. 2*. New York: The New Press, 1999.

———. *"Society Must Be Defended": Lectures at the College de France (1975–76)*. Translated by David Macey. New York: Picador, 2003.

Frankowski, Alfred. "Beyond the Dissensus Schema." In *Syndicate Philosophy*, symposium on *The Post-Racial Limits of Memorialization: Toward a Political Sense of Mourning* by Alfred Frankowski. First published in the online symposium. *Syndicate Philosophy*, https://syndicate.network/symposia/philosophy/the-post-racial-limits-of-memorialization/ 05/15/17.

———. *The Post-Racial Limits of Memorialization: Toward a Political Sense of Mourning*. Lanham, MD: Lexington Books, 2017.

Frankowski, Alfred and Lissa Skitolsky. "Lang's Defense and the Morbid Sensibility of Genocide Studies." *Journal of Genocide Research* 20, no. 3 (2018): 423–428. https://doi.org/10.1080/14623528.2018.1445420

Freud, Sigmund. *Beyond the Pleasure Principle.* New York: W. W. Norton & Company, 1990.

Fricker, Miranda. *Epistemic Injustice: Power and the Ethics of Knowing.* New York: Oxford University Press, 2009.

Gordon, Lewis R. "Fanon, Philosophy, and Racism." In *Racism and Philosophy*, edited by Susan E. Babbitt and Sue Campbell. Ithaca, NY: Cornell University Press, 2018.

Hadley, Susan and George Yancy, editors. *Therapeutic Uses of Rap and Hip-Hop.* New York: Routledge, 2012.

Jackson, Silas. Interviewed in: *When I Was a Slave: Memoirs from the Slave Narrative Collection.* Edited by N. R. Yetman. New York: Dover, 2002.

Jacobs, Harriet. *Incidents in the Life of a Slave Girl.* New York: Dover, 2000.

Jones, Janine. "The Impairment of Empathy in Goodwill Whites for African-Americans." In *What White Looks Like: African-American Philosophers on The Whiteness Question*, edited by George Yancy. New York: Routledge, 2004.

Katz, Mark. *Groove Music: The Art and Culture of the Hip-Hop DJ.* New York: Oxford University Press, 2012.

Lacan, Jacques. *The Seminar of Jacques Lacan: The Four Fundamental Concepts of Psychoanalysis (Vol. Book XI).* New York: W. W. Norton & Company, 1998.

Lang, Berl. *Genocide: The Act as Idea.* Philadelphia: Pennsylvania University Press, 2017.

Lemkin, Raphael. "Nature of Genocide." *New York Times*, June 14, 1953.

Levi, Primo. *Survival in Auschwitz.* Translated by Stuart Woolf. New York: Touchstone, 1995.

Lorde, Audre. *Sister Outsider: Essays and Speeches.* "Uses of the Erotic: The Erotic as Power." Berkeley, CA: Crossing Press, 1984.

Mills, Charles. *The Racial Contract.* New York: Cornell University Press, 1997.

Moshman, David. "Conceptual Constraints On Thinking about Genocide." *Journal of Genocide Research* 3, no. 3 (2001): 431–450. DOI: 10.1080/14623520120097224.

Orejuela, Fernando. *Rap and Hip Hop Culture.* New York: Oxford University Press, 2014.

Patterson, William. *The Man Who Cried Genocide: An Autobiography.* New York: International Publishers, Co., 1971.

Perry, Imani. *Prophets of the Hood: Politics and Poetics in Hip Hop.* Durham, NC: Duke University Press, 2004.

Peterson, James Braxton. *The Hip-Hop Underground and African American Culture: Beneath the Surface.* New York: Palgrave Macmillan, 2014.

Pitts, Andrea J. "Decolonial Praxis and Epistemic Injustice." In *The Routledge Handbook of Epistemic Injustice*, edited by Ian James Kidd, José Medina, and Gaile Pohlhaus, Jr. New York: Routledge, 2017.

Rankine, Claudia. "The Condition of Black Life Is One of Mourning." *The New York Times Magazine*, June 22, 2015.

Rose, Tricia. *Black Noise: Rap Music and Black Culture in Contemporary America*. Middletown, CT: Wesleyan University Press, 1994.

———. *The Hip Hop Wars: What We Talk About When We Talk About Hip-Hop—and Why It Matters*. Philadelphia: Basic Books, 2008.

Saucier, P. Khalil and Tryon P. Woods. "Hip Hop Studies in Black." *Journal of Popular Music Studies* 26, no. 2 (2014): 268–294. https://doi.org/10.1111/jpms.12077.

Schloss, Joseph G. *Breaking Beats: The Art of Sample-based Hip-hop*. Middletown, CT: Wesleyan University Press, 2014.

Spence, Lester K. *Stare in the Darkness: The Limits of Hip-hop and Black Politics*. St. Paul: University of Minnesota Press, 2011.

Taylor, Paul. *Black is Beautiful: A Philosophy of Black Aesthetics*. Hoboken, NJ: Wiley-Blackwell, 2016.

Thomas, Michael. "Sensibility in Section 80: Kendrick Lamar's Poetics of Problems." In *Kendrick Lamar and the Making of Black Meaning*, edited by Christopher Driscoll, Monica Miller, and Tony Pinn. London: Routledge, 2019.

Yancy, George. *Backlash: What Happens When We Honestly Talk About Racism in America*. Lanham, MD: Rowman & Littlefield, 2018.

———. *Black Bodies, White Gazes: The Continuing Significance of Race*. Lanham, MD: Rowman & Littlefield, 2008.

———. "Dear White America." *The Stone, The New York Times*, December 24, 2015.

Index

2Pac. *See* Shakur, Tupac
5th Ward Boys, 104, 105

aesthetics, 4, 6, 26, 31, 34, 59, 69, 110, 151, 154, 161, 167, 168
Agamben, Giorgio, 96
Agent Orange, 67, 68
Alcoff, Linda Martin, 8
Alim, H. Samy, 11; *Roc the Mic Right: The Language of Hip-Hop Culture*, 44, 45
All Lives Matter, 69
Amery, Jean, 117; "At the Mind's Limits," 117, 118
Angel Haze, 122, 123
anti-black racism, 2, 4, 8–10, 15, 19, 20, 27, 34, 35, 37, 39–41, 49, 71, 77, 80, 82, 84, 92, 99, 128, 136, 137, 139, 140, 154, 155, 159–62, 164, 166, 168, 169
anti-black violence: and murder, 12, 18, 23, 31, 43, 53, 71–73, 95, 106, 107, 119, 141, 149, 150, 152; and police brutality, 12, 18, 23, 56, 69, 84, 94, 119, 141, 148–50, 153; systemic, 5, 6, 10, 12, 14, 17, 37, 39, 53, 59, 61, 82, 95, 99, 135, 161; as tragic, 20, 66, 126, 132, 149; as traumatic violence, 10, 12, 14, 16, 19, 22, 57, 59, 87, 90, 94, 114, 116, 117, 119–22, 126, 128, 132, 155, 163; in the United States, 2, 20, 21, 48, 81–83, 85, 86, 95, 143, 162, 163. *See also* genocide; mass incarceration
Arendt, Hannah, 100; *The Origins of Totalitarianism*, 100, 101
Audible Mainframe, 113, 114

Baldwin, James, 5
Bates, 27, 129
Bauer, Yehuda, 100
Beastie Boys, 47
Bell, Derrick, 166; *Faces at the Bottom of the Well: The Permanence of Racism*, 166, 167
Belle, Kathryn Sophia, 129; "Queen Bees and Big Pimps: Sex and Sexuality in Contemporary Hip-Hop," 133n9
Berkowitz, Michael, 91; *The Crime of My Very Existence: Nazism and the Myth of Jewish Criminality*, 95–99
Bey, Yasiin, 53–56, 59, 149
Black Lives Matter (BLM), 13, 69, 143, 151, 168
BL Shirelle, 27, 129
Brand Nubian, 42, 78, 88, 89, 142, 151
break-beat, 15, 57–60

Brown, Michael, 43, 72
Burgos, Adam, 2; *Political Philosophy and Political Action: Imperatives of Resistance*, 2
Butler, Judith: *Endangered/Endangering: Schematic Racism and White Paranoia*, 43, 93, 94, 168. See also King, Rodney

Card, Claudia, 84, 87, 94; *Confronting Evils*, 95; "The Paradox of Genocidal Rape Aimed at Enforced Pregnancy," 109n20
Caruth, Cathy, 11, 70–72; *Unclaimed Experience: Trauma, Narrative, and History*, 60, 61
chattel slavery, 7, 79
civil rights, 1, 6, 7, 13, 32, 62, 151, 152, 167; Civil Rights Act, 62; movement, 35, 147, 167
Civil Rights Congress (CRC): *We Charge Genocide: The Crime of the American Government against the Negro People*, 21, 82–84, 102, 109n12
color line, 8, 40, 48, 49, 92, 137, 140. See also Du Bois, W. E. B.
CRC. See Civil Rights Congress
critical race theory, 8, 24, 136, 151

Dave East, 61
the death drive, 71–73. See also Freud, Sigmund
Dead Prez, 1, 113
Diallo, Amadou, 149, 150
dominant discourse, 7, 8, 13, 18–20, 31, 35, 40–49, 53, 55, 56, 68, 73, 102, 107, 114, 116–18, 122, 135, 136, 142, 143, 148, 155, 160, 163, 164
DonChristian Jones, 27
Dotson, Kristie, 8
Du Bois, W. E. B., 8, 35, 49, 65; *The Souls of Black Folk*, 5, 6, 92, 93
Dynasty, 27

EMDR. See Eye Movement Desensitization and Reprocessing

Eminem, 47, 144
empathy: in cognitive science, 140, 141; and emotional contagion, 23, 138–41, 143; musical, 135, 138, 139, 143, 155, 161; white impairment of, 32, 33, 36, 37, 55, 73, 102, 129–32, 135–41, 163, 164
episteme, 42–45, 66, 67, 89, 133, 143, 144, 147, 151, 155, 165. See also Foucault, Michel
epistemology of ignorance. See Mills, Charles
Eye Movement Desensitization and Reprocessing (EMDR), 16, 17, 21, 22, 116, 120–23, 130, 163

Fanon, Franz, 5; *Black Skin, White Masks*, 28n16, 40, 41, 79, 93
Federal Bureau of Investigation (FBI), 3
First Amendment, 3
flashbacks, 14, 16, 59–61, 66, 115, 121, 122
flow, 20, 32, 39, 63, 120, 137, 143
Floyd, George, ix, 147
Foucault, Michel, 42, 55, 65; "The Confession of the Flesh," 50n13; *Nietzsche, Genealogy, and History*, 98; "Society Must Be Defended," 43
Frankfurt School, 147
Frankowski, Alfred, 7, 21, 81, 85, 86; *The Post-Racial Limits of Memorialization: Toward a Political Sense of Mourning*, 29n26, 152–54
Freud, Sigmund, 115; *Beyond the Pleasure Principle*, 71–73
Fricker, Miranda: epistemic injustice, 20, 48–50

Gang Starr, 12, 13
genocide: and American slavery, 7, 77, 78, 80, 81, 84, 87, 89, 90, 100, 101; anti-black, 10, 12, 13, 22, 24, 42, 78, 86, 88, 89, 94, 113, 131, 133, 135, 142, 159, 162, 168; legal classification of, 81, 82; as mass murder, 73, 82, 83, 87; Nazi,

77, 96, 97, 100, 147; scholars and scholarship, 7, 21, 78, 80–82, 89, 108, 162
Gordon, Lewis R., 41; "Fanon, Philosophy, and Racism," 41, 42

Hadley, Susan, 13, 116
HHNL. *See* Hip-Hop Nation Language
Hill, Lauryn, 22, 53, 127
hip-hop: and the church, 4; and commercial success, 11, 12, 46, 47, 53, 54, 168; as EMDR, 16, 17, 21, 22, 116, 120, 123, 130; and empathy, 5, 19, 20, 32–37, 129, 130–33, 135, 138–42; and the erotic, 14, 15; and Hip-Hop Nation culture, xii, 1; as political resistance, 4, 13, 31, 114, 150, 151, 167, 169; and PTSD, 16, 17, 22, 59–61, 119–31; and sexism, 129; and the underground, 11, 12–14
Hip Hop for Respect, 149
Hip-Hop Nation Language (HHNL), 44, 45, 55, 56. *See also* Alim, H. Samy
Holocaust, 21, 77, 78, 80–82, 84, 86, 96, 100, 102, 162

Ice Cube, 12, 13, 149
Iggy Azalea, 47
Immortal Technique, 89, 90

Jacobs, Harriet: *Incidents in the Life of a Slave Girl*, 73
JAY-Z, 53, 62–64
J. Cole, 131
Jim Crow, 38, 81–83, 88, 89
Jones, Janine: "The Impairment of Empathy in Goodwill Whites for African-Americans," 28n13, 32–36, 46, 136, 138

Katz, Mark: *Groove Music: The Art and Culture of the Hip-Hop DJ*, 64–67
Kid Cudi, 150
King, Rodney, 43, 93
Knox, Jamal. *See* Mayhem Mal
KRS-One, 38, 39, 70

Kweli, Talib, 53, 149

Lacan, Jacques: *The Four Fundamental Concepts of Psychoanalysis*, 69
Lang, Berl: *Genocide: The Act as Idea*, 81–83
Lemkin, Raphael, 81–85; *Axis Rule*, 109n12; "Nature of Genocide: Confusion with Discrimination Against Individuals Seen," 84, 85
Levi, Primo, 106
Lifers Group, 80
Lil' Pump, 132
Lorde, Audre: "Uses of the Erotic: The Erotic as Power," 14, 15
Ludacris, 106, 114
Lupe Fiasco, 113, 126

Machine Gun Kelly, 47
mass incarceration, 32, 34, 38, 69, 70, 81, 85, 87–89, 95, 97, 104, 105, 107, 127, 161
Mayhem Mal, 3, 147, 165
Meek Mill, 35, 61, 67, 118, 136
Mills, Charles: epistemology of ignorance, 6–8, 149; *The Racial Contract*, 6–8
Mos Def. *See* Bey, Yasiin
Moshman, David, 100
mourning, 72, 143, 149–54, 164, 165. *See also* Frankowski, Alfred; Rankine, Claudia

Nas, 1, 53–54, 150
N. W. A., 3, 141, 149

Ortiz, Joell, 89, 90

Patterson, Orlando, 84, 94. *See also* social death
Perry, Imani, 129
Peterson, James Braxton: *The Hip-Hop Underground and African-American Culture: Beneath the Surface*, 62
Pitts, Andrea J.: "Decolonial Praxis and Epistemic Injustice," 49

prison: as Hell, 103–5, 138; industrial complex, 11, 90, 104, 113; reform, 35, 87, 89, 90, 98
Post Traumatic Stress Disorder (PTSD), 14, 16, 17, 20–22, 59–61, 69, 70, 114–31, 135, 163, 164
Public Enemy, 4, 80, 148

racial caste system, 32, 57, 80, 85, 89, 147, 161, 162, 164, 168
racial democracy, 4, 8, 21, 22, 33, 37, 49, 55, 57, 87–89, 93, 116, 119, 142, 162, 164
Rankine, Claudia: "The Condition of Black Life Is One of Mourning," 151, 152
rhythm, 15, 39, 40, 58, 59, 61, 120, 131, 140
Rose, Tricia: ideological insubordination, 63
Run-DMC, 4, 103
Run the Jewels, 68

sample, 62, 63, 67
Saucier, P. Khalil, 165–69; "Hip Hop Studies in Black," 165, 166, 168, 169
Schloss, Joseph G.: *Breaking Beats: The Art of Sample-Based Hip-Hop*, 57, 58, 61
scratch, 12, 57, 59–61, 64–70, 144, 163
sensibility: disruption of, 5, 7, 8, 10, 12–14, 18, 20, 22–24, 44, 46, 48, 54, 58, 60–65, 90, 96, 107, 136–38, 143, 144, 153, 154, 160, 163–65; of genocide, 21, 78, 80, 82, 85–88, 90, 92, 95, 96, 99, 102, 162, 163; neoliberal, 6, 24, 58, 59, 132, 133, 160; post-racial, 6, 10, 12, 13, 15, 20, 24, 27, 58, 89, 126, 144, 148, 152, 160, 163, 165, 168; white, 2–9, 13, 17–26, 31, 33, 35–37, 40–42, 44–50, 55, 56, 61, 68, 71, 73, 79, 84, 85, 89, 90, 92, 93, 102, 107, 114, 115, 120, 125, 135–39, 141–44, 147–49, 154, 155, 161, 164, 165

Shakur, Tupac, 5, 31–35, 49, 53, 56, 57, 62–65, 72, 73, 77, 86, 87, 94, 95, 102, 103, 113, 129, 130, 138, 140, 150
social death, 83, 84, 87, 92, 94, 95, 99, 102, 107, 151–54. *See also* Card, Claudia
Soren, Tabitha, 31–35
Spence, Lester K., 165–68; *Stare in the Darkness: The Limits of Hip-Hop and Black Politics*, 165, 166, 168

Taylor, Paul C.; *Black is Beautiful: A Philosophy of Black Aesthetics*, 4, 59, 65, 167
testimony: and politics, 4, 10, 11, 21, 49, 50–54, 67, 80, 87–90, 101, 102; and PTSD, 22, 113–18, 123–33; and white sensibility, 24, 33–36, 72–74, 136–44
the Thirteenth Amendment, 119
trauma: theory, 16, 22–24, 60, 67, 70, 164. *See also* anti-black violence; Post Traumatic Stress Disorder (PTSD)
A Tribe Called Quest, 67, 68

United Nations Convention on the Prevention and Punishment of the Crime of Genocide, 21

the Veil, 6, 36, 48, 49, 92, 93, 135, 137. *See also* the color line; Du Bois, W. E. B.

War on Drugs, 11, 32, 34, 63, 131
West, Kanye, 105, 151
Woods, Tryon P., 165–69; "Hip-Hop Studies in Black," 165, 167–69
Wu-Tang Clan, 157, 162

Yancy, George, 9, 13, 14, 30n33, 46, 116, 136, 137; *Backlash: What Happens When We Talk Honestly about Race in America*, 29n17, 37, 38; "Dear White America," 29n17, 37, 93, 109n17
YoungBoy Never Broke Again, 61

About the Author

Dr. Lissa Skitolsky is currently serving as the 2020–2021 Simon and Riva Spatz Visiting Chair in Jewish Studies at Dalhousie University in Halifax, Nova Scotia. Prior to moving to Canada, Dr. Skitolsky taught as an associate professor of philosophy at Susquehanna University and as an assistant professor of philosophy at Luther College. Her scholarship in the fields of genocide studies and continental philosophy focuses on illustrating the connection between discourse and sensibility in the normalization of state-sanctioned, systemic violence against racialized and gendered groups. Her work also identifies discursive and nondiscursive strategies of resistance against the moral indifference and willful ignorance also central to the repetition of state violence.

www.ingramcontent.com/pod-product-compliance
Lightning Source LLC
Chambersburg PA
CBHW050906300426
44111CB00010B/1400